Carl Sandburg

a reference guide

A
Reference
Guide
to
Literature

Ronald Gottesman
Editor

Carl Sandburg

a reference guide

DALE SALWAK

G.K.HALL &CO.

70 LINCOLN STREET, BOSTON, MASS.

Library of Congress Cataloging-in-Publication Data

Salwak, Dale
      Carl Sandburg: a reference guide / Dale Salwak.
          p. cm. -- (A Reference guide to literature)
      Includes index.
      ISBN 0-8161-8821-1
      1. Sandburg, Carl, 1878-1967--Bibliography. I. Title.
II. Series.
Z8781.5.S25 1988
[PS3537.A618]
016.811'.52--dc19   88-12048
                              CIP

This publication is printed on permanent/durable acid-free paper
MANUFACTURED IN THE UNITED STATES OF AMERICA

For Steve and Nancy Kelley

Contents

The Author

Dale Salwak is professor of English at Southern
California's Citrus College. He was educated at Purdue
University and then the University of Southern Califor-
nia under a National Defense Education Act competitive
fellowship program. His publications include literary
biographies of John Wain and A.J. Cronin; reference
guides to Kingsley Amis, John Braine, A.J. Cronin and
John Wain; and four collections: Literary Voices:
Interviews with Britain's "Angry Young Men", Mystery
Voices: Interviews with British Writers, The Life and
Work of Barbara Pym, and Philip Larkin: The Man and
His Work. He is currently completing a study of
Kingsley Amis, for which he was awarded a National
Endowment for the Humanities grant in 1985. In 1987
Purdue University awarded him its Distinguished Alumnus
Award.

Preface

As a leading figure in American literature, and as one of the most prolific writers of his time, Carl Sandburg inspired a massive amount of critical commentary--much of it knowledgeable, some of it obtuse, almost all of it interesting to scholars and to students of the man and his work. The purpose of this guide is to give the reader for the first time a clear picture of how Sandburg's writings looked to his American and, in some instances, British contemporaries and later readers. His reputation in Europe and in other non-English-speaking countries is, in itself, the subject for another full study; therefore, the foreign scholarship included is necessarily limited to that cataloged in the various bibliographical publications in the United States.

The selections that make up the body of this book begin with Philip Green Wright's foreword to Sandburg's first publication, In Reckless Ecstasy (1904.1); they end with a descriptive note on The Love Letters of Lilian Steichen and Carl Sandburg (1987.5), published twenty years after his death. Between the two are more than one thousand samplings of critical opinions, reflecting the fluctuations of Sandburg's reputation. A representative selection of critical comment drawn from many sources--newspapers, periodicals, journals, pamphlets, volumes of belles lettres, book-length studies, dissertations, versified tributes and parodies, private letters, conversations preserved for us by diarists or correspondents, literary gossips or faithful recorders of table talk--has been compiled to achieve that purpose. Although this reference guide cannot be called a definitive bibliography, it is as exhaustive a study of Sandburg scholarship as I could assemble.

To increase the usefulness of this book, several editorial devices have been employed. Within each year, the materials themselves have been arranged alphabetically and numbered consecutively. Each item begins with a bibliographic reference which includes the critic's name (when known), the title and date of the publication in which the item is to be found, and the appropriate pages. References and cross-references are to those numbers (thus "1939.14" refers to the fourteenth entry for the year 1939). This code is employed within the text to refer to reprints and replies; it is also used in the index at the back of the guide. The index is inclusive, with authors, titles, and subjects interfiled. All annotations are descriptive, not evaluative. In the few cases where I was unable to see the item cited, I have placed an asterisk before the entry and included in the annotation a note indicating the source of the work. References to the Nation are to the American periodical except where the city of publication is given as London. In the abstracts of interviews, bibliographies, major critical studies, and biographies, I have emphasized scope except in the case of very brief items.

This work owes much to many institutions and individuals. A major debt is to the compilers of earlier Sandburg bibliographies, including Gay Wilson Allen (1972.1), Jerome Green (1963.8), Fred P. Millett (1944.5), William P. Schenk (1936.20), Thomas Sculer Shaw (1948.21), Mark Van Doren (1969.14; 1974.1) and William White (1976.15), as well as the compilers of the Sandburg entries in the MLA International Bibliographies and the bibliographies in American Literary Scholarship. For their kind assistance in gathering materials, I should also like to thank the research assistants at the following libraries: the Huntington at San Marino, California; Rice University; University of California at Los Angeles and Irvine; University of Illinois at Urbana-Champaign, and University of Southern California. I am also indebted to Mickey Sharpsteen of the Hayden Memorial Library, Citrus College; to Professor Ronald Gottesman of the University of Southern California; and to my parents, Professor Stanley and Frances H. Salwak.

One last debt is acknowledged in the dedication.

Introduction

Carl Sandburg's reputation is based on a flood of literary
production—more than thirty-five books of poetry, nonfiction and
fiction, biography and autobiography, songs and children's stories,
along with many contributions to periodicals and anthologies, fore-
words, introductions, and foreign editions. His honors included two
Pulitzer Prizes, one for prose in 1940 (Abraham Lincoln: The War
Years), and one for poetry in 1950 (Complete Poems); honorary degrees
from fourteen universities both in the United States and abroad; and
two Gold Medals, one from the American Academy of Arts and Letters
for history and biography (1952), and another from the Poetry Society
of America for poetry (1953). Six high schools and five elementary
schools were named for him, poems were written about him, and two
presidents—Franklin Delano Roosevelt and Ronald Reagan—quoted him.
When he died at age eighty-seven, he was given a special service at
the Lincoln Memorial and eulogized as "more than the voice of
America. . . . He was America" (1967.3). At the time, his value to
twentieth-century American letters seemed assured.

Twenty years after his death, however, his critical reputation is
far from settled. To his admirers, he is an idealist, a fighter, a
philosopher, a dreamer, a tender yet powerful poet, always with something to say, always worth listening to and reading. To his de-
tractors, he is simpleminded, sentimental, gross, tiresome, sub-
literary, and unreadable. Many have agreed with Kenneth Rexroth,
who wrote that after about 1925 "there is nothing of value. . . .
Sandburg the historian, novelist, autobiographer, writer of children's stories simply does not exist for literature" (1958.12). In
looking over eighty-three years of critical commentary, we find a
full range of appraisals, from condemnation to high praise, and a
broad base of criticism. Few readers react to his work with in-
difference. To even begin to understand what Sandburg means to
American letters, historian J.G. Randall noted, "one must put
together the statements of men all over America" (1949.29). In
sketching the history of his critical reputation, I can present here
only some of the principal figures.

Harriet Monroe gave Sandburg's poetry its first serious audience when in March 1914 she published nine of his poems in her experimental magazine, Poetry. For that group of poems, including the now famous "Chicago," he won the $200 Helen Haire Levinson Prize, and two years later he published his first volume, Chicago Poems.

Critics were caught by surprise. Here was "tradition-shattering poetry" (1916.1), "alive, stirring, human" (1916.2), one of the "most original books which the age has produced" (1917.2). Many readers suggested that Sandburg might be the great democratic poet called for by Whitman. They noted that his confident use of common American speech, his social interest and sincerity, and his affirmation of the common man were exactly the correction that conventional poetry needed to revitalize it.

But not all reviewers were as impressed as these excerpts indicate. Amy Lowell, for example, acknowledged his virility and tenderness, his originality and strength, but objected to the propagandistic overtones in his poetry: "the lyricist in him has a hard time to make itself heard above the brawling of the marketplace" (1917.2). She predicted that his future would depend on whether the poet or the propagandist dominated. Other reviewers noted that Sandburg had the imagination of a poet but lacked any skill in communicating his vision to the reader (1916.6); that his vision of Chicago was "hideous" and "uninspired" (1916.10); that he should discipline his writing and pare his style of its excesses (1916.8); that because of the free verse form his work was "chaotic" (1918.6). One reviewer even questioned whether it was poetry at all (1916.2).

Two years later Sandburg followed with Cornhuskers. Inevitably critics hastened to compare it to his first volume, and most of them found in it a gain in power: greater depth and responsiveness to contemporary jargon, a tenderness and mysticism, a tempered social interest that asserted itself with less effort, a keener imagination, a more certain artistry (1929.8). Whereas many critics held the view that Sandburg was now in the front rank of American poets, others felt that his outspoken idealism prevented him from being a poet at all. The Review of Reviews praised him for revealing the "vitality and strength of the English tongue as it was in its beginning" (1919.5). The New York Times Book Review, on the other hand, noted the melancholy mood of the book and attributed it to "the racial soberness of the Scandinavian" (1919.4).

By 1920, when the "renaissance" of American literature was gaining momentum, Sandburg had reached the maturity of his power as a poet. He was twice recognized by national awards, and his next volume, Smoke and Steel, confirmed for many readers his position as one of two major living poets, the other being Robert Frost. Louis Untermeyer hailed the book as "an epic of modern industrialism and a mighty paean to modern beauty" (1920.14). Amy Lowell predicted that posterity would rank Sandburg "high on the ladder of poetic

achievement" and added: "Reading these poems gives me more of a
patriotic emotion than ever 'The Star-Spangled Banner' had been able
to do. This is America and Mr. Sandburg loves her so much that suddenly we realize how much we love her, too" (1920.12).

Other critics, however, saw the collection as a strong but uneven
work. Some complained that Sandburg had no sense of the past or
vision of the future (1920.7), that he was producing too much too
fast (1921.9), that he was suffering from a monotonous recurrence of
certain themes. The reviewer for the London Times asked if his work
constituted "a high and right art" (1920.4). But whether in praise
or disparagement, on one point most critics agreed: Sandburg was a
completely American poet, the Poet of the People.

When Slabs of the Sunburnt West appeared in 1922, critics noticed
immediately a change in style. Now the poet was using the catalog,
the repetitive accrual of images in parallel forms, the quotation of
American slang and platitudes. Many readers found these devices
irritating, his work incoherent, and his vocabulary dated. Clement
Wood wrote that Sandburg was writing in "unfamiliar rhythms, and a
vocabulary that tomorrow will speak only to the archaeologist"
(1922.23). The New York Times Book Review warned that he was in
danger of becoming "the Professional Chanter of Virility" (1922.1).
And another accused him of being "sketchy, repetitious, rather weary"
and wondered anew if the Poet of the People could in fact write
poetry at all (1929.8).

Those who admired Sandburg, on the other hand, found much to
praise in this volume. Walter Yust writing for the Double Dealer
likened reading the poems to listening to a symphony (1922.24).
Raymond Holden in the New Republic called him "personality, genius,
perspicacity, fire, love of life" (1922.13). Malcolm Cowley, in the
Dial, pointed to Sandburg's verse as "highly organized, [producing
effects] as complex and difficult sometimes as those of Swinburne's
most intricate ballades" (1922.8).

Mixed reviews continued to appear with the publication of Good
Morning, America, in 1928. He was compared, again, to Whitman. He
was praised, also again, for his humor and vision, and the rhythm of
his verse. But Percy Hutchinson, among others, chided that Sandburg
demonstrated no real growth as a poet, that he could not, or would
not, "discipline either his art or himself" (1928.11). The New
Republic encouraged more criticism and less "rhapsody and amused
tolerance" from his readers (1928.23). And another wrote that
Sandburg's social democracy was "a rubber-stamp idea, and comradeship
a lazy, undisciplined thought" (1930.2). But the consensus was that
"sunburned Carl Sandburg, in love with the earth," had found the
subject and the style vigorous and free enough for "a Continental
plateau and the Great Divide" (1928.27).

To many reviewers, Sandburg's next volume, The People, Yes (1936), marked the culmination of his work as a poet. Generous praise was given for his vision of the American people as heroic, for his lusty humor and vivid irony, for his optimism, for his success in rendering "the authentic accents of his brother" (1936.9). Stephen Vincent Benét called the book "a frescoe and a field of grass and a man listening quietly to all the commonplace, extra things that people say" (1936.5). Willard Thorp later referred to it as "a strange and powerful book" (1948.27). And Selden Rodman wrote that one-quarter of these poems were, along with the best of Emerson, Thoreau, Melville, Dickinson, Twain, Faulkner, and Frost, "the writing that has taught America the sound of its own voice" (1950.22). It was to be his last major book of poetry.

Although the core of Sandburg's artistic genius is his poetry, he wrote much else. His commentaries on events during World War II (Storm Over the Land, 1942, and Home Front Memo, 1943) were widely praised for their narrative skill, insight, intelligence, sympathy, and theme of heroism. He collected and sang folk songs, and his The American Songbag (1927) became recognized as one of the first serious attempts to assemble and record the authentic songs of the American people. Sandburg also wrote two volumes of children's tales-- Rootabaga Stories (1922) and Rootabaga Pigeons (1923)--and a histori- cal novel (Remembrance Rock, 1948), which he set in America from the arrival of the Pilgrims to the onset of World War II. Sandburg would never garner a reputation for the above writings comparable to what he achieved as poet and biographer, but this work was, together with his lecturing, one of the vehicles by which he earned his living.

Sandburg succeeded in creating one of his most memorable charac- ters through the medium of prose in Abraham Lincoln: The Prairie Years (1926) and Abraham Lincoln: The War Years (1939). The criti- cal reception given to both volumes was among the best he ever received. The work was called an American Epic, a chronicle of an important historic period, a representative story of America, a memorial to pioneer times. Critics praised Sandburg's "indefatigable thoroughness" (1940.6), his "staggering accomplishment" (1939.1), the "strength, scope and beauty" of his writing (1939.2), his "vital and stimulating" approach to Lincoln's life (1926.33). Of great satis- faction to many readers was Sandburg's ability to see the humanity, the simplicity, the doubts and uncertainties, and loneliness of Lincoln. Allan Nevins saw it as "homely but beautiful, learned but simple, exhaustively detailed but panoramic . . . [occupying] a niche all its own, unlike any other biography or history in the language" (1968.32). Henry Commager Steele wrote: "[Sandburg] has realized that Lincoln belongs to the people, not to the historians, and he has given us a portrait from which a whole generation may draw under- standing from the past and inspiration for the future" (1940.7). More than one reviewer commented on the happy conjunction of the perfect writer and the perfect subject. On 12 February 1959, the

150th anniversary of Lincoln's birth, Sandburg was the first private
citizen to be invited to deliver an address before a joint session
of Congress.

If we can still read Sandburg with profit, why then has he been
disparaged by so many who determine literary reputations? There are
perhaps three main reasons for this history, and the first reason
stems from literary fashion. For the New Critics his poetry held few
interesting ambiguities, intentional or unintentional. There were no
puzzles, no obscure allusions, no "levels of meaning" within them.
Whereas admirers proclaimed him "a latter-day Whitman, objectors
cried that their six-year-old daughters could write better poetry"
(1916.4). One needed only to turn to the poetry of Pound or Eliot,
they said, and the contrast was clear.

Yet another dynamic at play in the shaping of Sandburg's critical
reputation has to do with his mellow optimism and faith in the future.
Oscar Cargill saw this attitude as a positive good, a sign of moral
and intellectual growth, and a by-product of Sandburg's research and
writing on Lincoln (1950.8). But according to Kenneth Rexroth and
others, the poet's oversized enthusiasm kept him out of sympathy with
the main poetic influences in an age of pessimism. In his optimistic
faith, Sandburg failed to fulfill the authentic social role of the
poet. Thus we find these critics preferring the early discontented
Socialist over the later optimistic singer of folk wisdom.

A third factor that has told against Sandburg's repute is more
difficult to assess. Some critics were unable to find either literary or intellectual grace in a man whose books were read by millions,
who always headed the best-seller lists, and who lived a financially
comfortable life. Gay Wilson Allen said that Sandburg suffered from
the "curse of success" (1972.1), and that critics found his "love
affair with the people" a source of irritation. Such a poet must not
be very good, it was thought. He must be writing to the lowest level
of the public's comprehension on subjects that are dull, common, or
insignificant. "His own degree of sensitivity and his power to
render human feeling must both be very low" (1979.5).

Readers interested in tracing in greater detail the development
of Sandburg's critical reputation will want to consult the following
writers: Paul Ferlazzo (1979.5), John G. Fletcher (1920.11), Louis
Untermeyer (1923.20; 1936.23), T.K. Whipple (1928.27), Harriet Monroe
(1932.8), Oscar Cargill (1950.8), Daniel G. Hoffman (1950.14), Gay
Wilson Allen (1960.1; 1974.4), Jerome Green (1963.8), Roy Prentice
Basler (1969.1), David Perkins (1976.13), Louis D. Rubin, Jr.
(1977.7) and Richard Crowder (1978.3). Of the numerous full-length
biographical and critical studies of the life and work that have been
attempted, the following are recommended: Gay Wilson Allen (1972.1),
North Callahan (1970.1; 1987.1), Richard Crowder (1964.2), Karl
Detzer (1941.4), Hazel Durnell (1965.1), Harry Golden (1961.5),
Joseph Haas and Gene Lovitz (1967.12), Jeffrey Hacker (1984.3), Grace

Hathaway Melin (1973.7), Lilla S. Perry (1981.7), Helen Sandburg (1978.18), Paula Steichen (1969.12; 1982.8), William A. Sutton (1968.42), Mark Van Doren (1969.14), and Bruce Weirick (1924.12). Obviously of special importance to anyone interested in Sandburg's life are his autobiographies (Always the Young Strangers, 1953; Breathing Tokens, 1978), and two collections of letters (1968, 1987). For additional biographical material and tributes to the man and his work by some of those people who knew him best, the reader will also want to consult special issues of the Journal of the Illinois State Historical Society (1952.29; 1953.19, 31) and the Lincoln Herald (1968.16).

Writings by Carl Sandburg

In Reckless Ecstasy (1904)
Incidentals (1907)
The Plaint of a Rose (1908)
Joseffy (1910)
Chicago Poems (1916)
Cornhuskers (1918)
The Chicago Race Riots, July, 1919 (1919)
Smoke and Steel (1920)
Slabs of the Sunburnt West (1922)
Rootabaga Stories (1922)
Rootabaga Pigeons (1923)
Abraham Lincoln: The Prairie Years (1926)
Selected Poems (1926; edited by Rebecca West)
Carl Sandburg (1926; edited by Hughes Mearns)
The American Songbag (1927; editor)
Abe Lincoln Grows Up (1928)
Good Morning, America (1928)
Steichen, the Photographer (1929)
Potato Face (1930)
Early Moon (1930)
Mary Lincoln: Wife and Widow (1932; with Paul Angle)
The People, Yes (1936)
Abraham Lincoln: The War Years (1939)
Storm over the Land: A Profile of the Civil War Taken Mainly from
    Abraham Lincoln: The War Years (1942, 1943)
Home Front Memo (1943)
The Photographs of Abraham Lincoln (1944; with Frederick Hill
    Meserve)
Remembrance Rock (1948)
Lincoln Collector: The Story of Oliver R. Barrett's Great Private
    Collection (1949)
Complete Poems (1950, 1970)
The New American Songbag (1951)
Always the Young Strangers (1953)
Prairie-Town Boy (1955)
The Sandburg Range (1957)
Harvest Poems, 1910-1960 (1960)

Wind Song (1960)
Honey and Salt (1963)
The Wedding Procession of the Rag Doll and the Broom Handle and Who
   Was in It (1967)
The Letters of Carl Sandburg (1968; edited by Herbert Mitgang)
Breathing Tokens (1978; edited by Margaret Sandburg)
Ever the Winds of Chance (1983; edited by Margaret Sandburg and
   George Hendrick)
The Poet and the Dream Girl: The Love Letters of Lilian Steichen and
   Carl Sandburg (1987; edited by Margaret Sandburg)

Writings about Carl Sandburg, 1904–87

1 WRIGHT, PHILIP GREEN. "Foreword." In In Reckless Ecstasy, by
   Charles A. Sandburg. Galesburg: Asgard Press.
      Calls the young Sandburg a modern Viking and praises him
   for his force and virility, his soul's kinship with all that is
   beautiful and terrible in nature, and his enthusiasm, which is
   that of "one who is witnessing the sunrise for the first time."

1 ANON. "New Lamps for Old." Dial 56 (16 March):231-32.
      Reacts to Sandburg's poems published in the 14 March issue
   of Poetry. "The typographical arrangement for this jargon
   creates a suspicion that it is intended to be taken as some form
   of poetry." Calls the verse "nothing less than an impudent
   affront to the poetry-loving public." (See reply in 1914.2)

2 MONROE, HARRIET. "The Enemies We Have Made." Poetry 4 (May):
   63.
      Reacts to charges made against Sandburg in the Dial (see
   1914.1). Defends her choice and asks, "Whom and what has The
   Dial discovered?" Refers to the "intellectual life of this vast,
   chaotically rich region" and to "a great opportunity" in Sandburg's choice of subject. Excerpted: 1977.10.

3 _____. "Poetry's Banquet." Poetry 4 (April):26-27.
      Reports on Sandburg's appearance at a banquet to honor
   William Butler Yeats, held at the Cliff-Dwellers Club in Chicago.
   Sandburg read his poem "Limited."

1915

1 HECHT, BEN. "Slobberdom, Sneerdom, and Boredom." Little
   Review 2 (June-July):25.
      Finds in Sandburg a sustaining of "a dying faith in Walt
   [Whitman], humanity, and vers libre in general." Sandburg
   stirred up considerable excitement with the reading of his Billy
   Sunday poem at the Walt Whitman dinner held at the Grand Pacific
   Hotel.

1916

1 ANON. "Nonfiction." Booklist 13 (October):23.
      Review of Chicago Poems. Calls it "tradition-shattering
   poetry" that gives "a vivid picture of the crudity and power of
   Chicago" while offending many lovers of poetry as it was. Predicts that Sandburg will endure, however, and this phase will
   pass.

2 ANON. "Notable Books in Brief Review." New York Times Book
   Review, 11 June, p. 242.
      Review of Chicago Poems. Sandburg's best is very good, but
   the worst is "dull and shapeless." Finds throughout the book a
   feeling of responsibility for the faults in our civilization.
   Although some is not poetry, the book is "all alive, stirring,
   human." Excerpted: 1985.5.

3 ANON. "Poetry for Vacation Reading." American Review of
   Books 53 (June):761.
      Review of Chicago Poems. On the one hand, likens these
   poems to a Rodin sculpture; on the other, their outline is in-
   determinant, blending with a "primal mist out of which all life
   and eternity are shapen."

4 ANON. "A Straightforward Poet." Independent 87
   (18 September):425.
      Review of Chicago Poems. "In methods of observation and
   manner of expression [Sandburg] is intrinsically a poet, tho
   [sic] as to technique and substance he often angers us." Notes
   some similarities between Sandburg and Whitman.

5 BRADLEY, WILLIAM ASPENWALL. "Four American Poets." Dial 61
   (14 December):528-29.
      Review of Chicago Poems. Comments on Sandburg's "brutality
   and violence of expressions," much of which he finds to be "alien
   and artificial." There are two Sandburgs: the clever reporter
   ("rather gross, simpleminded, sentimental, sensual man among
   men") and the true artist ("highly sensitized impressionist")
   belonging with the Imagists.

6   BRAITHWAITE, WILLIAM STANLEY. "Chicago Poems." Boston
     Transcript, 13 May, p. 6.
          Review of Chicago Poems. Concedes Sandburg's "tenderness"
     and "visual strength" but calls the collection "a book of ill-
     regulated speech that has neither verse nor prose rhythms." Says
     that Sandburg has the imagination of a poet but lacks any skill in
     communicating his vision to the reader.

7   BUEHRMANN, ELIZABETH. "Portrait of Carl Sandburg." Little
     Review 3 (April):3.
          Reprint of a silhouette photograph of Sandburg.

8   FIRKINS, O.W. "American Verse." Nation (London) 103
     (17 August):152.
          Review of Chicago Poems. Finds here two divergent aspira-
     tions as Sandburg reaches out simultaneously toward "the brawny
     and the lissome." Too often the poet's images of man are so like
     "the mud" that his submergence produces "no effect of tragic
     incongruity." Concludes that he must learn how to discipline his
     writing and pare his style of its excesses. Excerpted: 1985.5.

9   FREDERICK, JOHN T. "Carl Sandburg's 'Chicago Poems.'"
     Midland 2 (June):189-93.
          Review of Chicago Poems. Perceives the genuine originality
     of the book and calls it "a permanent contribution to the liter-
     ature of the Middle West and of America." When the twentieth-
     century growth of humanity is studied, people will read this
     book.

10   HACKETT, FRANCIS. "Impressions." New Republic 8
     (28 October):328-29.
          Review of Chicago Poems. Praises Sandburg's use of
     Whitmanesque free rhythms and imagism. Finds here an "exquisite
     realization of the scenes" and none of the "laxity that comes
     from splitting attention several ways." But remains unimpressed
     by Sandburg's vision of Chicago; it is "hideous" and "un-
     inspired." Reprinted: 1918.4. Excerpted: 1985.5.

11   KREYMBORG, ALFRED. "To Sandburg." Poetry 8 (June):158.
          Addresses a poem to Sandburg.

12   LOWELL, AMY. "Carl Sandburg." Poetry Review 1 (July):46.
          Review of Chicago Poems. Comments on Sandburg's virility
     and tenderness, music, irony, and use of nature, and calls this
     one of the "most original books which the age has produced."
     Sandburg is one of the most important poets writing in America
     today.

13   M[ONROE], H[ARRIET]. "Reviews: Chicago Granite." Poetry 8
     (May):90-93.
          Review of Chicago Poems. Comments on Sandburg's heroism,
     his use of free verse (akin to his own "slow speech" and "massive
     gait"), his honesty. Although he is predominantly loud, there
     appears a suggestion of pity and delicacy. His speech is "torn
     out of the heart." Excerpted: 1924.6, 25. Reprinted: 1932.8.

14   UNTERMEYER, LOUIS. "Books: Enter Sandburg." Masses Review
     8 (July):30.
          Review of Chicago Poems. Sandburg's hate might overbalance
     the power of his work were it not exceeded by "the fiercer viril-
     ity of his love." Calls him "a feeler rather than a thinker."
     Weaknesses are seen in occasional "artificiality of expression
     and gesture." Overall, this "intensely personal" volume is
     "vivid with the health of vulgarity" and has the "strength of
     sorrow as well as the gaiety of strength." He is an artist.
     Excerpted: 1919.9; 1923.20.

15   ZWASKA, CAESAR. "Modernity Exposed--and Gone One Better."
     Little Review 3 (August):9-11.
          Review of Chicago Poems. In one book Sandburg has "gone
     the entire range of a life today." He understands the failures
     and the lies and exposes the cause. He is both a "humanitarian
     poet" and an "artist-poet."

                              1917

1   ARENS, EGMONT H. "To Carl Sandburg." Poetry 10 (August):
     279.
          Poem about Sandburg.

2   LOWELL, AMY. "Edgar Lee Masters and Carl Sandburg." In
     Tendencies in Modern American Poetry. New York: Macmillan,
     pp. 200-232.
          Calls Sandburg a lyricist but objects to the propagandistic
     overtones in his poetry. Although the war poems are strong, con-
     vincing, and poetic, his proletarian and revolutionary sympathies
     are disturbing. Calls Chicago Poems "an imaginative conception
     of real grandeur" and one of the most original books produced in
     this age. But he lacks Edgar Lee Masters's "broad artwork."
     Reprinted: 1921.5. Responded to: 1949.10.

3   REED, EDWARD BLISS. "Recent American Verse." Yale Review 6
     (January):417.
          Review of Chicago Poems. Praises as the best the section
     entitled "Fogs and Fires," because of its unrhymed measures "as
     fine as Henley's [and with] mood and vision touched with beauty."

1918

1 ANON. "Cornhuskers." Booklist 15 (December):98.
Review of Cornhuskers. This collection will add to
Sandburg's reputation as author of Chicago Poems. Finds most
notable "The prairie" and "The four brothers, notes for war
songs (Nov. 1917)."

2 ANON. "A Little Sermon on Free Verse." Outlook 120
(18 December):619.
Review of Cornhuskers. Sandburg belongs in the "front
ranks" of contemporary American poets. His vision is so com-
pelling that the reader often does not care what the lines are.

3 COOK, HOWARD WILLARD. "Carl Sandburg." In Our Poets of
Today. New York: Moffat, Yard, pp. 129–35.
In Chicago Poems, Sandburg "glories" in free verse. His
lines are sometimes "almost primeval" in their intensity, but
they are American "to the core." In form and expression they
echo Whitman. Includes brief biography. Reprinted: 1929.3.

4 HACKETT, FRANCIS. "Illuminations." In Horizons: A Book of
Criticism. New York: B.W. Huebsch, pp. 305–10.
Reprint of 1916.10.

5 KREYMBORG, ALFRED. "Reviews: Carl Sandburg's New Book."
Poetry 13 (December):155–61.
Review of Cornhuskers. Finds influences of Whitman
(catalogs, imagism), O. Henry (colloquialisms), and Lincoln
("homely outlook and gesture"), but Sandburg is himself. He is
life. No theory is imposed on him. He is primarily a lyricist.

6 PHELPS, WILLIAM LYON. The Advance of English Poetry in the
Twentieth Century. New York: Dodd, Mead, pp. 289–91.
Chicago Poems has been overrated. Finds in it the raw
material of poetry rather than the finished product. Although
feeling and appreciation are there, it is not enough to lift it
above being pretentious. The book leaves the impression of being
"chaotic in form and content." Nevertheless, Sandburg has a
gift for "effective poetic figures of speech," and this will
enable him to surpass the "average excellence" exhibited here.
Includes brief biography.

7 UNTERMEYER, LOUIS. "Strong Timber." Dial 65 (5 October):
263–64.
Review of Cornhuskers. Finds here a gain in power over
Chicago Poems, a greater depth and responsiveness to contemporary
jargon, a tenderness and mysticism coupled with a tempered social
criticism that asserts itself with less effort. Includes a reprint of 1916.14. Reprinted: 1919.9; 1923.20. Excerpted:
1985.5.

5

1919

1   AIKEN, CONRAD. "Poetic Realism: Carl Sandburg." In
Skepticisms: Notes on Contemporary Poetry. New York:
Knopf, pp. 143–48.
Comments on Sandburg's originality, vigor, harshness,
sensuousness, ethical irony, and sentimentality. Concludes that
the sociologist gets in the way of the poet. Like Frost,
Masters, Gibson, and Masefield, he searches for "color and pathos
in the lives of the commonplace" but is less selective. Sandburg
writes the way he does because he simply cannot do better.
Reprinted: 1968.2.

2   ANON. "Casual Comment." Dial 67 (12 July):28.
Review of Cornhuskers. This is a book of "deft ideas" and
"poetical revolution." Evaluates the split of the Pulitzer Prize
between this volume and Margaret Wideemer's The Old Road to
Paradise.

3   ANON. "Cornhuskers." Boston Transcript, 11 January, p. 9.
Review of Cornhuskers. Calls Sandburg "an undeniable
ideality whose very passion for his ideals prevents him from
being a big poet."

4   ANON. "Mr. Sandburg's Poems of War and Nature." New York
Times Book Review, 12 January, p. 13.
Review of Cornhuskers. This is a melancholy book but an
improvement over the force, crude beauty, and primitive strength
of Chicago Poems. Attributes the mood to Sandburg's "racial
soberness." Hopes he will overcome his "naive materialism of the
self-made Socialist" and his portrait of an indifferent Nature.
Excerpted: 1985.5.

5   ANON. "Poetry and Verse Technic." American Review of Reviews
59 (January):107.
Review of Cornhuskers. Through Sandburg the reader feels
"the vitality and strength of the English tongue as it was in the
beginning." There is no doubt about his vision, imagination, and
sense of beauty. But he blurs the illusion of life because of a
lack of form.

6   FIRKINS, O.W. "Pathfinders in America." Nation 108
(4 January):20–21.
Review of Cornhuskers. Sees much of the black smoke of
Chicago Poems softened and turned to blue here. Sandburg has
"his good moments, his lease of inspiration, his dole of phrase.
But often, very often, he plans effects he cannot execute." He
lacks "confirmative particulars."

7   FRANK, WALDO DAVID. "Chicago." In Our America. New York:
     Boni & Liveright, pp. 150-53.
          Brief biographical sketch and commentary on Chicago Poems
     and Cornhuskers. "Carl Sandburg is aware of himself: that means
     aware of life: that means in love." His words are "luminous."
     Reprinted: 1922.11.

8   LIPPMANN, WALTER. "Introductory Note." In The Chicago Race
     Riots, July, 1919, by Carl Sandburg. New York: Harcourt,
     Brace & Howe, p. iv.
          Mentions Sandburg's firsthand, sympathetic account: "moved
     not alone to indignation . . . but to thought." Reprinted with
     added preface: 1969.7.

9   UNTERMEYER, LOUIS. "Carl Sandburg." In The New Era in Ameri-
     can Poetry. New York: Henry Holt, pp. 95-109.
          Finds in Sandburg's poems "another phase of the new and
     definitely American spirit." Beneath the brutality, he is possi-
     bly "the tenderest of living poets." Most critics have overlooked
     his power to make "language live." Finds in Chicago Poems, for
     example, "a gigantic, youthful personality and an older, alien
     will to mount." Mentions Sandburg's passion against injustice
     and economic horrors, and says that his finest gift as a poet is
     "the sharp and sympathetic gift of the etcher with his firm,
     clean-cut and always suggestive line." Reprinted: 1923.20.
     Includes excerpt from 1916.14 and reprint of 1918.7. Responded
     to: 1927.8.

10   ____. "Considers It on State Street, Chicago, Illinois" and
     "Guessers by C-rl [sic] Sandb-rgh [sic]." In Collected
     Parodies. New York: Harcourt, Brace, pp. 112, 303.
          Two parodies of Sandburg from 1919.

11   WILKINSON, MARGARET O. New Voices. New York: Macmillan,
     pp. 55-57, 180-82, 192, 217-18, 408-45.
          Views Sandburg as one of the "radical poets." The poems,
     like the man, are virile and tender. Of value is the truth of
     their thoughts and emotions. Sandburg always writes "close to
     the heart of the folk, whence the best poetry comes." Discusses
     his rhythm, radicalism, symbols, "magical design," eloquence,
     candor, and wisdom. Reprinted with revisions: 1935.2.

                              1920

1   ANON. "Chicago Race Riots." Booklist 16 (February):154.
          Brief review of The Chicago Race Riots. Calls this "a
     serious and intelligent investigation."

                                7

2   ANON. "The Negro Problem in America." Spectator (London) 124
      (10 July):51-52.
         Brief review of The Chicago Race Riots.

3   ANON. "Smoke and Steel." Booklist 17 (November):63.
         Review of Smoke and Steel. Sandburg transmutes life today
      into words, "sometimes very beautiful, sometimes very ugly,"
      panoramically or sketchily, in formal speech or slang.

4   ANON. "Smoke and Steel." Times Literary Supplement (London),
      9 December, p. 816.
         Review of Smoke and Steel. Takes issue with Sandburg's
      rejection of the traditions of English poetry. His slang strains
      too hard to be contemporary; his irritation with the past too
      often leads him to be too ready to use the ugly. Beauty is used
      only for contrast. His poems are dominated by an almost reckless
      determination to be American. But the energy here is impressive,
      and the poems succeed in attaining what they set out to accom-
      plish. Questions whether Sandburg's work constitutes "a high and
      right art." Reprinted: 1921.2.

5   ANON. "Somersaults for God's Sake." Nation 111 (December):
      621.
         Review of Smoke and Steel. Sandburg is growing in power.
      "Not so many readers will be able to explain the genius with
      which he chooses details, communicates the flavor of postures
      and movements, compresses words within metaphors."

6   BENJAMIN, PAUL L. "A Poet of the Common-Place." Survey 45
      (2 October):12-13.
         Considers Sandburg, Frost and Robinson to be our greatest
      poets. Comments on his critical judgment and "masterly tech-
      nique" in Chicago Poems, Cornhuskers, and Smoke and Steel.

7   BRAITHWAITE, W[ILLIAM] S[TANLEY]. "Smoke and Steel." Boston
      Transcript, 16 October, p. 7.
         Review of Smoke and Steel. Sandburg lacks a sense of the
      past and a vision of the future. This is a pity, for he has "by
      nature the qualities of spirit which, if fused and blended"
      properly, would make some of "the loveliest and most convincing
      poems of our day."

8   C[ARNEVALI], E[MANUEL]. "The Sandburg-Sarett Recital."
      Poetry 15 (February):271-72.
         Reports on Sandburg's readings and sung ballads in Chicago,
      21 December 1919. "Sandburg is a kingly reader. His reading is
      exactly as beautiful as his poetry and his person. He is one of
      the most completely, successfully alive human beings I ever saw."

9   CLARK, C.C. "Bolshevik Verse." Theosophical Quarterly 17
     (January):233.
        Cites "Southern Pacific" as an example of "counterfeit
     poetry." Finds in this poem the motif of malice, deriving from
     Sandburg's "envy and ignoble ambition." These verses do not
     represent "the present glorious trend of American literature and
     American life," although we are asked to believe the contrary.

10   DEUTSCH, BABETTE. "A Roughneck Mystic." New York Evening
     Post Literary Review, 27 November, p. 6.
        Review of Smoke and Steel. Calls Sandburg a "roughneck
     mystic" whose vivid use of slang helps fill the gap that followed
     the collapse of poetic diction. Compares Sandburg to Whitman and
     the fifteenth-century French poet François Villon.

11   FLETCHER, JOHN G. "Some Contemporary American Poets."
     Chapbook 2 (May):15-19.
        Discusses the difficulties that beset the critic in
     attempting to approve the values of Sandburg's work. Comments
     on Sandburg's variety of experience, his message of endurance,
     his vision, and his use of the Blakeian "mystic method" of seeing
     "through realities, not with realities." Divides the work into
     acceptable aspects (such as his mystical quality) and deplorable
     aspects ("bombast," propaganda, and "short-winded rhythms"). The
     distinguishing fact about Sandburg is that he is the son of an
     unlettered Swedish immigrant.

12   LOWELL, AMY. "Poetry and Propaganda." New York Times Book
     Review, 24 October, p. 7.
        Examines Sandburg as poet and propagandist in Chicago
     Poems, Cornhuskers, and Smoke and Steel. Concludes that he has
     "dared greatly" and that "posterity, with its pruning hand, will
     mount him high on the ladder of poetic achievement." Reprinted:
     1921.5. Responded to: 1927.8. Excerpted: 1985.5.

13   SHERMAN, STUART P. "Poetic Personalities." Yale Review 10
     (April):632-33.
        Review of Smoke and Steel. "Among the radical individual-
     ists Carl Sandburg is . . . by all odds the most positive and
     agreeable voice." His latest volume is an improvement. "Progress
     from this point must be towards more impersonal and more definite
     forms." Reprinted: 1921.22.

14   UNTERMEYER, LOUIS. "Smoke and Steel." New Republic 25
     (15 December):86, 88.
        Review of Smoke and Steel. Calls this Sandburg's first
     "completely successful long poem" in which he establishes himself
     as a living major poet (along with Frost). He is a reporter
     turned mystic. His mood, accent, and image are held at "a glow-
     ing pitch, fused in a new intensity." But there is a danger here:
     his thought directs him, "so that he becomes the instrument

rather than the artist." In spite of this, the book is "an epic of modern industrialism and a mighty paean to modern beauty." Excerpted: 1921.8; 1985.5.

15   WILSON, EDMUND. "The Anarchists of Taste—Who First Broke the Rules of Harmony with the Modern World." Vanity Fair 11 (November):65.
     Comments on the influence of Chicago on Sandburg's verse and speculates what might have happened had he been born and raised in France. Coming from the city, there is in his verse "no ecstasy of beauty here, no calm and high reflection. . . . There is nothing in Chicago to encourage a sensitive lover of life." Free verse is the proper vehicle of expression for one coming from the cramped, untrained, and starving poetic feeling of our time. Free verse is appropriate for his "half journalistic impressions of the modern world." When he tries to write a bona fide lyric poem, however, "the form is less adequate."

16   WYATT, EDITH F. "The Chicago Race Riots." New Republic 22 (17 March):98–99.
     Review of The Chicago Race Riots. Everyone who is interested in America's race problem should read this book. "Especially every Chicagoan ought to read it."

1921

1   ANDERSON, SHERWOOD. "Sketch of Carl Sandburg." Bookman 54 (December):360–61.
     Finds beneath the "He man" another Sandburg, "a sensitive, naive, hesitating man." Excerpted: 1985.5.

2   ANON. "The Poet of American Industrialism." Living Age 308 (22 January):231–34.
     Reprint of 1920.4.

3   BAILEY, M.E. "The Chicago Race Riots." Bookman 52 (January): 303.
     Review of The Chicago Race Riots. Sandburg's personal narration and comment "makes vivid" his statistics and analysis. He is able to bring the general problem of race down to "more specific terms."

4   CARNEVALI, EMANUEL. "Our Great Carl Sandburg." Poetry 22 (February):266–72.
     Review of Smoke and Steel. After Whitman, Sandburg is in words and metaphors the "wealthiest writer" America ever read. Praises his tone ("tender and motherly"), lessons (of "health and strength"), and slang ("purely and originally American"). But his "perfect book" is yet to come. This work lacks "lust and desire." Many are not poems but statements.

5   LOWELL, AMY. "Edgar Lee Masters and Carl Sandburg." In
    Tendencies in Modern American Poetry. Boston and New York:
    Houghton Mifflin, pp. 200-232.
        Reprint of 1917.2; 1920.12. Responded to: 1921.5; 1927.8.

6   _____. "The Poems of the Month." Bookman 53 (September):
    404-6.
    Brief review of Smoke and Steel.

7   ROSENFELD, PAUL. "Carl Sandburg." Bookman 53 (July):389-96.
        Finds it unfortunate that Sandburg "puts blinders on his
    mind" and does not let life have its full way with him. He has
    failed to refine his material, exercise self-criticism, and be-
    come more than the "rudimentary artist" he seems to be. In the
    spirit of Whitman, however, Sandburg is a "poet priest" for
    America, and he has done for the American language what Synge did
    for the speech of the Gaelic peasantry. Reprinted: 1924.10.

8   UNTERMEYER, LOUIS. "Lyric Fire." Bookman 52 (January):362.
        Review of Smoke and Steel. Calls this both "an epic of
    modern industrialism and a mighty paean to modern beauty."
    Sandburg and Sona Teasdale (in Flame and Shadow) are "united by
    an attention to life that is, first of all, lyrical." Includes
    excerpt from 1920.14.

9   WILSON, ARTHUR. "Sandburg: A Psychiatric Curiosity." Dial
    70 (January):80-81.
        Review of Smoke and Steel. Sandburg has lost what made him
    great--"the ability to determine when he has written something
    good." These poems lack the "certitude of genius." Sandburg is
    "a factory hand in the very hell he abominates." Excerpted:
    1985.5.

10 WOOD, CLEMENT. "Smoke and Steel." New York Call, 9 January,
    p. 6.
        Review of Smoke and Steel. Sandburg is a "misty, rather
    than descriptive or truly evocative poet." He is "the antithesis
    of the imagist demand for sharply evoked image. . . . We see the
    smoke, and miss the steel."
    1985.5.

11 YUST, WALTER. "Carl Sandburg, Human Being." Bookman 52
    (January):285-90.
        Sandburg talks of trying to achieve "a kind of freedom" in
    writing comparable to Nora's fight for something in Ibsen's A
    Doll's House.

1922

1   ANON. "Sandburg's Virile Slabs." New York Times Book Review
    and Magazine, 4 June, p. 11.
        Review of Slabs of the Sunburnt West. Warns that Sandburg
    is "in danger of becoming the Professional Chanter of Virility."
    In this book of "decided merit," Sandburg's excellence comes "not
    in the virile portions, but in those quieter, more restrained
    moments." He is unable to sustain his mood in the long poems.

2   ANON. "Shelf of Fairy Tales." New York Times Book Review,
    19 November, p. 10.
        Review of Rootabaga Stories. Speaks of "the cadences of
    his prose, so often implicit of poetry."

3   BENÉT, W[ILLIAM] R[OSE]. "A Shelf of Poetry." Literary
    Review (New York Post), 22 July, p. 820.
        Review of Slabs of the Sunburnt West. Whether or not
    Sandburg's work endures, his words are "strikingly alive, his
    irony rasps, the impression sinks deep."

4   BOYNTON, P.H. "American Authors of Today. IV. The Voice of
    Chicago: Edgar Lee Masters and Carl Sandburg." English
    Journal 11 (December):610, 617-20.
        In Chicago Poems, Sandburg "treats life frankly because on
    the whole he likes it and believes in it." He describes things
    as they are. His "brutality" is not objectionable. Includes
    brief biographical background. Reprinted: 1924.2; 1925.1.

5   BRITTEN, CLARENCE. "Speaking of By-Products." New Republic
    33 (27 December):126-27.
        Review of Rootabaga Stories. These stories are drawn from
    "some of the stuff going to waste in his poetry factory." The
    collection is poetical, even though it is not printed that way.

6   BRYNNER, WITTER. "The Great Iron Cat--To Carl Sandburg."
    Fugitive 1 (December):110-11.
        Poem addressed to Sandburg.

7   CLARK, ARTHUR MELVILLE. In The Realistic Revolt in Modern
    Poetry. Oxford: Basil Blackwell, pp. 17-24.
        In chapter 4, describes Sandburg and T.S. Eliot as examples
    of "extreme Whitmanists." Having rejected traditional back-
    grounds, they have disqualified themselves from the fellowship of
    poets.

8   COWLEY, MALCOLM. "Two American Poets." Dial 73 (November):
    562-67.
        Review of Slabs of the Sunburnt West. Praises Sandburg's
    diction. In contrast with H.L. Mencken whose interest in the

American language was scholarly and objective, Sandburg "never
wrote an American dictionary, but he does something more
hazardous and exciting: he writes American." His language is
"freshly acquired in which each word has a new and fascinating
meaning." The effects in these poems are "as complex and difficult sometimes as those of Swinburne's most intricate ballades."

9   ELIOT, T.S. "London Letter." Dial 76 (May):512.
     "Some of [Sandburg's] smaller verse is charming; but it
appears to be rather an echo of Mr. Pound, who has done it
better."

10   F., J. "Carl Sandburg Again." Bookman 55 (July):521.
     Review of Slabs of the Sunburnt West. Finds a mellowing in
this book. "To the old music and understanding comes sweetness."
Advises the reader to read the poems aloud for that is "the only
way to understand the deep music that is the essence of this
great poet of common hopes and emotions."

11   FRANK, WALDO DAVID. "Chicago." In The New America. Intro-
     duction by Hugh Walpole. London: Jonathan Cape, pp. 150-53.
     Reprint of 1919.7.

12   GUITERMAN, ARTHUR. "Chanters and Singers." Independent 109
     (5 August):53-54.
     Review of Slabs of the Sunburnt West. "No assortment of
verbal Roman candles and pinwheels and other interjectional
fireworks, no quantity of Whitmanesque catalogues, can supply the
place of coherent and cohering sentences, whether in prose or
verse." Despite the praise of the intelligentsia, this work is
not perfect.

13   HOLDEN, RAYMOND. "Slabs of the Sunburnt West." New Republic
     32 (30 August):26.
     Review of Slabs of the Sunburnt West. Sandburg is a poet
of "great distinction" who gives "color and substance to the
facts of human life." Praises his "personality, genius, perspicacity, fire, love of life." Urges that he leave the Chicago
Daily News; otherwise, this fine poet is "certain to die with his
promise unfulfilled." This collection is on a lower level of
excellence than Chicago Poems because he "can make a false note
seem a true one." Excerpted: 1985.5.

14   LOEBER, WILLIAM. "Reviews: The Literary Tough." Double
     Dealer 3 (February):105-7.
     Examines Chicago Poems, Cornhuskers, and Smoke and Steel in
light of Felix E. Schelling's contention that Sandburg--"the
intellectual tough"--can be ignored because he finds ugly things
and writes about them in an ugly way (see 1922.21). But
Sandburg owes no apology. Out of 441 poems, 199 are tough and
242 are not. He writes "just how it feels for him to be

alive." If his words shock the sensitive, that is not his
limitation but the academic's. Finds the essential Sandburg to
be "gripped by indignation" with a sense of "beauty, joy, grief."
He is able to talk for people and "in the words of their mouths."

15   [LOWELL, AMY.] Dear Sir (or Dear Madam): A Critical Fable.
     Boston and New York: Houghton, Mifflin, pp. 29-33.
        Offers an amusing portrait, in verse, of Sandburg, calling
     him "a strange, gifted creature."

16   MANLY, JOHN MATTHEWS, and EDITH RICKERT. "Carl Sandburg." In
     Contemporary American Literature: Bibliographies and Study
     Outlines. New York: Harcourt, Brace, pp. 275-77.
        The authors offer brief biographical background and sug-
     gestions for reading Sandburg. Includes primary and secondary
     bibliography to 1922. Reprinted and revised: 1929.9.

17   MAYNARD, THEODORE. "Amy Lowell, Carl Sandburg and Edgar Lee
     Masters: The Fallacy of Free Verse." In Our Best Poets:
     English and American. New York: Henry Holt, pp. 194-215.
        Discusses the uneven, disparate elements in Sandburg's
     poetry. Sees a mellowing quality entering the poems.

18   M[ONROE], H[ARRIET]. "His Home Town." Poetry 20 (September):
     332-38.
        Review of Slabs of the Sunburnt West. Praises
     "Washington Monument by Night" (the best), "At the Gates of
     Tombs" (humor both sad and grotesque), "Primer Lesson," and
     "Harsk, Harsk" (good for one or two readings). But regrets
     that the organization of the other poems is not tighter, more
     coherent. The title poem lacks intensity of feeling. Favors
     "The Windy City" because it has more plan and shape than earlier
     poems of similar length.

19   MUSSEY, MABEL H.B. "Books for the Younger Reader." Nation
     115 (6 December):618.
        Review of Rootabaga Stories. Implies that no intelligent
     child could make much sense of this collection.

20   POUND, EZRA. "Ezra Pound on Sandburg." Double Dealer 3
     (May):277-78.
        Responds to William Loeber's study (see 1922.14) to ask
     whose fault it is that Sandburg is a "tough." Wonders why some
     university has not offered him a fellowship "to browse in its
     library and polish his language."

21   SCHELLING, FELIX E. "Carl Sandburg--Rebel." In Appraisements
     and Asperities as to Some Contemporary Writers. Philadelphia
     and London: J.B. Lippincott, pp. 73-78.
        Much of the imagery in Smoke and Steel is "remarkably
     original" in irony and the grotesque. He is "a man without

pose, . . . earnest and manly." His "brutality" is admirable.
(See 1922.14, 20.)

22   SHERMAN, STUART P. "A Note on Carl Sandburg." In Americans.
     New York: Scribner's, pp. 239-45.
         Sandburg is a radical poet whose Slabs of the Sunburnt West
     is difficult to read as a meditation on "God, civilization, and
     immortality." The obscurity in his poems is due to mixed liter-
     ary allegiance and his writing for the "literary smart set"
     rather than for the taxi drivers and clerks with whom he sympa-
     thizes. He is in danger of "leaving his readers with a sense
     either that his conception of the nation is illusory or that
     both he and they inhabit a world of illusions." Includes reprint
     of 1920.13.

23   WOOD, CLEMENT. "A Homer from Hogwallow." Nation 115
     (26 July):96-97.
         Review of Slabs of the Sunburnt West. Finds a kinship in
     word selection with Wylie, Frost, and Robinson. Calls him a
     "word artist" whose method and vocabulary limit his audience. He
     strays further than any American poet from the accepted poetic
     vocabulary. This is the paradox of Sandburg. "If you are
     attuned, receptive, you lay him down with . . . emotional
     thrill." If you inspect his "slang-dipped" lines, none of the
     "magic and beauty" is to be found. Predicts that college cur-
     riculums of 1950 "may bracket his work with Beowulf or the Ancren
     Riwle, as old American or Early Hogwallowan." Excerpted:
     1985.5.

24   YUST, WALTER. "Reviews: Slabs of the Sunburnt West."
     Double Dealer 4 (August):104-6.
         Review of Slabs of the Sunburnt West. Likens reading the
     poems to listening to a symphony. "I sit and wait for meanings."
     Finds here "unspeakable intimations" concerning life, vivid pic-
     tures, deepest irony, and "unique courage to break through syn-
     tactical as well as literary tradition." For these reasons
     three-quarters of the book is rewarding.

                                1923

1   ANON. "Hyacinths and Biscuits." Christian Century 40
     (29 March):390-91.
         Brief review of Rootabaga Pigeons.

2   ANON. "Rootabaga Pigeons." Literary Review, 10 November,
     p. 230.
         Review of Rootabaga Pigeons. Finds these stories "a shade
     inferior in quality" compared to Rootabaga Stories. "Yet for all
     that, Carl Sandburg has invented a new and rootedly American kind
     of fairy story."

3   ANON. "Rootabaga Stories." Dial 74 (February):210.
      Brief review of Rootabaga Stories.

4   AUSTIN, MARY. The American Rhythm. New York: Harcourt,
      Brace, pp. 17, 32.
        Studies the development of verse forms from the primitive
poetic beginnings of the American Indian tribal dances, notes the
rhythmic patterns in Smoke and Steel, and groups Sandburg with
Whitman and others. Reprinted with addenda: 1930.8.

5   B., L. "Rootabaga Pigeons." Freeman 8 (12 December):335.
        Review of Rootabaga Pigeons. Adults may find these stories
charming, but a child of ten will lay the book down "with a
solemn headshake of bored dissatisfaction."

6   BONNER, M.G. "Rootabaga Pigeons." International Book Review,
      23 November, p. 60.
        Review of Rootabaga Pigeons. This is close to the work of
a genius, although some of the writing is "uneven." "It is as
though Carl Sandburg brushed aside every old idea upon which to
build a story and proceeded to make his own out of new materials
which he had discovered."

7   No entry

8   GLASS, EVERETT. "Carl Sandburg." Laughing Horse 1, no. 8:7.
        A parody in verse entitled "I Took Two Friends to a Bull-
fight" with comments on Amy Lowell and Sandburg.

9   HANSEN, MARY. "Carl Sandburg: Poet of the Streets and of
      the Prairie." In Midwest Portraits: A Book of Memories and
      Friendships. New York: Harcourt, Brace, pp. 17-91.
        Covers many of the significant aspects of Sandburg's work
to demonstrate that he was genuine. Describes his Elmhurst
workman, quotes him about his youth, and provides biographical
background. In his use of free verse, Sandburg sought freedom
from both the scholarly mind (set on classical concepts and con-
ventions) and the popular mind (nourished on stereotyped
standards of rhythm and meter).

10   LEE, MUNA. "Reviews." Double Dealer 5 (January):38.
        Review of Rootabaga Stories. As a storyteller, Sandburg
shares affinities with Andersen and Harris. His stories vary
greatly in mood. Some are "unnecessarily harrowing" for a
child's imagination. His fairy tales have "strictly proletarian
fairies."

11   LINDSAY, NICHOLAS VACHEL. So Keep Going to the Sun.
      Memphis: Mrs. Dicken's Bookshop.
        Published by the author to celebrate Sandburg's visit to
the Goodwyn Institute, New York City, 17 November.

12 MacLEAN, A.M. "Rootabaga Pigeons." New York Tribune, 14 October, p. 31.
Review of Rootabaga Pigeons. Finds much novelty in these stories of "eccentric, imaginative beings, bizarre happenings, fascinating turns of language."

13 MARKEY, GENE. "Carl Sandburg" and "Carl Sandburg and J.C. Squire." In Literary Lights: A Book of Caricatures. New York: Knopf, pp. 7, 49.
Two caricatures that depict Sandburg calling upon the Poetry Society of America and reviving the ancient Whistler-Ruskin controversy with Squire.

14 MELCHER, FREDERIC G., comp. "American First Editions: Number 17 . . . Carl Sandburg, 1878." Publisher's Weekly 103 (20 January):149.
Lists first editions of Sandburg's works from Chicago Poems through The Chicago Race Riots with printer's errors in Slabs of the Sunburnt West.

15 MOORE, ANNE C. "Opening the New Children's Books." Bookman 58 (October):188.
Review of Rootabaga Pigeons. Those who found pleasure in Rootabaga Stories will find still more in this collection. Those who did not like the first book should read this one before forming "a final opinion as to the value of Carl Sandburg's contribution to American children's books." The stories are "unequal in content and form" and some of them were not written for children. But some are bound to survive because they are works of art.

16 ____. "The Rootabaga Country." Nation 117 (5 December):651.
Review of Rootabaga Pigeons. "Sandburg's nonsense is fresh nonsense." Has much in common with Edward Lear, but "he is not an imitator of anybody." Finds here much "genuine creative art."

17 NAAR, CONSTANCE. "Back to Rootabaga." New Republic 36 (14 November):313.
Brief review of Rootabaga Pigeons.

18 PHELPS, WILLIAM LYON. "As I Like It." Scribner's Magazine 73 (April):503.
Review of Rootabaga Pigeons. Calls this "a charming, quaintly nonsensical, and highly imaginative" book, better than Smoke and Steel or Chicago Poems.

19 SMITH, HENRY JUSTIN. Deadlines: Being the Quaint, the Amusing, the Tragic Memoirs of a Newsroom. Chicago: Covici-McGee, pp. 113-23.
Reminisces about Sandburg's work as a journalist in Chicago.

20 UNTERMEYER, LOUIS. "Carl Sandburg." In American Poetry since
1900. New York: Henry Holt, pp. 67-87.
Discusses the strengths and weaknesses of each volume of
verse. Calls Sandburg the "emotional democrat" of American
poetry, the "laureate of industrial America." His blend of
"beauty and brutality" is his most "endearing quality." Includes
excerpt from 1916.14 and reprint of 1919.9.

21 VAN DOREN, CARL [C.]. "Flame and Slag: Carl Sandburg, Poet
with Both Fists." Century 106 (September):786-92.
Discusses Sandburg's passion and frequent prosiness. Com-
plains that he is unable or unwilling to write consistently, so
that he throws off poetry that is either "slag" or "flame." But
in the flames one finds beauty, tenderness, and irony mated with
rapture, and so Sandburg is "a genius." Reprinted: 1924.11.

1924

1 BARTLETT, A.H. "Voices from the Great Inland States:
Illinois." Poetry Review 15 (March-April):101-4.
Sandburg's poetry is "a dramatic attack on the grim facts
of life with a vivid sense of beauty."

2 BOYNTON, PERCY H. "The Voice of Chicago: Edgar Lee Masters
and Carl Sandburg." In Some Contemporary Americans: The Personal Equation in Literature. Chicago: University of Chicago
Press, pp. 50-71.
Reprint of 1922.5. Reprinted: 1925.1.

3 CONKLING, GRACE. "Six Books for Children." Yale Review,
n.s. 13 (January):409-10.
Review of Rootabaga Pigeons. The stories are told in "a
rhythmic prose as highly organized as Mr. Sandburg's
poetry. . . . He uses old words as they have never been used
before and new words of his own."

4 DELL, FLOYD. "To Carl Sandburg." In Looking at Life. New
York: Knopf, pp. 258-60.
Comments on Sandburg's tone ("abrupt and vivid"), subjects
("everyday American"), girls (the possibility for something better than everyday life). Sandburg wants the world to do for
itself what he has done about it in his poems: "Stop being dis-
couraged and cynical, quit being afraid of dirt and ugliness, and
trust in its secret dreams."

5 JONES, LLEWELLYN. "Carl Sandburg: Formalist." American
Review 2 (July-August):356-62.
Examines Sandburg's use of form and theme in his poetry.

6 M[ONROE], H[ARRIET]. "Comment: Carl Sandburg." Poetry 24
   (September):320-26.
      Considers Sandburg's themes, emotional impulse, and art,
   and defends his poetic technique.. "He is bent on the business,
   in the deepest sense a poet's business, of seeing our national
   life in the large—its beauty and glory, its baseness and shame."
   He has widened the rhythmic range of English poetry. Includes
   excerpt of 1916.13. Reprinted: 1926.25. Excerpted: 1924.7.

7 _____. "The Free-Verse Movement in America." English Journal
   13 (December):701-2.
      Discusses Sandburg as essentially a lyric poet. His
   rhythms are as "personal as his slow speech and massive gait."
   His subjects are "intensely local and personal." He has never
   written in "exact metrics." Includes excerpt from 1924.6.

8 MUNSON, GORHAM B. "The Single Portent of Carl Sandburg."
   Double Dealer 7 (October):17-26.
      Surveys Sandburg's first four books of poetry and concludes
   that he has written "a large and undeniable amount of dross."
   But he has points of interest and one rare quality—his
   "mysticism"—seen in the remarkable Slabs of the Sunburnt West.
   Discusses his personality, values, vocabulary, and improved
   technique. It is impossible to label his work as a whole beyond
   saying that "it is slack and immediate expression."

9 RASCOE, BURTON. "Carl Sandburg." Literary Review 5
   (27 September):1-2.
      Describes Sandburg's physical features and surveys his
   formative years to help explain his temperament and his "humanitarian radicalism." Notes that he is freeing himself of social
   criticism and propaganda and is becoming "fanciful, imagistic and
   elegiac." His one weakness is a "deficient critical sense." But
   he seems to intimate more, and this is a strength. He speaks for
   the people to whom Whitman wanted to appeal. "Sandburg has remained at heart one of them." Includes details of a visit with
   him at the Daily News office in Chicago.

10 ROSENFELD, PAUL. "Carl Sandburg." In Port of New York:
    Essays on Fourteen American Moderns. New York: Harcourt,
    Brace, pp. 65-81.
       Sandburg is "sure of living." Discusses his themes and
    artistry and the uncertainty of his development. Finds a
    "weariness" in Slabs of the Sunburnt West and a "wish to evade
    feeling" in Rootabaga Stories. Includes reprint from 1921.7.
    Reprinted: 1961.16.

11 VAN DOREN, CARL. "Flame and Slag: Carl Sandburg." In Many
    Minds. New York: Knopf, pp. 136-50.
       Reprint of 1923.21.

12   WEIRICK, BRUCE. "The Contemporary Renaissance." In From
     Whitman to Sandburg in American Poetry: A Critical Survey.
     New York: Macmillan, pp. 193-95, 210-21.
          Rates Sandburg as the leading Midwest poet. Calls him a
     "humanitarian revolutionist" and, perhaps, "the greatest American
     poet since Whitman," of whom he is a descendant.

                                1925

1   BOYNTON, PERCY H. "Voice of Chicago--Edgar Lee Masters and
     Carl Sandburg." In Some Contemporary Americans: The Personal
     Equation in Literature. Chicago: University of Chicago
     Press, pp. 50-71.
          Reprint of 1922.5; 1924.2.

2   CARNEVALI, EMANUEL. "Our Great Carl Sandburg." In A Hurried
     Man. Paris: Three Mountains Press, pp. 233-40.
          Review of Smoke and Steel. Summarizes the images and mes-
     sage in each poem. Praises Sandburg's tenderness, pity, lesson
     of "health and strength," use of slang, and depiction of nature
     in "beautiful words." But he suffers from unnecessary repeti-
     tion, an "unsympathetic boisterousness," as well as a lack of
     "poetic spirit" and "lust and desire." Instead of being wise,
     Sandburg "sees if he can trick wisdom into a phrase or two." He
     is "the poet of America's good qualities."

*3   FRANKENSTEIN, ALFRED V. Syncopating Saxophones. N.p.:
     R.O. Ballou, pp. 73-78.
          Cited in 1963.8.

4   HANSEN, HARRY. "Carl Sandburg: Poet of the Prairies."
     Pictorial Review 26 (September):2, 114-18.
          Biographical article. Stresses parallels between Sandburg
     and Lincoln such as their concern with plain people, their care-
     ful choice of words, and their straightforward manner.

*5   _____. Carl Sandburg: The Man and His Poetry. Girard,
     Kans.: Haldeman Julius.
          Cited in 1963.8.

6   JONES, LLEWELLYN. "Carl Sandburg: Formalist." In First
     Impressions: Essays on Poetry, Criticism, and Prosody. New
     York: Knopf, pp. 53-68.
          Shows Sandburg's conscious use of "quantitative syllable
     rhythm" and discusses his content, satire, and children's sto-
     ries. Tries to dispel the stereotype of Sandburg as a rough,
     radical free-verse prose-poet. Often he is "an aesthetic poet."

7   KREYMBORG, ALFRED. "Chicago." In Troubadour: An Auto-
     biography. New York: Boni & Liveright, pp. 279-85.
          Memoir in which Sandburg's "free spiritual voice," "his
     intuition for the lyric impulse of the land," his unassuming
     manner, and his work as journalist are all recommended. Re-
     printed: 1957.6.

8   VAN DOREN, CARL [C.], and MARK VAN DOREN. "Carl Sandburg
     1878--." In American and British Literature since 1890. New
     York: Appleton-Century, pp. 22-27.
          Discusses Sandburg's early verse (through Slabs of the
     Sunburnt West). See 1939.18 for a broader study with consider-
     able attention devoted to Sandburg's development as a poet.

9   WALSH, ERNEST. "Seventeen Poems: Carl Sandburg." This
     Quarter 1 (Spring):74.
          Poem dedicated to Sandburg.

10   WOOD, CLEMENT. "Carl Sandburg: A Hymn from Hogwallow."
     In Poets of America. New York: E.P. Dutton, pp. 246-61.
          Chicago Poems was strong, but the succeeding volumes have
     deteriorated.

                              1926

1   AIKEN, CONRAD. "Sentiment of the Quotidian." New Republic 49
     (8 December):86-87.
          Review of Selected Poems of Carl Sandburg. Summarizes
     Rebecca West's preface (see 1926.41) and calls Sandburg a
     "sentimentalist." Contrary to West's opinion, the poet never
     strikes profoundly into the "inner life" of any of his working
     folk. "He is essentially a lover of surfaces" and therefore like
     Vachel Lindsay he does not endure rereading. Excerpted: 1985.5.

2   ANON. "Books in Brief." Nation 123 (10 November):487.
          Review of Selected Poems of Carl Sandburg. Calls him the
     "loquaciously introspective genius of the Middle West."

3   ANON. "Carl Sandburg in England." Living Age 329
     (3 April):72-73.
          Review of Selected Poems of Carl Sandburg. Praises his
     optimism and absence of sentimentality. Like Whitman, his out-
     look is virile and modern, but Whitman "never wrote anything of
     such sheer beauty as the poem 'Lost!'"

4   ANON. "Sandburg and Stallings." Bookman 63 (May):261.
          Brief review of Selected Poems of Carl Sandburg.

5   ANON. "Selected Poetry." Booklist 23 (December):124.
        Brief review of Selected Poems of Carl Sandburg. Calls
this a "judicious selection."

6   No entry

7   BABCOCK, CHARLOTTE F. "Carl Sandburg." Forum 76
     (September):432-33.
        Poem about Sandburg.

8   BARTON, WILLIAM E. "The Abraham Lincoln of the Prairies."
     World's Work 52 (May):102-5.
        Review of Abraham Lincoln: The Prairie Years. Although
there is not much new material here, the book is notable because
Sandburg gives "new atmosphere and color" to his portrait of
Lincoln and picture of the times. Sandburg's "background of
experience" and "poetic temperament" qualify him to write notable
history, not a biography, and so this is "real literature" in
which there is an "unimportant mistake" on every page.

9   BONNER, M.G. "Nonfiction." International Book Review,
     26 May, p. 383.
        Review of Abraham Lincoln: The Prairie Years. This is a
superb work in which Sandburg succeeds in capturing fully "the
appealing personality of Lincoln."

10   BROWN, R.C.E. "Nonfiction." North America 223 (26 June):353.
        Review of Abraham Lincoln: The Prairie Years. Sandburg's
"vividly human portrait" of Lincoln is given "a richly peopled
background." This picture has "vitality, realism, sympathy and
discrimination." It holds the reader's attention and commands
respect.

11   COOK, S.L. "Abraham Lincoln: The Prairie Years." Boston
     Transcript, 6 February, p. 2.
        Review of Abraham Lincoln: The Prairie Years. Undoubtedly
it has done Sandburg much good to write this "able, rugged book."

12   FARRAR, JOHN. "Carl Sandburg's Masterpiece." Bookman 63
     (March):86.
        Review of Abraham Lincoln: The Prairie Years. Sandburg
could be "the supreme American novelist" of his period. He com-
bines the depth of Dreiser with "a stronger grasp of broad
aspects of human character and a limpid, graphic style." The
biography's success is probably due to the fact that Sandburg
and Lincoln are so alike. Carlyle and Macaulay immediately come
to mind.

13   G., B. "A Poet from the Mid-West." Boston Transcript,
     6 October, p. 4.
         Review of Selected Poems of Carl Sandburg. Questions
     whether Sandburg writes poetry at all, "unless we violently and
     without warrant tear the word poetry from its roots in the past."
     His verse lacks form. In his view of life, he reminds us of
     James Whitcomb Riley.

14   GARD, WAYNE. "Abraham Lincoln: The Prairie Years."
     International Book Review 4 (February):189.
         Interview in which Sandburg talks about his purpose in
     writing Abraham Lincoln: The Prairie Years. He wanted to
     "restore him to the common people." The simplicity of style,
     pictorial quality of his words, and directness and economy of his
     narrative suggest the epics of Homer.

15   GHENT, W.J. Review of Abraham Lincoln: The Prairie Years.
     Outlook 142 (24 February):296.
         Sandburg "vividly recreates the man and shows him moving
     about in the midst of his environment." Sandburg's "luminous
     realism" is probably unsurpassed by any other writer who has
     attempted the same.

16   HANSEN, HARRY. "The First Reader." Book World, 12 October,
     p. 4.
         Review of Selected Poems of Carl Sandburg. Sandburg's
     relationship with Whitman is overworked by critics. His mind
     has grown gradually more conservative. The reader must clear
     his mind of pedantry in order to be moved by Sandburg's music,
     rhythm, and authentic singing.

17   HARMON, LUCY. "A Study of the Vocabulary of Carl Sandburg."
     M.A. thesis, University of Chicago, 24 pp.
         Examines Sandburg's use of the vernacular in his poetry and
     relates his vocabulary to theme and artistry.

18   H[ARRINGTON], W[ILLIAM] E. "Book Reviews." Sewanee Review 34
     (October–December):506–8.
         Review of Abraham Lincoln: The Prairie Years. Calls this
     a new kind of biography, a "living epic of the frontier."
     Sandburg tells with "dignity and beauty" the story of the prairie
     settlement, cotton, and factory slavery. "Against this back-
     ground the personality of Lincoln is relative, intimate, smacking
     of the soil and freedom.

19   HAYDEN, K.S. Review of Abraham Lincoln: The Prairie Years.
     Annual of the American Academy 126 (July):164.
         Sandburg's biography lives. It is more than an ordinary
     biography; it is "a captured atmosphere, a portrait done with
     the exquisite, patient care, the intent reverence, the elusive
     tenderness of a Rembrandt."

20   HILL, FRANK ERNEST. "Selected from Carl Sandburg." New York
      Herald Tribune Books, 10 October, p. 4.
          Review of Selected Poems of Carl Sandburg. Calls this a
      "satisfactory" volume and praises Sandburg's fine use of idiom,
      his rhythm, heart, and philosophy. Finds him limited as a
      prophet (or seer) in music and power. "He has worked originally,
      he has improved and refined part of what he took, and he has
      given a gift as definitive as Whitman's, if smaller, to an
      America that Whitman foresaw, but never knew." Excerpted:
      1985.5.

21   M., L.B. "The Frontier Book Shelf." Frontier 7 (November):
      [26].
          Review of Abraham Lincoln: The Prairie Years. Sandburg
      brings his subject to life with "great" detail and a "loving
      exactness." Only he could have written this book because he is
      "a poet, an idealist, a rough man of the people, a man of the
      Middle West."

22   McBRIDE, H. "The Lincoln of the Plains." Dial 80 (June):
      513-16.
          Review of Abraham Lincoln: The Prairie Years. Summarizes
      Sandburg's viewpoints and comments on his style and organization
      of materials.

23   MEARNS, HUGHES, ed. "Carl Sandburg." In Carl Sandburg. The
      Pamphlet Poets. New York: Simon & Schuster, p. 5.
          Says that these poems represent Sandburg in "a variety of
      strong and tender moods." They are "a distillation of a rich
      American experience." Behind all his writing is the theme of
      "an astonishing life among men and things." His speech is of
      the common man. Includes primary bibliography and brief bio-
      graphical information.

24   MENCKEN, H.L. Prejudices. New York: Knopf, p. 86.
          Rates Sandburg the best of those in the new poetry move-
      ment, as well as the "soundest and most intriguing."

25   MONROE, HARRIET. "Carl Sandburg." In Poets and Their Art.
      New York: Macmillan, pp. 29-38.
          Reprint of 1924.6 with excerpt from 1916.13.

26   MOORE, ANNE C[ARROLL]. "The Children's Lincoln." New York
      Herald Tribune Books, 21 February, p. 8.
          Review of Abraham Lincoln: The Prairie Years. The mean-
      ings and surprises in this book are for readers of any age. The
      biography is "full of familiar stories in new settings, it is
      soaked with facts and it is also saturated with beauty."

27 _____. "Nonfiction." <u>Bookman</u> 63 (April):209.
   Review of <u>Abraham Lincoln: The Prairie Years</u>. "A veri-
table mine of human treasure from which to read aloud or to pore
over by oneself."

28 MORRISON, C.M. "New Books." <u>Literary Review</u>, 13 February,
   p. 1.
   Review of <u>Abraham Lincoln: The Prairie Years</u>. This is a
biography of the nation and the story of the world of that time.
"The Midlands of Yesterday knew the real Lincoln. Carl Sandburg
has given him back to America and its Midlands."

29 PEARSON, EDMUND. "The Book Table." <u>Outlook</u> 144 (10 November):344.
   Review of <u>Selected Poems of Carl Sandburg</u>. These are
poems, although sometimes they are too much of the "sweat-and-
hairy-chest school of literature." Whether poetry or prose,
"they are remarkable and magnificent."

30 R., D. Review of <u>Abraham Lincoln: The Prairie Years</u>.
   <u>Independent</u> 116 (13 February):193.
   Calls this "the best, the noblest" poem that Sandburg has
yet written. In spiritual value, insight, interpretation, feeling, and sense, it is also the "best picture" of Lincoln we have.

31 ROBERTS, R.E. "Sandburg and Lincoln." <u>New Statesman</u> 27,
   supp. (5 June):iii.
   Review of <u>Abraham Lincoln: The Prairie Years</u>. Calls this
"a masterpiece" which suits its subject. The book requires few
alterations or omissions.

32 ROBINSON, L.E. "New Biographies of Lincoln." <u>Yale Review</u> 16
   (October):183-85.
   Review of <u>Abraham Lincoln: The Prairie Years</u>. Says that
this is an unorthodox biography because it is the work not of a
trained biographer but of an artist.

33 SHERMAN, STUART P. "Carl Sandburg's Lincoln." <u>New York
   Herald Tribune Books</u>, 7 February, pp. 1, 3.
   Review of <u>Abraham Lincoln: The Prairie Years</u>. Discusses
Sandburg's portrayal of the Lincoln myth. The effect is "vital
and stimulating." It is a book to "'live in.'" The underlying
idea is "rationalistic and liberal." The book allows us to
become better acquainted with Sandburg as well as with Lincoln.
Reprinted: 1927.10. Excerpted: 1985.5.

34 SHERWOOD, ROBERT E. "When Lincoln Rode the Circuit." <u>New
   York Times Book Review</u>, 14 February, p. 1.
   Review of <u>Abraham Lincoln: The Prairie Years</u>. Calls this
an "intensely individual" achievement in which Sandburg gives
"greater play to his own lyrical imagination." His guesses about

Lincoln are "far better than most." It is important as a piece
of creative writing but not necessarily as a contribution to
Lincoln literature.

35   SKINNER, CONSTANCE LINDSAY. "Songs that Give Reason for
     Singing." North American Review 223 (December):26-27, 698-99.
        Review of Selected Poems of Carl Sandburg. At his worst,
Sandburg is "diffuse, clownish or vulgar." At his best, he is
"an inescapable and irresistible emotional force." The book is
a "treasure."

36   STAPLES, ARTHUR G. "Carl Sandburg: Poet and Newspaperman."
     In Bowdoin College: An Institute of Modern Literature at
     Bowdoin College, Brunswick, Maine, from May 5 to May 16, 1925,
     in Commemoration of the Centennial Year of the Graduation of
     the Class of 1825. Lewiston, Maine: Lewiston Journal,
     pp. 55, 69-74.
        Reports on a "stirringly emotional evening" with Sandburg
at Bowdoin Institute. He is the product of the life and action
of newspaper people. In performance, he uses "the emotions of
the voice as a spur to the imagination." His voice is of "rich
and mystic music." Summarizes Sandburg's views on realism and
romanticism and his definition of art. Sandburg, like
Longfellow, can be rough or gentle when he wants to be.

37   STRACHEY, J. ST. L. "New Books." Spectator 136 (May):911.
     Review of Abraham Lincoln: The Prairie Years.

38   UNTERMEYER, LOUIS. "Carl Sandburg." Saturday Review of
     Literature 3 (30 October):251.
        Review of Selected Poems of Carl Sandburg. Sandburg is
"the laureate of industrial America" whose works comprise the
fragments of a wandering yet somehow unified saga." Finds
annoying Sandburg's "gnomic idiom," his reliance on abstraction
or cryptic mannerisms. Feels that he has not received his due
as a craftsman. His rhythms are "masterly." Sees a definite
development in the work. (See 1939.5.)

39   VAN DOREN, MARK. "First Glance: The Prairie Years." Nation
     122 (10 February):149.
        Review of Abraham Lincoln: The Prairie Years. Sandburg
has presented the elements of Lincoln's mystery "more subtly and
more completely" than has anyone else. In spite of the occa-
sional poetry, the book is "amply and profoundly beautiful."

40   WEST, REBECCA. "The Voice of Chicago." Saturday Review of
     Literature 3 (4 September):81-83.
        Like Robert Burns, Sandburg is a national poet because he
writes of the "real America." He expresses the monumental big-
ness and fecundity of the central states. His image is so vast
that it requires a thousand poems. "The main determinant of his

art is the power of his native idiom to deal with the inner life
of man." Reprinted: 1926.41. Responded to: 1927.6, 8.

41   WEST, REBECCA, ed. "Preface." In Selected Poems of Carl
     Sandburg. London: Jonathan Cape; New York: Harcourt, Brace,
     pp. 15-28.
        Reprint of 1926.40. Excerpted: 1985.5.

42   WHITE, W.A. Review of Abraham Lincoln: The Prairie Years.
     New York World, 7 February, p. 6m.
        "No one but a poet with a poet's patience and a poet's
     understanding heart could have written this book." Sandburg's
     Lincoln takes on "reality, strong, rank, pungent, gorgeous
     reality."

43   WILLIAMS, STANLEY THOMAS. The American Spirit in Letters.
     New Haven: Yale University Press, p. 304 and passim.
        Brief reference to Sandburg as "an apotheosis of the immi-
     grant." Finds in his poetry that "every hindrance of conven-
     tional thought and form collapses." He is Whitman's "most
     tempestuous progeny." His Lincoln biography was "bizarre."

44   WOOD, CLEMENT. Poets of America. New York: E.P. Dutton,
     p. 261.
        Argues that Sandburg has enough vision, affirmation,
     melody, and contact with unsung life to become the day's leading
     poet. But finds in his poetry an unending vocabulary, belliger-
     ence, and obsession with the uncouth.

45   WOODBURN, J.A. "Book Reviews." American Political Science
     Review 20 (August):674-77.
        Review of Abraham Lincoln: The Prairie Years. Finds
     interest on every page. As storyteller, realist, interpreter,
     and artist, Sandburg never leads the reader astray. Excerpted:
     1985.5.

46   WOOLF, LEONARD. "Out of the Wilderness." Nation and
     Athenaeum 39 (1 May):130.
        Review of Abraham Lincoln: The Prairie Years. Sandburg's
     biography gives the reader "an overpowering sense of reality"
     in Lincoln's character.

47   WYATT, EDITH [F.]. "Lincoln at Home." New Republic 46
     (17 March):116-17.
        Review of Abraham Lincoln: The Prairie Years. Finds here
     many "swift and poetic characterizations" of men and women and a
     fine tone of scrupulous truth." The economic history in the book
     is Sandburg's "greatest prose contribution." Its most moving
     poetic value is "its power in making Lincoln's thought a part of
     the world-thought of the future."

1927

1   ADAMS, FRANKLIN P. "Sandburg's Songbag." Saturday Review of
Literature 4 (3 December):365.
. Review of The American Songbag. This "fascinating garland"
has been compiled with "passionate reverence and loving enthusiasm." Calls it "a vigorous job, done caressingly."

2   ANON. "Brief Notices." Poetry 31 (October):53.
Review of Selected Poems of Carl Sandburg. If critics of
Sandburg have dealt with him inadequately, it is because most of
them have "minds incapable of dealing adequately with realities."

3   BROCK, H.I. "Our Native Songs Are Only Rarely Truly Native."
New York Times Book Review, 18 December, pp. 6, 19.
Review of The American Songbag. Calls this a "very bulky
collection indeed." Comments on the words and music.

4   COBLENTZ, STANTON A. "The Repudiation of the Beautiful." In
The Literary Revolution. New York: Frank-Maurice, pp. 91–92.
The modern tendency among writers has been "to sully and
obscure the beautiful." Refers to Sandburg and the influence on
his poetry of the city and streets full of people. Reprinted:
1969.2.

5   DEUTSCH, BABETTE. "The Voice of the Land." New York Herald-
Tribune Books, 4 December, p. 3.
Review of The American Songbag. Sandburg recognizes that
"it was not so much in the individual vision as in the racial
experience which is the stuff of common balladry that the history
of the nation was to be found." This is an excellent collection
deserving of respect. "It is packed with beauty and information." Finds fault only with the arrangements. Sometimes the
melodies have been "prettified and spoiled."

6   FRANK, FLORENCE KIPER. "Rebecca West's Chicago." New
Republic 49 (19 January):252.
In a letter comments on West's introduction to Sandburg's
poems (see 1926.40, 41). West "adds rather to her reputation as
brilliant fictionist than to her prestige as social interpreter."

7   GOSTELOW, WILLARD F. "Carl Sandburg." Prairie Schooner 1
(October):291–98.
Survey of Sandburg's career.

8   JONES, HOWARD MUMFORD. "Backgrounds of Sorrow." Virginia
Quarterly Review 3 (January):111–23.
Review of Selected Poems of Carl Sandburg. Responds to
Louis Untermeyer (see 1919.9), Amy Lowell (see 1920.12; 1921.5),
and Rebecca West (see 1926.40, 41). Says the total impression of
Sandburg is not one of brutality or coarseness but "of a brooding

and mystic gentleness." His profoundest belief is that the
"universe is mainly cruel and capricious, that meaning is given
it only by the lives of men." To call Sandburg a national poet
is "to confuse all literary values." Since Chicago Poems he has
developed from "rebellion through scepticism to resignation." In
the later volumes there is a richness in fantasy, in lyricism, in
a satisfaction with "beauty for its own sake." For many readers
the central difficulty is his diction, but if examined carefully
readers will find in the volumes "an extraordinary freshness and
variety of diction, a command over words." Although he suffers--
from a monotonous recurrence of certain themes, a predictable
view about the proletariat, stylistic idiosyncrasies, and pessimism about the view that art is eternal--overall he is "the most
richly endowed of all our living poets, and the most unpredicta-
ble." His command of words is as original as Shakespeare's.

9   LOVETT, ROBERT MORSS. "Books." Dial 82 (February):153-56.
      Review of Selected Poems of Carl Sandburg. Sandburg's
great theme is "human experience." His chief power is "that of
entering sympathetically into the experience of others." Finds
West's introduction to be "artificial."

10 SHERMAN, STUART [P.]. "Carl Sandburg's Lincoln." In The Main
      Stream. New York and London: Scribner's, pp. 8-16.
      Reprint of 1926.33.

11 SIMON, R.A. Review of The American Songbag. New York Evening
      Post, 10 December, p. 14.
      In this "neatly assembled" anthology with "well-made"
arrangements, Sandburg's notes are "short and helpful, although I
should have preferred a little less 'wistful' orchestration."

12 VAN DOREN, MARK. "First Glance: The American Songbag."
      Nation 125, supp. (7 December):646.
      Review of The American Songbag. Sandburg's Lincoln biog-
raphy and this collection have a common origin in his feeling
that contemporary American poetry, perhaps including his own, was
not getting at the heart of the people. This collection is a
contribution to American history "in an entirely serious sense."

1928

1   ADAMS, FRANKLIN P. "Sandburg's Songbag." Saturday Review of
      Literature 4 (3 December):365.
      Review of The American Songbag. Calls this a "glorious,
beautiful, brimming, singable, abundant compilation." Sandburg
has gathered these songs "with passionate reverence and loving
enthusiasm. . . . It is a vigorous job, done caressingly."

2   AIKEN, CONRAD. "Those Unknown Singers." <u>Dial</u> 84 (May):
    425-27.
        Review of <u>The American Songbag</u>. This is a book about the
    America Sandburg loves. But these folk songs are at the lowest
    level, reflecting spiritual poverty in their crudeness.

3   ANON. "Better Books for All-Round Reading." <u>World Tomorrow</u>
    11 (December):522.
        Review of <u>Good Morning, America</u>. Finds here "the inimi-
    table Sandburg."

4   ANON. "New Books Await the Children." <u>New York Times Book</u>
    <u>Review</u>, 23 September, p. 10.
        Review of <u>Abraham Lincoln Grows Up</u>. Finds the viewpoint
    throughout to be, "in general, rather mature for any but fairly
    well-developed minds."

5   No entry

6   BRICKNELL, HERSCHEL. "The Literary Landscape." <u>North</u>
    <u>American Review</u> 226 (December):unpaged advertiser.
        Review of <u>Good Morning, America</u>. This book is typical of
    Sandburg, which means that "a good deal of it resembles prose."

7   CRAWFORD, JOHN. "Good to Feel the Warmth of Sandburg." <u>New</u>
    <u>York Evening Post</u>, 3 November, p. 9m.
        Review of <u>Good Morning, America</u>. Sandburg intensifies and
    makes dramatic the everyday aspects of experience. These lyrics
    are "whimsical impressions, brusquely humorous salutations,
    wistful questionings, nature sketches, minor epics in homespun
    philosophy, and emphatic 'yeas.'"

8   DEUTSCH, BABETTE. "Seen During a Moment." <u>New York Herald-</u>
    <u>Tribune Books</u>, 21 October, p. 2.
        Review of <u>Good Morning, America</u>. Sandburg shares with
    Whitman certain feelings about the world: perplexity, mystery,
    "pitying tenderness." But his rare dry humor and "sense of
    transience" keeps him from falling into Whitmanesque sentimen-
    tality. He is among those men who are "struggling to realize
    this nation." Excerpted: 1985.5.

9   HANSEN, HARRY. "Lincoln Comes Home." In <u>Further Adventures</u>
    <u>in Essay Reading</u>. Edited by Thomas Ernest Rankin, Amos R.
    Morris, Melvin T. Stone, and Carlton F. Wells. New York:
    Harcourt, pp. 44-54.
        Calls <u>Abraham Lincoln: The Prairie Years</u> a "remarkable
    book" because of Sandburg's "rich emotion," his "understanding of
    the significance of isolated facts," and his ability to make
    Lincoln's character live.

10   HOLCOMB, ERNEST LOLITA. "Whitman and Sandburg." English
      Journal 17 (September):549-55.
          Similarities between Whitman and Sandburg are found in
      terms of "fidelity to the here and now," "concrete pictures,"
      realism, "Americanisms," and freedom. Contrasts their poems and
      concludes that Sandburg is a "surer master of his art" in his
      more effective use of contrast, his more unified and compact
      expression, his avoidance of sentimentality, and his emphasis of
      "divinity" over "dirt" in his poetry.

11   HUTCHINSON, PERCY. "Carl Sandburg Sings Out, 'Good Morning,
      America.'" New York Times Book Review, 21 October, p. 2.
          Review of Good Morning, America. In his endeavor to be
      "distinctively national," Sandburg became parochial and therefore
      largely defeated "the very end he so earnestly sought." The
      tragedy of Sandburg is that he cannot, or will not, "discipline
      either his art or himself." Views Good Morning, America as "a
      salutation to America, an appreciation, an exhortation and a
      prophecy." Excerpted: 1985.5.

12   KARSNER, DAVID. "Carl Sandburg." In Sixteen Authors to One:
      Intimate Sketches of Leading American Story Tellers. Illus-
      trated by Esther M. Mattsson. New York: Lewis Copeland,
      pp. 145-55.
          Finds in the poetry "a portrait of Sandburg himself."
      Covers his life and his views on Lincoln, politics, songs,
      children's stories, and the life of a writer.

13   KISSACK, ROBERT A. "Ballads in Print." Bookman 67 (March):
      101.
          Brief review of The American Songbag.

14   LOWELL, AMY. "To Carl Sandburg." In Selected Poems of Amy
      Lowell. New York: Houghton, Mifflin, pp. 84-85.
          Poem about Sandburg.

15   MENCKEN, H.L. "American Folk-Song." American Mercury 13
      (March):383.
          Review of The American Songbag. "The volume would lose
      three-fourths of its peculiar interest if there were no Sandburg
      in it." His commentary is "charming." Points out a few errors.

16   MERRIAM, DORIS S. "Book Shelf." Frontier 8 (March):141, 143.
          Review of The American Songbag. Many of the songs are
      "weirdly unexpected," but all are of value as a contribution to
      song and folk history of America.

17   MUNSON, GORHAM B. Destinations: A Canvass of American Liter-
      ature since 1900. New York: J.H. Sears, pp. 3, 101.
          As a member of the "Middle Generation" of poets, Sandburg
      represents "the romantic spirit in full insurgence." But he has

failed to develop. His later books are a repeat of his earlier ones.

18 NEVINS, ALLAN. "Abe Lincoln Grows Up." Saturday Review of Literature 5 (10 November):346.
       Brief review of Abraham Lincoln: The Prairie Years. Praises Sandburg's "panorama of Western life." Comments on his "minute fidelity" to detail, his "warmly human sympathy."

19 NILES, ABBE. "Sandburg's Reliques." New Republican 54, supp. (21 March):170.
       Review of The American Songbag. Calls this "the supreme American song-collection." It benefits from Sandburg's "love and knowledge of songs in their dual aspect, as literature, and as things to be sung."

*20 PAELIK, MARTIN. "Smoke and Steel." Englische Studien 62 (March):415–20.
       Review of Smoke and Steel. Cited in 1963.8.

21 POUND, LOUISE. "America Sings." Yale Review, n.s. 18 (September):202–3.
       Review of The American Songbag. Here Sandburg acknowledges his indebtedness to American ballads and songs. His own poetry, "with its free and swinging rhythms, echoes the spirit of the songs he has brought together in his collection."

22 REDFIELD, MARGARET PARK. "Book Reviews." American Journal of Sociology 33 (March):819–22.
       Review of The American Songbag. This "work of art" gives expression to the "sentiments and emotional attitudes" of an entire nation. The grouping is "graceful."

23 SEAVER, EDWIN L. "Hyacinths and Biscuits." New Republic 57 (5 December):76.
       Review of Good Morning, America. Since 1914, Sandburg has had nothing new to say and, worse, he is saying it with less vigor. More criticism and less "rhapsody and amused tolerance" from his readers might have helped him. He is still unable to establish values and articulate criticism of his America.

24 T., J.D. "More Americans for Your Christmas List." Outlook and Independent 150 (19 December):1375.
       Review of Good Morning, America. Obscurities in his poetry arise from an attempt to reconcile the ugly and the beautiful. The reader fails to understand the impulse behind the poetry because of the "maze of words," the "strange union of incongruities," the "inconsistent thoughts" and "unknown emotions."

25 VAN DOREN, MARK. "The Tender Swede." Nation 127
    (31 October):456-57.
        Review of Good Morning, America. Comments on Sandburg's
    humor, "talkiness," and "love of American lingo." But finds no
    difference between "'a hard old earth' and 'a sweet young
    earth'"--attributable, no doubt, to Sandburg's "tender brain."

26 WHIPPLE, LEON. "Poets Americano." Survey Graphic 61
    (1 November):169.
        Review of Good Morning, America. Calls this "a paean to
    this great gorgeous shield of American earth." His free rhythms
    serve his vision "with more beauty and honesty" than anybody
    since Whitman.

27 WHIPPLE, T.K. "Carl Sandburg." In Spokesmen: Modern Writers
    and American Life. New York: D. Appleton, pp. 161-83.
        Examines Sandburg's first four volumes and defines his
    aesthetic limitations. The impression they leave is "one of much
    power ill controlled." The work is varied but "uneven and un-
    certain, . . . a medley of high poetry, flat prose and shown
    counterfeit." Comments on his sensitivity, zest for living,
    "power of realization," sensuous experience, melancholy, emo-
    tional instability, contemplative mind, tragic sense of life,
    and agnosticism. "His seems to be a deeply religious nature
    which has never found a religion." He is a "yea-saying psalmist"
    in form but most important in feeling. Reprinted: 1963.23;
    1978.21.

1929

1   CHAPIN, ELSA, and THOMAS RUSSELL. A New Approach to Poetry.
    Chicago: University of Chicago Press, pp. 41-42, 48, 66-67,
    82, 89.
        Examines how form is essential to a full interpretation
    of a poem. Rewrites "Nocturne in a Disabled Brickyard" and
    "Fog" as prose and shows that form is dictated by content in
    "Grass."

2   COMPTON, CHARLES H. "Who Reads Carl Sandburg?" South
    Atlantic Quarterly 28 (April):190-200.
        Surveys one hundred recent readers of Sandburg's poetry at
    the St. Louis Public Library and summarizes their opinions.
    Finds a correspondence between their estimation of his place in
    American literature and that of literary critics. Concludes
    that the poetry goes down deep into the life of this century.
    His readers "in the most part have the same street addresses as
    the characters of Sandburg's own creations." Excerpted:
    1934.2.

3   COOK, HOWARD WILLARD. "Carl Sandburg." In Our Poets of
    Today. New York: Dodd, Mead, pp. 129–35.
        Reprint of 1918.3.

4   FERRIS, HELEN. "Books to Delight Our Youngest Readers."
    Bookman 70 (29 November):309.
        Review of Rootabaga Country. Praises Peggy Bacon's illus-
    trations. "No artist could have caught more aptly the spirit of
    Carl Sandburg's stories than she."

5   GOLDSMITH, SOPHIE. "The Harvest of Children's Books." Nation
    129 (20 November):600.
        Review of Rootabaga Country. Admirers of Sandburg will
    welcome these selected tales. Praises the new illustrations.

6   GREGORY, HORACE. "Sandburg's Salutation." Poetry 33
    (January):214–18.
        Review of Good Morning, America. Sandburg and America are
    one. His function is "the business of making articulate the
    speech of inarticulate masses." What Robert Burns has done for
    Scotland, Sandburg has done for Chicago and the Middle West.
    Both have taken poetry out of the complexly formal category.
    Examines Sandburg's slow and natural growth as a poet, his
    broad appeal, his "real strength which lies in the minute com-
    monplaces, expressing many moods, ideas and desires of many
    people."

7   HERRMANN, EVA. On Parade: Caricatures by Eva Herrmann.
    Edited by Erich Posselt. New York: Coward-McCann,
    pp. 130–33.
        One caricature of Sandburg and a primary bibliography for
    the years 1915–28.

8   KREYMBORG, ALFRED. "Springfield, Spoon River and the
    Prairies." In Our Singing Strength: An Outline of American
    Poetry (1620–1930). New York: Coward-McCann, pp. 382–94.
        Unlike Masters, Sandburg knows how to sing. In his poetry
    we find a combination of "reality and romance, truth and beauty,
    speech and song." He is the pioneer West's "foremost singer."
    With Good Morning, America, Sandburg shows a firmer handling of
    the materials of life, but he is "dangerously repetitious" in
    places. The best pages of Chicago Poems are his portraits of
    the worker. Cornhuskers represents an advance: broader adven-
    tures, keener imagination, more certain artistry. Smoke and
    Steel is his "finest volume," for the man and the artist have
    reached maturity. Slabs of the Sunburnt West is inferior:
    "sketchy, repetitious, rather weary." Includes brief biographi-
    cal background beginning with his contributions to Poetry in
    1914. Reprinted: 1934.4.

9   MANLY, JOHN MATTHEWS, and EDITH RICKERT. "Carl Sandburg."
    In Contemporary American Literature: Bibliographies and Study
    Outlines. Introduction and revision by Fred B. Millett. New
    York: Harcourt, pp. 275-77.
        Reprint of 1922.16 with updated material.

10 REICHARD, GLADYS A. "Book Reviews." Journal of American
    Folklore 42 (January-March):81-82.
        Review of The American Songbag. This is a book "to be
    enjoyed, not analyzed." These songs are for any mood, "no matter
    how depressed or exalted," with or without a musical instrument.

11 WILLIAMS, WILLIAM CARLOS. "Good . . . For What?" Dial 86
    (April):250.
        Review of Good Morning, America. Sums up Soviet poet
    Mayakovsky's opinion of Sandburg and then calls Sandburg "a
    writer of excellent hokkus." His "profuseness . . . is a surge
    of pain." Notes technical improvements over the earlier work.
    In spite of the faults, the "songs are its strengths."

                                1930

1   AMIDON, BEULAH. "'Tween Age." Survey 65 (15 December):341.
        Review of Early Moon. Says that Sandburg's poetry "tells
    more than the words say."

2   ANON. "Book Reviews." Sewanee Review 38 (April-June):255.
        Review of Good Morning, America. Sandburg is now "a
    factory hand, writing poems mechanically on a quantity basis."
    He lacks quality in his thought and expression. Democracy is "a
    rubber-stamp idea, and comradeship a lazy, undisciplined
    thought."

3   ANON. "Mr. Sandburg's Stories." New York Times Book Review,
    25 May, p. 8.
        Review of Potato Face. Says that the adolescent imagina-
    tion functions badly here. Stories take the shape of "inchoate
    allegory, either so obvious as to be dull or so inobvious as to
    be meaningless." Narrator has the wrong audience. Rootabaga
    Stories was richer in "imaginative delights."

4   ANON. Review of Early Moon. Booklist 27 (December):167.
        Brief review with comments on the "perfect" illustrations.

5   ANON. Review of Early Moon. Christian Century 47
    (12 November):1388.
        Sandburg is unique. His imitators copy his "formlessness
    without his insight or his imagination."

                                35

6 ANON. Review of Potato Face. Booklist 26 (June):358.
   Brief review with praise for the themes and style of
writing.

7 ANON. "Sandburg's Poetry." Saturday Review of Literature 7
   (11 October):206.
      Review of Early Moon. Calls this "a charming and haunting
selection."

8 AUSTIN, MARY. The American Rhythm: Studies and Re-
   expressions of Amerindian Songs. Boston and New York:
   Houghton Mifflin, pp. 17, 32.
   Reprint of 1923.4 with addenda.

9 BRENNER, RICA. "Carl Sandburg." In Ten Modern Poets. New
   York: Harcourt, Brace, pp. 119–48.
      Relates Sandburg's life to his poetry. Finds in his poems
two moods, "social and lyrical." As Sandburg expressed the
larger personality of America, he became the poet of America and
"the creator of a new body of American folk song."

10 EVANS, NANCY. "The Poetry of Things." New York Herald-
    Tribune Books, 2 November, p. 8.
       Review of Early Moon. Writing these poems must have
brought great satisfaction to the poet. Readers will understand
them.

11 JEWELL, EDWARD A. "New Books on Art." New York Times Book
    Review, 19 January, p. 16.
       Review of Steichen, the Photographer. Sandburg's text is
an "interesting narrative," but he is inclined to be "noisy" and
play "blind man's bluff with the English language."

12 JONES, LLEWELLYN. "Nonsense and Sentiment." New York Times
    Book Review, 6 April, p. 3.
       Brief review of Potato Face.

13 LANDON, KATHERINE. "New Books for Children." Bookman 72
    (November):249.
       Review of Early Moon. Discusses the enduring values of
these poems.

14 LOWELL, AMY. "Poetry and Propaganda." In Poetry and Poets:
    Essays. New York: Houghton Mifflin, pp. 148–60.
       In Smoke and Steel, Sandburg is both poet and propagandist.
His future will depend upon which finally dominates the other,
but the danger of propaganda is growing larger. Calls him a
"tortured . . . lover of humanity in travail." His "exag-
gerated misery" seldom produces good poetry. Dislikes the
colloquialisms and slang here; he uses them where they should
not be used. When he sees life as a poet, his poems are

"potentially adequate." When he sees it as a "biased senti-
mentalist," he injures life and himself. "Either this is a very
remarkable poet, or he is nothing."

15   MOORE, ANNE C. "Distinctive Children's Books." Atlantic
     Monthly 145 (December):28.
          Brief review of Early Moon. Calls this a collection of
     "beauty and wisdom."

16   NASH, J.V. "Carl Sandburg, an American Homer." Open Court 44
     (October):633–39.
          Praises Sandburg's early verse and examines his style,
     technique, and themes.

17   PATTEE, FRED LEWIS. The New American Literature 1890–1930.
     New York: Century, pp. 281–83.
          Divides Sandburg's career into four periods: that showing
     the influence of society and Whitman; that characterized by un-
     couthness; that in which he becomes esoteric and unintelligible;
     and a fourth period of distinctive prose work. Concludes that
     Sandburg's writings show too much sociology and too little
     artistry.

18   ROSENFELD, PAUL. "Carl Sandburg and Photography." New
     Republic 61 (22 January):251–52.
          Review of Steichen, the Photographer. Praises the photo-
     graphs but criticizes Sandburg for failing in his job as nar-
     rator. Responded to: 1930.20 with reply by Rosenfeld.

19   SMITH, MYRON B. "Light and Shade." Saturday Review of
     Literature 6 (8 February):714.
          Brief review of Steichen, the Photographer. In spite of
     some "intimate and irrelevant" information, Sandburg tells the
     story "with a poetic understanding of another creative spirit."
     Comments on the photographs.

20   STRAND, PAUL. "Steichen and Commercial Art." New Republic
     62 (19 February):21.
          Responds in a letter to Paul Rosenfeld's review of
     Steichen, the Photographer (see 1930.18). Takes issue with the
     statement that the book is "tilted to deny spirit." Wishes
     Rosenfeld had said more on the thesis of the book and shown that
     the photographs are "clearly intended to illustrate and prove
     it." Says the thesis proclaims "commercial art to be the great
     art of today, and all else, generously lumped under the category
     of 'art for art's sake,' to be born dead." Rosenfeld responds:
     "If I centered on Sandburg and not on Steichen, it was only for
     the reason that Sandburg was once a spiritual force, and his
     words still bear weight."

1   BLANKENSHIP, RUSSELL. "The New Poetry: Carl Sandburg." In *American Literature As an Expression of the National Mind*. New York: Henry Holt, pp. 605-13.
Predicts that Sandburg may be cited for beginning "a new and individual poetic form." Comments on the "living beat and surge" of Chicago Poems, his diction ("very vivid slang" and "easy, colloquial style"), his depiction of Chicago (interested primarily in the people), and his humanitarianism (fundamentally a "true mystic of the machine age"). "The Chicago poet stands in poetry where Dreiser stands in fiction." Includes brief biographical information.

2   DICKINSON, ASA DON. *The Best Books of Our Time, 1901-1925*. New York: H.W. Wilson, pp. 121-22.
Lists Chicago Poems, Cornhuskers, Smoke and Steel, and Slabs of the Sunburnt West.

3   HERZBERG, MAX J. "Introduction and Notes." In *Abraham Lincoln Grows Up*, by Carl Sandburg. New York: Harcourt, Brace, pp. v-viii.
Discusses Sandburg's lifelong interest in Lincoln.

4   PUTNAM, SAMUEL. "Postface." In *A Gentleman Decides*, by Sis Willner. Chicago: Black Archer Press, pp. 76-78.
Sees parallels between Willner and Sandburg (author of the preface to the book). "Each has that hard, cold quality which is of Chicago . . .; but scrape the steely surface, and you will find that each is . . . mellow." Praises Sandburg's preface as "a charming sonata, played . . . as a prelude to a gracious evening."

5   SONNENSCHEIN [pseud., Stallybrass], WILLIAM SWAN. *The Best Books: A Reader's Guide and Literary Reference Book*. 3d ed. London: George Routledge, p. 2820.
Lists Chicago Poems, Selected Poems, Smoke and Steel, Slabs of the Sunburnt West, and Good Morning, America.

6   WILLNER, SIS. "To Carl Sandburg, Who Said:." In *A Gentleman Decides*. Chicago: Black Archer Press, pp. 15-16.
Poem dedicated to Sandburg.

1   CALVERTON, V.F. *The Liberation of American Literature*. New York: Charles Scribner's Sons, p. 414.
Sees Sandburg's poetry as completely American, a response to a growing consciousness of nationality.

2   No entry

3   CRAVEN, AVERY. "Sandburg's Friendly Study of Mary Lincoln."
     New York Herald-Tribune Books, 27 November, p. 1.
         Review of Mary Lincoln: Wife and Widow. In this "sane and
     well-reasoned story," Sandburg helps put the controversy to rest
     and Mary Lincoln "in her right position." "His art is nowhere
     better employed than in picturing the broken old lady alone with
     her memories in candle light and shadows." Says that "high art
     and sound learning . . . are combined to give one of the best
     books in this field."

4   DUDLEY, DOROTHY. Forgotten Frontiers: Dreiser and the Land
     of the Free. New York: H. Smith and R. Haas, pp. 15-20.
         Relates how Dreiser objected to Sandburg's seeming passion
     for social change and couldn't understand why he shied away from
     the explicit in matters of sex. But he admired Sandburg and
     tried to find a New York publisher for him. He praised
     Sandburg's elegance (amidst the commonplace) and his ability
     to choose the right word and put it in the right place.

5   DUFFUS, R.L. "Mary Todd's Part in the Making of Abraham
     Lincoln." New York Times Book Review, 4 December, p. 3.
         Review of Mary Lincoln: Wife and Widow. Says that
     Sandburg is unable to write about Mary Todd "with the spontaneous
     sympathy which he has for the personality of Lincoln himself."

6   GARRISON, W[INIFRED] E. "A Case for the Psychiatrist."
     Christian Century 49 (7 December):1517.
         Review of Mary Lincoln: Wife and Widow. Praises this book
     as "dispassionate and thoroughly documented." Sandburg's narra-
     tive is "carefully written." "The normal concern which the pub-
     lic might be expected to have about her life and character
     reduces itself to a melancholy interest in knowing what Lincoln
     had to put up with during the twenty-two years of their married
     life."

7   LEWISOHN, LUDWIG. Expression in America. London and New
     York: Harper, 496 pp., passim.
         Discusses Sandburg's failure "to differentiate between the
     fundamental and the accidental in human tradition," his comments
     on Shakespeare's sonnets, his naturalistic revolt, and his sub-
     ject matter. Reprinted: 1937.6.

8   MONROE, HARRIET. "Carl Sandburg." In Poets and Their Art.
     New York: Macmillan, pp. 29-38.
         Praises Sandburg's development since Chicago Poems. Dis-
     cusses his themes, "emotional impulse," and artistry. His finest
     lyrics rank as among the best in the English language. Includes
     a reprint of 1916.13.

9   RICKWORD, EDGELL. <u>Towards Standards of Criticism</u>. Edited by
     F.R. Leavis. London: Wishart, pp. 108–111.
         Sandburg's strengths lie in his "localization," in his
     having broken free from English tradition, in his having accepted
     his environment as material for his poetry, in his simplicity,
     and in his rhythm.

10   STOLBERG, BENJAMIN. Review of <u>Mary Lincoln: Wife and Widow</u>.
     <u>New York Evening Post</u>, 19 November, p. 7.
         Sandburg's "yarn-and-essay" misses the "whole fantastic
     tragedy of her life and marriage." This narrative reminds one of
     a Hans Christian Andersen children's story. Only in Paul M.
     Angle's edited collection of her letters do we find the genuine
     Lincoln. "To my mind quite inexcusably, Mr. Sandburg is
     obviously unfamiliar with the psychiatric and psychological
     literature, without which such a biography should never be
     attempted."

                                    <u>1933</u>

1   BRICKNELL, HERSCHEL. "The Literary Landscape." <u>North
     American Review</u> 235 (February):188.
         Review of <u>Mary Lincoln: Wife and Widow</u>. Sandburg tells
     the truth with "reasonable tenderness and sympathy." Calls the
     book "a real contribution" to our understanding of Mrs. Lincoln's
     bearing upon the development of her husband's character and
     therefore upon the history of America.

2   DELL, FLOYD. "Last Days in Chicago." In <u>Homecoming: An
     Autobiography</u>. New York: Farrar & Rinehart, p. 236.
         Relates how he read some of Sandburg's early poems. "They
     were all impressionistic, misty, soft-outlined, delicate."

3   HICKS, GRANVILLE. <u>The Great Tradition: An Interpretation of
     American Literature since the Civil War</u>. New York:
     Macmillan, pp. 241–42.
         Describes Sandburg as part of a pessimistic "middle genera-
     tion" that grew out of the muckraking decade. His work is futile
     because he is "unable to see how beauty and goodness can triumph
     over evil and squalor." Reprinted with revisions: 1935.1.

4   HOWE, M.A. DeWOLFE. "The Bookshelf." <u>Atlantic Monthly</u> 151
     (January):6.
         Review of <u>Mary Lincoln: Wife and Widow</u>. Because of its
     "excellent presentation" of material heretofore unavailable,
     this book is "a notable addition to Lincolniana."

5   KREYMBORG, ALFRED. "American Poetry after the War #1."
     English Journal 25 (March):175.
         Includes reference to Sandburg as a member of the midwest-
     ern group of poets--along with Vachel Lindsay and Edgar Lee
     Masters.

6   _____. "American Poetry after the War #2." English Journal
     25 (April):263-73.
         Notes that e.e. cummings extended Sandburg's love for
     American slang.

7   PARRY, ALBERT. Garrets and Pretenders: A History of
     Bohemianism in America. Rev. ed. New York: Covici-Friede,
     pp. 189-191, 195, 197.
         Refers to Sandburg's trip to Wheaton, Illinois, as a
     reporter, his younger years in Chicago among other literary
     giants, and the importance of his contributions to Poetry. In-
     cludes a sketch of the poet by Ivan Opffer.

8   PHELPS, WILLIAM LYON. "As I Like It." Scribner's Magazine 93
     (May):322.
         Brief review of Mary Lincoln: Wife and Widow. With "rare
     sympathy and tenderness" Sandburg has created a "fine portrait."

                              1934

1   ANON. "Harmony Helps Sandburg." Newsweek 3 (5 May):38.
         Review of the musical version of Good Morning, America.
     "The form is as new as the music and should not be confused with
     a cantata although it is written for male chorus and solo
     contralto. In some parts the music is as rough-hewn as the
     words, but reaches an appalling lyric quality toward the end."

2   COMPTON, CHARLES [H]. Who Reads What? New York: H.W.
     Wilson, pp. 52-69.
         Ascertains what classes of people are representative of
     Sandburg's readers, how they became interested, how well they
     like him, and why. Includes summaries of their opinions of his
     poetry. Includes excerpt of 1929.2.

3   EMERSON, DOROTHY. "Poetry Corner: Carl Sandburg."
     Scholastic 25 (22 September):11.
         Brief portrait of Sandburg, the man and the writer.

4   KREYMBORG, ALFRED. A History of American Poetry. New York:
     Tudor.
         Reprint of 1929.8.

5   LUCCOCK, HALFORD E. Contemporary American Literature and
Religion. Chicago and New York: Willett, Clark, 300 pp.,
passim.
Covers Sandburg's biographical background, religious
impulse, satire, and social criticism.

6   WALSH, ERNEST. "Carl Sandburg." In Poems and Sonnets of
Ernest Walsh. New York: Harcourt, Brace, p. 25.
Poem about Sandburg.

1935

1   BASLER, ROY PRENTICE. The Lincoln Legend: A Study in Changing Conceptions. Boston and New York: Houghton Mifflin,
pp. 14, 21, 25-27, 43, 138-41, 296.
Covers Sandburg's epic treatment of the river voyage, his
Lincoln poems, and The Prairie Years, which he calls an "adequate
literary treatment of the early life of Lincoln against its
proper background."

2   DEUTSCH, BABETTE. This Modern Poetry. New York: W.W.
Norton, pp. 53-56, 212-14, and passim.
In Chicago Poems, Sandburg answered Emerson's summons to
sing of America's common-man tradition. "His work is sensual,
tender, slightly sentimental, and alive with the idiom of the
plain people." Like Whitman and Frost, he cares about people,
but he "does not search their minds deeply." Like Whitman he is
sometimes verbose and sentimental. "But his delight in colloquial language, his feeling for slang as poetic diction of a
fresh sort, his sense of values in the cadences of common speech,
were a distinct contribution to American poetry." Contrasts his
work with that of e.e. cummings. In Sandburg's work, "the
pathetic tone" is paramount; in cummings's, the satirical.
Reprinted: 1969.3.

3   HICKS, GRANVILLE. The Great Tradition: An Interpretation of
American Literature since the Civil War. New York:
International Publishers, pp. 241-42.
Reprint with minor revisions of 1933.3.

4   WILKINSON, MARGUERITE [O.]. New Voices: An Introduction to
Contemporary Poetry. Rev. ed. New York: Macmillan,
pp. 55-57, 180-82, 192, 217-18, 303-304, 408-45.
Reprint of 1919.11 with updated material.

1936

1   ANON. "Poets and People." <u>Time</u> 28 (31 August):47.
        Review of <u>The People, Yes</u>. Sandburg makes the people "a
    hero worth a poet's tribute." Comments on his "deceptive in-
    formality," use of native phrases, and examples of "fresh,
    unstudied, lower-class humor." Sandburg comes close to fusing
    his philosophy and work into a sensible, symmetrical program.

2   ARVIN, NEWTON. "Carl Sandburg." <u>New Republic</u> 88
        (9 September):119-21.
        Although Sandburg has not aimed at being a metaphysical
    poet, "a troubled skepticism, an enervating indecisiveness" over-
    lie much of what he has written. Certain images--mist, fog,
    phantoms, ashes, and dust--are emblematic of his almost un-
    relieved uncertainty. His use of slang is a clarifier, but
    sometimes it is a "decoy" from the full truth. The books do
    have spirit, however, and Sandburg speaks for the people and
    writes for them as readers. Reprinted: 1937.1.

3   BEGAN, LOUISE. "Verse." <u>New Yorker</u> 12 (22 August):71-73.
        Review of <u>The People, Yes</u>. Sandburg is a mystic realist
    whose weaknesses are prettiness, sentimentality, and vagueness.
    With this volume, however, much of his weaknesses have vanished
    from his style and thinking. Calls it "sturdily written and
    closely coordinated for all its seeming lack of form."

4   BELITT, BEN. "The Majestic People." <u>Nation</u> 143 (22 August):
        215-16.
        Review of <u>The People, Yes</u>. This book proves that Sandburg
    is "thoroughly alive to the 'shock and contact of ideas' today."
    It is "a heroic book without a hero" that should be considered
    "entirely in terms of its 'revolutionary' content."

5   BENÉT, STEPHEN VINCENT. "Carl Sandburg--Poet of the Prairie
        People." <u>New York Herald-Tribune Books</u>, 23 August, pp. 1-2.
        Review of <u>The People, Yes</u>. In <u>Chicago Poems</u>, Sandburg is
    a "brutal realist," a "smasher of ideals," but always himself
    with "great sensitiveness and grace." His new volume is his
    "longest and most sustained piece of work" yet in verse. In
    these "memoranda of the people" Sandburg writes with "honesty and
    anger." Excerpted: 1985.5.

6   BENÉT, WILLIAM ROSE. "Memoranda on Americans." <u>Saturday</u>
        <u>Review of Literature</u> 14 (22 August):6.
        Review of <u>The People, Yes</u>. Discusses Sandburg's "vigor,"
    "hypnotic cadence," "ominous" tone, lack of cohesion and struc-
    ture, and failure to think through the situation in which modern
    civilization finds itself. He never tells us where the people
    are getting. "Sandburg is too interested in the half-tones of

humanity, the highlights of humor, the terse queerness."
Excerpted: 1985.5.

7   BOIE, MILDRED. "Book Reviews." North American Review 242
(Winter):421, 424.
Review of The People, Yes. Sandburg speaks directly of
immediate problems with "universal language." His hero is the
people. Comments on the book's curious "timeless timelessness,"
its lyricism, and its "general diffuseness and planlessness."

8   BOYNTON, PERCY H. "The Contemporary Scene: Criticism
Revitalized." In Literature and American Life for Students of
American Literature. Boston and New York: Ginn, pp. 820-24
and passim.
Comments on Sandburg's voice and attitude toward social
injustice in Chicago Poems, Cornhuskers, Smoke and Steel, and
Abraham Lincoln. Calls his voice "melodious vehemence, simply
used without a touch of elocution, but with a flexible command of
tone effects and the nicest feeling for the retard and the half-
pause." Sandburg treats life "frankly and without bitterness"
because on the whole he likes it and believes in it.

9   BRAGDON, ELSPETH. Review of The People, Yes. Springfield
Republican, 13 September, p. 7e.
Comments on the clichés of the people's speech in these
poems. "Like rain, they are received gratefully by the ear
which hears in them the authentic accents of his brother and the
cherished creations of his own phrasemongering."

10   EATON, ANNE T. "New Books for Boys and Girls." New York
Times Book Review, 31 May, p. 11.
Review of Rootabaga Stories. Says that these stories have
"their greatest charm for boys and girls when told or read
aloud, and storytellers will welcome this complete collection."
Excerpted: 1985.5.

11   GANNETT, LEWIS. Review of The People, Yes. New York Herald-
Tribune, 20 August, p. 15.
Although this may not be folk-poetry, "it is folk-wisdom
and folk-speech." Sandburg is at his best when he gives almost
a phonographic recording of "the barbaric yawps, the pinched
wisdom, the rough laughter, the warm heart of these United
States."

12   JACK, PETER M. "Carl Sandburg Writes in the True Accents of
the People." New York Times, 23 August, p. 3.
Review of The People, Yes. Finds interesting in this "book
of words" Sandburg's philology, history, politics, sociology,
psychology, and polemics, but perhaps only one-tenth is "poeti-
cally interesting." Praises Sandburg's use of the speech of the
people.

13   LONG, DANIEL. "People and THE People." Survey Graphic 25
      (December):692.
         Review of The People, Yes. Calls the sections "prose
      poems. . . . You either 'get' it or you don't."

14   LOVEJOY, ARTHUR O. The Great Chain of Being: A Study of the
      History of an Idea. New York: Harper, p. 317.
         Sandburg owes something to the evolutionism of the German
      romantics, for whom truths were revealed through a religion of a
      struggling, gradually self-revealing life force. Reprinted:
      1960.12.

15   MacLEISH, ARCHIBALD. "The Tradition of the People." New
      Masses 20 (1 September):25–27.
         Review of The People, Yes. Every radical should read this
      to learn that there is a living American tradition upon which a
      social revolution might be built. Our great tradition is a be-
      lief in people. A "revolutionary party" will achieve a "people's
      state" only by convincing the people of its belief in this tradi-
      tion. Excerpted: 1941.5.

16   MASTERS, EDGAR LEE. Across Spoon River: An Autobiography.
      New York: Farrar & Rinehart, 426 pp., passim.
         Records Sandburg's appearance 1 March 1914 at the Cliff-
      Dwellers Club in Chicago to honor Yeats. Disagrees with his
      vision of Chicago: it is too narrow and unfair to the city it-
      self. Finds in his earliest poems (1903) "a refreshing realism."

17   OAKES, VICTOR LOVITT. "A Western Bookshelf." Frontier and
      Midland 17 (Winter):136.
         Review of The People, Yes. Sandburg is nearer today to
      being "the two-fisted Carl Sandburg of his brawny shouldered
      early poems than he has ever been." Reading the book gives one
      a sense of exhilaration. It is unified and varied.

18   R., J. "Carl Sandburg's Firecracker." Christian Science
      Monitor, 2 September, p. 10.
         Review of The People, Yes. Four-fifths of this book is
      inarticulate and therefore cannot be considered poetry. His
      "violence too often tumbles the beautiful temples of poetry that
      he patiently labors to build." Finds here only a vague belief
      in the power of the people.

19   ROSENBERG, HAROLD. "Poets of the People." Partisan Review 3
      (October):21–26.
         Review of The People, Yes. Asks where the forms of Ameri-
      can poetry originated, and to what end they were conceived. Goes
      to Whitman for the answers and covers Sandburg's development.
      Notes his conversational dialect, lists, reiterated statements,
      isolated images, scientific phrases, prose rhythms, liberal
      quotes. This is Sandburg's best volume.

20   SCHENK, WILLIAM P. "Carl Sandburg--A Bibliography." Bulletin
      of Bibliography and Dramatic Index 16 (September-December):
      4-7.
          Primary and secondary listings through 1936.

21   SLOAN, M.B. "Carl Sandburg--A Portrait." University Review
      2 (Spring):151-54.
          Offers a summation of Sandburg's career to date and reviews
      his life briefly.

22   TAYLOR, WALTER FULLER. A History of American Letters. New
      York and Chicago: American Book, pp. 402-4, 585-86.
          Chicago Poems introduced "the decisive appearance of
      America's first significant poet of industrialism." Comments on
      Sandburg's Smoke and Steel (his most ambitious effort in the
      "poetizing of the machine age"), "Etchings," fables in pictures
      (most successful of his poems are "condensed fables"), style
      ("brief chants"). Includes primary and secondary bibliography,
      1904-30.

23   UNTERMEYER, LOUIS. Modern American Poetry: A Critical
      Anthology. New York: Harcourt, Brace, pp. 15-16, 211-14.
          Reviews Sandburg's development with comments on Chicago
      Poems ("full of ferment"), Cornhuskers ("more sensitive"), Smoke
      and Steel ("synthesis of its predecessors"), Slabs of the Sun-
      burnt West ("fresh fusing"), Good Morning, America ("his best and
      worst"), The People, Yes! ("energy" and "imagination"), and
      Remembrance Rock ("thin in plot, thick with data, . . . an ex-
      tended romance"). Like Frost, Sandburg was "true to things."
      Includes biographical details.

24   Z[ABEL], M[ORTON] D. "Sandburg's Testament." Poetry 49
      (October):33-45.
          Review of The People, Yes. Calls this "a guide-book on
      American themes" and "a manual of words and phrases, episodes and
      characters, conflicts and forces." Finds here a more serious
      purpose. His use of talent surpasses the earlier volumes. Like
      Leaves of Grass, this is a "vast retrospect of life and labor in
      America." He is a poet realist, folklorist and reporter. Had he
      worked harder at his social or moral philosophy, he would have
      been a greater poet. His poetic form is a "loose, amorphous,
      copious, semi-prose medium." Whitman, as prophet, had a visionary
      imagination. Sandburg, as historian, has a realistic imagina-
      tion. "Hardly a fifth of the volume is classified by any
      definition as poetry, although any definition of poetry must
      include the purpose and imagination that runs through its pages."
      Reprinted: 1937.9.

1937

1   ARVIN, NEWTON. "Carl Sandburg." In After the Genteel
    Tradition: American Writers since 1910. Edited by Malcolm
    Crowley. New York: W.W. Norton, pp. 79-87.
        Reprint of 1936.2.

2   BLACKMUR, R.P. "The Composition in Nine Poets." Southern
    Review 2 (Winter):565.
        Review of The People, Yes. Sandburg's work has the "air of
    coming from a mind that knows what it sees, believes what it
    sees, and is at home with what it sees." But he lacks an
    "objectively felt philosophy" and an intelligent form.

3   COFFIN, ROBERT P. "Poets of the People." Virginia Quarterly
    13 (Winter):126-31.
        Review of The People, Yes. Like Masters, Sandburg shows
    his strength as an orator. His bitterness is against "erring
    humanity." Both poets are "incurable believers in life."

4   DAVIDSON, EUGENE. "New Books in Review." Yale Review 26
    (Summer):820-21.
        Review of The People, Yes. Sandburg affirms his belief in
    democracy. Notes that "passion and an organic understanding" run
    through most of the book, and it might be better "to redefine
    poetry rather than to redefine the poet" when coming to terms
    with it.

5   DEUTSCH, BABETTE. "Poetry for the People." English Journal
    (College ed.) 26 (April):265-74.
        Appraises Sandburg in light of his desire to communicate
    with the "average wayfaring man." Although not so distinguished
    as other modern poets, he has different goals. Reports that
    Sandburg was quoted by President Franklin Delano Roosevelt--the
    first poet to be so honored since Theodore Roosevelt quoted E.A.
    Robinson.

6   LEWISOHN, LUDWIG. The Story of American Literature. New York
    and London: Harper, 496 pp., passim.
        Reprint of 1932.7.

7   LOGGINS, VERNON. "Revolution." In I Hear America: Litera-
    ture in the United States since 1900. New York: Thomas Y.
    Crowell, pp. 249-81.
        Calls Sandburg's poetry "the people become articulate."
    Compares him favorably to Whitman, and The People, Yes to Leaves
    of Grass.

8   RASCOE, BURTON. "Unconventional Portraits: Carl Sandburg." In Before I Forget. New York: Literary Guild of America, pp. 434–38.

    In appendix, Rascoe tells of his encounter with Sandburg at the Daily News office in Chicago. Comments on his physical appearance ("a brooding glowering look"), voice, likes and dislikes, and character ("his soul is kindly and his nature sentimental in its tendencies"). Likens him to Will Rogers. Discusses his "confused critical sense" and notes that his formative years bred in him "a humanitarian radicalism."

9   ZABEL, M[ORTON] D., ed. "Sandburg's Testament." In Literary Opinion in America: Essays Illustrating the Status, Methods, and Problems of Criticism in the United States since the War. New York: Harper, pp. 406–15.

    Reprint of 1936.24.

1938

1   LUNDERBERGH, HOLGER. "Carl Sandburg." American Scandinavian Review 26 (Spring):49–51.

    Brief appreciation of Sandburg, the man and the writer, with attention to his early poems and formative years.

2   MONROE, HARRIET. A Poet's Life: Seventy Years in a Changing World. New York: Macmillan, 488 pp., passim.

    Reports her shock when she read the first lines of "Chicago." But then she read on and sensed a novel but authentic voice. She decided to publish all nine poems Sandburg had submitted in Poetry, March 1914. Thus as editor she gave his poetry its first serious audience. Reports that Ezra Pound commented to her that he thought Sandburg had promise and a commendable purpose but that he did not yet know enough about writing.

3   ROSENBLATT, LOUISE M. Literature as Exploration. New York: D. Appleton-Century-Crofts, p. 260.

    Sandburg and other contemporaries "write about a life that the student can understand." For example, Sandburg's personal impact on a student might be stronger than Matthew Arnold's.

4   SMITH, BERNARD. Forces in American Criticism: A Study in the History of American Thought. New York: Harcourt, Brace, p. 350.

    Brief reference to Sandburg's contributions to Poetry and Amy Lowell's remarks about his poetry (see 1917.2; 1921.5).

5   TIETJENS, EUNICE. "My Friends the Poets." In The World at My
    Shoulder. New York: Macmillan, pp. 21, 38-42.
        Memoir of Sandburg in his younger days. Covers his work on
    Day Book, the "sweep and vitality" of Chicago Poems, his writing
    for Poetry, and The American Songbag.

                                 1939

1   ANON. "Carl Sandburg's Lincoln." Newsweek 14 (4 December):
    29-30.
        Review of Abraham Lincoln: The War Years. Finds virtue
    and fault in one fact--"it is long and all-inclusive." Calls
    this a "staggering accomplishment," which is rich in its re-
    creation of the times. Includes biographical information on
    Sandburg.

2   ANON. "Your Obt. Servt." Time 34 (4 December):84.
        Review of Abraham Lincoln: The War Years. Sandburg's now
    completed four-volume work "is a work whose meanings will not
    soon be exhausted, whose greatness will not soon be estimated."
    No American biography surpasses it in "wealth of documentation
    and fidelity to fact, . . . in strength, scope and beauty."
    Reprinted: 1940.6.

3   BENÉT, STEPHEN VINCENT. "Atlantic Bookshelf." Atlantic
    Monthly 164 (December):22.
        Review of Abraham Lincoln: The War Years. This is a
    biography of the Civil War. Its virtue is that Sandburg keeps
    his narrative within a contemporary frame of time and leaves the
    reader with "renewed faith in the democracy that Lincoln believed
    in and a renewed belief in the America he sought." Sandburg
    shows Lincoln clearly and fully. Every American should read
    this book. Excerpted: 1985.5.

4   BROOKS, CLEANTH. Modern Poetry and the Tradition. Chapel
    Hill: University of North Carolina Press, pp. 77-80, 101-2,
    119.
        Comments on Sandburg as a local colorist. His primary
    impulse is a rejection of the past and a repudiation of English
    poetic tradition. Thus he (like Whitman) epitomizes "wildness"
    in poetry, is crude in form, and is a writer of the elementary,
    undifferentiated "stuff of poetry." Reprinted: 1948.7.

5   CHRISMAN, LEWIS H. "Carl Sandburg, the Laureate of Industrial
    America." Religion in Life 8 (Winter):120-31.
        Stresses Sandburg's link with the people. Disagrees with
    Untermeyer's calling him the "laureate of industrial America"
    (see 1926.38). Sandburg is not a propagandist, sociologist, or
    intellectual. He is a poet whose concern is human beings. His

method is emotional, suggestive, questioning. Fundamentally,
he is an optimist.

6   COMMAGER, HENRY STEELE. "Lincoln Belongs to the People."
     Yale Review, n.s. 29 (December):374-77.
         Review of Abraham Lincoln: The War Years. Calls this an
     authentic biography in which Lincoln comes to life in a story
     that is "complex and fascinating." Best of all is Sandburg's
     "genius" for re-creating those who affected Lincoln. His por-
     trait is one from which a whole generation may draw "understand-
     ing of the past and inspiration for the future." Excerpted:
     1985.5.

7   ELTING, M.L. Review of Abraham Lincoln: The War Years.
     Forum 102 (December):iv.
         In spite of the myriad of incidents and "perfect torrent of
     details," Sandburg "smothers neither the life of his narrative
     nor the interest of his reader." At times wishes that Sandburg
     had given more of his own judgment. Excerpted: 1940.3.

8   FADIMAN, CLIFTON. "Sandburg Finishes Lincoln." New Yorker
     15 (2 December):114.
         Review of Abraham Lincoln: The War Years. Sandburg's work
     will endure as a source for anyone wanting to know what Lincoln
     was "thinking, doing, and feeling." Comments on his two styles:
     "plain, downright factual reporting" and a kind of "prose
     poetry, often moving, occasionally a little high-flown."

9   GANNETT, LEWIS. Modern Speeches on Basic Issues. Compiled
     by L.R. Sarrett and W.T. Foster. Boston: Houghton Mifflin,
     pp. 371-76.
         Includes Gannett's review of The People, Yes taken from a
     radio talk in 1936 over the NBC network. Some of Sandburg's
     lyrical lines are the kind of "tolling poetry" that sings and
     laughs in a memorably American way.

10   LERNER, MAX. "Lincoln as War Leader." New Republic 101
     (6 December):197-98.
         Review of Abraham Lincoln: The War Years. Praises the
     completed biography: "the democrat, the poet, the story-teller,
     the earthy Midwesterner, the singer of the people has managed
     somehow to write about another democrat who was also something of
     a poet in his way and a vast story-teller and an earthy Mid-
     westerner and a product of the popular mass." In historical
     literature there is nothing quite comparable to Sandburg's
     achievement. Excerpted: 1940.3. Reprinted: 1940.6.

11   LEWIS, LLOYD. "Carl Sandburg Sings the 'Lincoln-Music.'"
     New York Herald-Tribune Books, 3 December, p. 3.
         Review of Abraham Lincoln: The War Years. Calls this
     biography "the most catholic evaluation to date." His

description of how Lincoln wrote his papers, speeches, and letters "is as absorbing as it would be suddenly to come across the
revelation of just how Shakespeare wrote Hamlet." Sandburg makes
"eloquent use" of contemporary anecdotes and language. His
account is "as detailed as Dostoievsky, as American as Mark
Twain." Reprinted: 1940.6.

12   LOWDEN, CARL S. "Carl Sandburg Impressively Reviews Lincoln's
      War Years." Christian Science Monitor, 23 December, p. 10.
          Review of Abraham Lincoln: The War Years. Sandburg shows
      himself to be "a capable historian, but it is as the Lincoln
      biographer that he reveals mastery of high order." Calls this
      "a monumental work." Every American can read it with pride.

13   MABIE, JANET. "Carl Sandburg." Christian Science Monitor,
      7 October, p. 16.
          Interview in which Sandburg comments on what he gets from
      writing the Lincoln biography: "a degree of patience."

14   NEVINS, ALLAN. "Abe Lincoln in Washington." Saturday Review
      of Literature 21 (2 December):3-4, 20, 22.
          Review of Abraham Lincoln: The War Years. Finds similari-
      ties between this book and Douglas S. Freeman's biography of
      Robert E. Lee: "the same amplitude, the same panoramic quality,
      the same exhaustiveness in research." The most distinctive
      qualities in Sandburg's work are "pictorial vividness" and a
      "cumulative force of his detail." His portrait emphasizes three
      qualities in Lincoln's personality: "tenderness of heart,"
      "shrewd thrust and grasp of his mind," "moderation . . . of
      temper." The book's weaknesses include an overwhelming pile of
      details and facts of the times, lack of documentation, and diffi-
      culty in distinguishing between important and unimportant events.
      But the book does help us comprehend Lincoln's intellect and
      moral stature. Excerpted: 1985.5.

15   ROBINSON, L.E. "Sandburg's Lincoln." Nation 149
      (2 December):614.
          Review of Abraham Lincoln: The War Years. Sandburg's
      biography is an "outstanding contribution" because of its range
      of information and adaptability to leisurely reading "by reason
      of [its] style and chapter arrangement."

16   SHERWOOD, ROBERT E. "The Lincoln of Carl Sandburg." New
      York Times Book Review, 3 December, pp. 1, 14.
          Review of Abraham Lincoln: The War Years. In the first
      installment, Sandburg gave "greater play to his own lyrical
      imagination." Now, in this "folk biography," he stays with doc-
      umentary evidence and writes a work so great that it will require
      "great reading and great reflection before any true appreciation
      of its permanent value can be formed." His method is unlike
      that of any biographer since Homer. Reprinted: 1940.6.
      Excerpted: 1985.5.

17   UNTERMEYER, LOUIS. From another World. New York: Harcourt,
     Brace, pp. 315-17 and passim.
        Memoirs of his encounters with Sandburg. Discusses
     Masters, Lindsay, and Sandburg, and says that of the three, the
     latter is "the most powerful as well as the most panoramic."

18   VAN DOREN, CARL C., and MARK VAN DOREN. "Sandburg 1878--."
     In American and British Literature since 1890. Rev. ed.
     New York: D. Appleton-Century, pp. 32-37.
        Expands their discussion to include Good Morning, America
     and The People, Yes. Sandburg's chief trait is that "he is at
     once so bold and challenging toward adults and so sympathetic and
     affectionate toward the young." Many of his poems are "still
     rough or underdone." This is because he refuses help from any
     poetic method except his own. For Sandburg, language is more
     than syntax and diction. "It is the whole way a people has of
     expressing itself." Includes reprint of 1925.8.

19   VAN GELDER, ROBERT. "His Job Well Done, Sandburg Relaxes."
     New York Times, 11 December, p. 20.
        Interview with Sandburg in which he discusses his method
     of composing Abraham Lincoln: The War Years.

20   WOOLF, SAMUEL J. "Sandburg Talks of Lincoln." New York Times
     Magazine, 12 December, pp. 7, 14.
        Interview essay in which Sandburg discusses his writing of
     the Lincoln biography.

                                   1940

1   ANON. "Pulitzer History Award." Saturday Review of Litera-
     ture 22 (11 May):13.
        Covers Sandburg's winning the Pulitzer Prize for Abraham
     Lincoln: The War Years.

2   ANON. "Sandburg Denounces T.S. Eliot as Royalist and 'Close
     to Fascist.'" New York Herald-Tribune, 24 October, p. 18.
        Brief article in which Sandburg is quoted as saying that
     Eliot is close to the Fascists. See 1952.35.

3   AUSLANDER, JOSEPH. "A Poet Writes Biography." English
     Journal 29 (May):347-55.
        Discusses Sandburg's lifelong interest in Lincoln. Dis-
     agrees with critics who say that Sandburg is "a vague, impracti-
     cal sort of fellow whose existence is principally in the world of
     the imagination." His Lincoln biography is great scholarship,
     "definitive and noble." "Every American carries in his heart an
     unwritten biography of Lincoln. Sandburg has written that biog-
     raphy." Includes excerpts from 1939.7, 10.

4   BASLER, ROY P[RENTICE]. "Book Reviews." American Literature
     12 (May):264-66.
         Review of Abraham Lincoln: The War Years. Calls this "a
     dual masterpiece, a comprehensive history . . . and a compre-
     hensive biography of President Lincoln, skilfully blended and
     mutually illuminated." Although its total effect is less
     satisfying than The Prairie Years, as a work of art Sandburg
     achieves "the epic portrayal of an era in modern civilization
     with Man as its hero."

5   BEARD, CHARLES A. "The Sandburg Lincoln." Virginia Quarterly
     Review 16 (Winter):112-16.
         Review of Abraham Lincoln: The War Years. Notes that
     Lincoln is portrayed here not as the "mighty hero" but as a "poor
     limited mortal," steadfast in his purpose. Says that "an air of
     grave thoughtfulness hangs over the lightest words." Reprinted:
     1940.6.

6   BEARD, CHARLES A., ed. The Lincoln of Carl Sandburg: Some
     Reviews of "Abraham Lincoln: The War Years." New York:
     Harcourt, 48 pp.
         Includes reprints of 1939.2, 10, 11, 16; 1940.5, 7.

7   COMMAGER, HENRY STEELE. "Lincoln Belongs to the People."
     Yale Review, n.s. 29 (Winter):374.
         Review of Abraham Lincoln: The War Years. Praises this as
     "the greatest of all Lincoln biographies," appropriate from the
     pen of a poet. It is "genuine, simple, broad, humane, dramatic,
     poetic, thoroughly American in its muscular, idiomatic words, in
     its humor, in its catholicity and democracy." Reprinted: 1940.6.

8   JONES, EDGAR DeWITT. "The People's Lincoln." Christian
     Century 57 (3 January):21-22.
         Review of Abraham Lincoln: The War Years. This book is
     "bewildering" in its bigness. Considers it as a painting
     ("colossal"), a building ("massive"), as music ("grand and
     majestic"), as poetry ("epic, magnificent in form and sweep").

9   LEWIS, LLOYD. "The Many-Sided Sandburg." Rotarian 56 (May):
     44-46.
         Brief biographical essay in which he presents Sandburg as
     "the foremost American poet since World War 1."

10   LUCCOCK, HALFORD E. American Mirror: Social, Ethical and
     Religious Aspects of American Literature, 1930-1940. New
     York: Macmillan, pp. 28, 233-35.
         Sandburg answered Whitman's call to "flood himself with
     the immediate age." He has "real faith in people" and writes
     with "a biting anger" of profiteers.

11   MILLETT, FRED B. Contemporary American Authors. New York:
     Harcourt, Brace, pp. 139–40, 557–61.
        Calls Sandburg a more conscious artist than either Lindsay
     or Masters, but less successful than Frost in his use of collo-
     quial speech.

12   ORIANS, G. HARRISON. A Short History of American Literature
     Analyzed by Decades. New York: F.S. Crofts, pp. 292, 307.
        Brief discussion of the characteristics of Sandburg's
     poetry.

13   ORTIZ-VARGAS, ALFREDO. "Perfiles anglo-americanas." Revista
     Ibero-americana 4 (November):163–76.
        In Spanish. Includes a profile of Sandburg's career.

14   RAMSDELL, CHARLES W. "Carl Sandburg's Lincoln." Southern
     Review 6 (Winter):439–53.
        Review of Abraham Lincoln: The War Years. Discusses
     Sandburg's method, occasional confusions, research, errors,
     uneven writing, sketches of personalities, depiction of Lincoln's
     spiritual growth, lack of historical training. Calls this the
     "longest and most detailed" life of Lincoln. Sandburg has tried
     to do "an extremely difficult job with entire honesty." But he
     has not escaped entirely from the Lincoln legend.

15   THOMPSON, KATHERINE. "Portrait of Sandburg." Scholastic 36
     (6 May):25, 28.
        Brief description of Sandburg as poet including biographi-
     cal details.

16   WELLS, HENRY. New Poets from Old. New York: Columbia
     University Press, p. 212.
        Although Sandburg is one of today's representative poets,
     "his feeling for the relation of words and music represents a
     cultural development extending far back not only into American
     but into the English and European past."

17   WOOLF, S[AMUEL] J. "Sandburg Talks of Lincoln." Scholastic
     36 (5 February):21.
        Brief interview in which Sandburg relates the writing of
     his biography of Lincoln.

                              1941

1   ANON. "Old War Horse in New Harness: Carl Sandburg as a
     Columnist." Newsweek 17 (7 April):59–60.
        Reports that Sandburg will return to writing a column for
     the Chicago Times Syndicate on 5 April. Includes biographical
     background.

2 BENÉT, STEPHEN VINCENT, and ROSEMARY BENÉT. "Sandburg: Son of the Lincoln Countryside." New York Herald-Tribune Books, 14 December, p. 8.
     Biographical data and personal relationships. Sandburg is identified with people and democracy and is related to Emerson's "The American Scholar." Includes a brief review of his career.

3 CARGILL, OSCAR. Intellectual America. New York: Macmillan, pp. 262, 287, 323.
     Refers to Sandburg's influence on Eliot, MacLeish and Sherwood Anderson. Reprinted: 1968.6.

4 DETZER, KARL WILLIAM. Carl Sandburg: A Study in Personality and Background. New York: Harcourt, Brace, 210 pp.
     Writes of Sandburg as an individual, his methods of working, and the influence of his interest in Lincoln.

5 MacLEISH, ARCHIBALD. "Mr. Sandburg and the Doctrinaires." In A Time to Speak. Boston: Houghton Mifflin, pp. 36-41.
     Excerpt from 1936.15.

6 MATTHIESSEN, F.O. American Renaissance: Art and Expression in the Age of Emerson and Whitman. London and New York: Oxford University Press, pp. 592-93.
     Comments on Whitman's influence on Sandburg, who "responded whole-heartedly to [his] desires for this country." His Lincoln biography is "the only one to equal Whitman's depth of feeling for the land." Sandburg has opened up new material from the Middle West. But on most occasions, "his descriptions are left even rougher than Whitman's." His mysticism is cloudy. Unlike Whitman's, Sandburg's faith does not spring from a "profound acceptance of natural order." He sees life as "anarchy, swept by uncontrollable forces." Yet he also celebrates the city's "beautiful energy." This "confused state of mind is a symptomatic response to our social choas."

1942

1 ANON. "Sandburg--from Poetry to Politics." Business Week 653 (7 March):7.
     Brief item about Sandburg's interest in the American political scene. The UAW hopes to pit him against "labor-baiter" Rep. Clare Hoffman.

2 BEAL, ELIZABETH. "Young People." Library Journal 67 (1 November):958.
     Review of Storm over the Land. This is a "most fascinating account" of the Civil War, a "true picture" of the life of the times in terms "most young people will understand."

3   GREGORY, HORACE, and MARYA ZATURENSKA. A History of American
    Poetry 1900-1940. New York: Harcourt, Brace, p. 217.
        Relates Sandburg the man to Sandburg the poet. Discusses
    his creation of "a unified literary personality with which he
    provides an atmosphere for his verses." Finds in his verse a
    binding rhythmical unity.

4   KAZIN, ALFRED. "America! America!" In On Native Grounds:
    An Interpretation of Modern American Prose Literature. New
    York: Harcourt, Brace, pp. 395-98.
        In Sandburg's biography of Lincoln we see an example of
    "the new nationalism." To read it is "to know the supreme happi-
    ness of being alive again in the past."

5   KINIERY, PAUL. "Books of the Week: History." Commonweal 37
    (30 October):48.
        Review of Storm over the Land. This book "will make the
    Civil War come to life." Sandburg deals with the war "directly,
    clearly and honestly."

6   LAWSON, EVALD BENJAMIN. "That Man Knows Lincoln." Lutheran
    Companion, 12 February, p. 13.
        Review of Abraham Lincoln: The War Years. Only Sandburg,
    as a man of the common people, could write sympathetically such
    a story. Includes an anecdote of the poet's visit to Lawson's
    home and his comments on how he wrote the biography.

7   LEECH, MARGARET. "Profile of 'The War Years.'" Nation 155
    (2 December):420-21.
        Review of Storm over the Land. Calls this "a swift and
    straightforward story." Although it lacks "the magnificence" of
    the original volumes, Sandburg has eliminated "their formidable
    length and occasional turgidness."

8   LEWIS, LLOYD. "The Sandburg Digest." New York Herald-Tribune
    Books, 25 October, p. 7.
        Review of Storm over the Land. "The book is not, as a
    whole, what it would have been had Sandburg written it all new
    from cover to cover." But he has retained "the impressionistic
    story of the great war," and the people who experienced it come
    alive. Praises the illustrations and photographs.

9   NEVINS, ALLAN. "The American Spirit in War." Saturday
    Review of Literature 25 (31 October):3.
        Brief review of Storm over the Land. Praises Sandburg's
    narrative skill, "poetic insight," "penetrating interpretation,"
    human sympathy, and theme of heroism in this "'profile' or rapid,
    graphic sketch."

10   SCANDRETT, R.B., Jr. "New Books." Survey Graphic 31
     (December):601.
        Brief review of Storm over the Land.

11   SCOGGIN, MARGARET C. "1942 Books for Young People." Library
     Journal 67 (15 October):893.
        Review of Storm over the Land. Calls this "startlingly
     contemporary in feeling." Sandburg shows an age like our own
     "torn by doubts, hampered by political bickerings, confused by
     professional rivalries, and yet, sustained by Lincoln's faith."

12   VAN GELDER, ROBERT. "An Interview with Mr. Carl Sandburg."
     New York Times Book Review, 31 May, pp. 2, 14.
        Sandburg discusses the writing of Abraham Lincoln: The War
     Years.

13   WILLIAMS, WILFRED. "New Books." Churchman 156 (15 December):
     19.
        Review of Storm over the Land. Includes summary and brief
     discussion of Sandburg's themes.

                                 1943

1   ANON. "Briefly Noted." New Yorker 19 (25 September):85.
        Review of Home Front Memo. Praises many of the pieces as
     "warm and moving." Others, however, are "blighted by a self-
     consciously bad syntax that threatens to become Mr. Sandburg's
     worst mannerism."

2   ANON. "Grant's 'Attrition': Anticipating Foch." Times
     Literary Supplement (London), 29 May, p. 268.
        Review of Storm over the Land. Calls this "an excellent
     summary from the Northern point of view." Sandburg portrays
     battles graphically, but "vital factors are too often over-
     looked."

3   BOAS, RALPH R. "Sandburg's Early Lynching." Explicator 1
     (June), item 67.
        Responds to W.E.R.'s request that someone explicate this
     "difficult to interpret" poem (Explicator 1 [March], item Q22).
     Christ is the "comprehensive symbol of man." The social message
     is clear: "the all-embracing love of God as manifested in His
     Son's comprehensive human quality."

4   BORLAND, HAL. "Sandburg Speaking." New York Times Book
     Review, 26 September, p. 9.
        Review of Home Front Memo. Calls this a "readable record,
     a complete and eloquent one." Every American can read with
     pride this record of what our poets have been doing and saying
     "while the fires of hate were sweeping the world."

                                  57

5   BRAGDON, MARSHALL. Review of Home Front Memo. Springfield
    Republican, 2 October, p. 6.
       Comments on the "ramblings and unevenness" of this collec-
    tion. But finds running through it "the curious unity of a great
    American who, like Daniel Boone, is never 'lost' though sometimes
    'bewildered.'"

6   COUSINS, NORMAN. "Medicine for the Chicago Anarchists."
    Saturday Review of Literature 26 (9 October):12.
       Editorial review of Home Front Memo. Reads it as social
    comment, as "magnificent diffusion." Warns against reading
    Sandburg "primarily as a hayseed philosopher and poet, a shaggy,
    higgledy-piggledy wandering minstrel of democracy." To read him
    in this way may obscure "the real stature of one of the soundest
    and wisest thinkers of our time."

7   DERLETH, AUGUST. Review of Home Front Memo. Book Week,
    26 September, p. 4.
       Finds here some of the "most memorable work" Sandburg has
    done. The "man on the street" will read this with understanding
    because Sandburg has put into "simple, direct and memorable prose
    what he himself has been thinking but has not been able to
    articulate." Calls this "an important contribution to the war
    effort."

8   LEWIS, LLOYD. Review of Home Front Memo. Weekly Book Review,
    17 October, p. 5.
       Sandburg is in the war for "democracy, singing and swing-
    ing." Praises him for risking his reputation in controversy, for
    coming out of the poet's ivory tower "when his beloved democracy
    is endangered."

9   POSTE, Pvt. LESLIE I. "Subject Books." Library Journal 68
    (15 September):724.
       Review of Home Front Memo. Praises this as a "comprehen-
    sive collection" and important documentary record of "the feel-
    ings of a troubled American citizen in midst of the war."

10 ROVERE, RICHARD H. "The War Years." New Republic 109
    (22 November):725.
       Review of Home Front Memo. This is tedious, repetitious,
    "inferior stuff." But does find Sandburg's "warmth, gentleness
    and sound feeling for American life."

11 T., M.J. "Sandburg on the Home Front." Christian Science
    Monitor, 16 October, p. 11.
       Review of Home Front Memo. Calls Sandburg a "poet-
    philosopher." The collection may be read as "current comment
    written for posterity." Its effect is "curiously interesting."

12   WELLS, HENRY W.   "New America."   In The American Way of
      Poetry. Columbia Studies in American Culture, no. 13. New
      York: Columbia University Press, pp. 135-47 and passim.
          Discusses Sandburg as representative of the spiritual un-
      folding of the West, his achievements as poet and biographer, and
      his work with regard to its national and sectional implications.
      Places him as champion of the proletarian, spokesman for the
      whole country, partisan for the underprivileged, believer in a
      planned economy, and pastoral poet. "Of all our American poets
      writing today, Sandburg best expresses the spiritual urges of the
      entire American people. More effectively than any other poet, he
      voices the social hopes and aspirations of a united and demo-
      cratic America." Includes discussion of Chicago Poems, The
      People, Yes, and Slabs of the Sunburnt West. Reprinted: 1964.11.

                              1944

1   ADAMS, J. DONALD. The Shape of Books to Come. New York:
      Viking Press, p. 145.
          Classifies Sandburg with those writers who win and keep
      audiences by "vitalized creation" rather than by making obeisance
      to the private gods of the cognoscenti.

2   ANON. "Off the Hollywood Wire." New York Times, 11 June,
      pt. 2, p. 3.
          Announces that Sandburg has signed a contract with Metro-
      Goldwyn-Mayer for "a biographical novel of American life, manners,
      and morals" to be called An American Cavalcade.

3   ELGSTROM, A.H. "Carl Sandburg." Ord och Bild (Stockholm) 3
      (Winter):528-39.
          Profile of Sandburg as a man and writer.

4   GERTZ, ELMER. "Profile of Carl Sandburg." Lincoln Herald 46
      (June):28-31, 39.
          Recalls his earlier contacts with Sandburg and then their
      meeting at Chi Kaming Goat Farm in 1943. Discusses his speech
      and his collections of manuscripts, photographs, and memorabilia
      on Lincoln; summarizes his comments on poets, politics, philos-
      ophy, and journalism.

5   MILLETT, FRED B. Contemporary American Authors: A Critical
      Survey and 219 Bio-Bibliographies. New York: Harcourt,
      Brace, pp. 139-40, 557-61.
          Overview in which he calls Sandburg "a more conscious and
      critical craftsman" than either Lindsay or Masters. His verse
      is "untraditional and unacademic" and his colloquialism differs
      from Frost's. In The People, Yes, he has attempted his "largest
      subject, a re-creation in popular language of the mind and heart

of the American people." Includes biographical information and
primary/secondary bibliography through 1938.

6   TAIPALE, A.K.M. Nykyajan Amerikkalaisia kirjailijoita: Carl
    Sandburg, Theodore Dreiser, Sinclair Lewis. Helsingissa:
    Kustannuosakeyhtio Otava, 131 pp., passim.
        In Finnish. References to Sandburg's work as a writer, the
    development of his career, and the reception given to his work in
    Europe.

1945

1   CRAWFORD, B.V., A.C. KERN, and M.H. NEEDLEMAN. Outline His-
    tory of American Literature. New York: Barnes & Noble,
    p. 132.
        Brief references to Sandburg as a poet of secondary
    importance.

2   TATE, ALLEN, ed. Sixty American Poets, 1896-1944. Washing-
    ton, D.C.: Library of Congress, p. 114.
        Compares Sandburg to Whitman and sees him as a "throwback
    to the wandering jongleur."

1946

1   CROWDER, RICHARD [H.]. "Sandburg's Caboose Thoughts."
    Explicator 4 (May), item 52.
        Examines "Caboose Thoughts" and sees the narrator as "the
    simple, 'human' philosopher."

2   DUDLEY, DOROTHY. Forgotten Frontiers: Dreiser and the Land
    of the Free. New York: Beechhurst Press, pp. 415-20.
        Reports that in 1918 Edgar Lee Masters showed Sandburg's
    poems to Theodore Dreiser, who then recommended them to H.L.
    Mencken and to all other unconventional editors of his acquain-
    tance. "He said explicitly they were wonderful."

3   FISHER, DOROTHEA FRANCES. American Portraits: Pictures by
    Enit Kaufman. New York: Henry Holt, pp. 136-40.
        Portraits of Sandburg.

4   GREGORY, HORACE, and MARYA ZATURENSKA. "Carl Sandburg." In
    A History of American Poetry, 1900-1940. New York: Harcourt,
    pp. 242-51.
        Judges Sandburg's accomplishments by focusing on his in-
    fluence, the critical judgments his contemporaries have passed
    upon his work, and his position in national letters. Ascribes
    more influence to Lincoln's "Gettysburg Address" than to any
    other literary source on Sandburg's style. Dismisses The People,

Yes as a jumble in which "the kind of knowledge that can be
gained by referring to the files of The World Almanac [was]
thrown and heaped together half humorously."

5   HOFFMAN, FREDERICK J., CHARLES ALLEN, and CAROLYN F. ULRICH.
The Little Magazine: A History and a Bibliography.
Princeton: Princeton University Press, 450 pp., passim.
    Covers the history of Sandburg's contributions to little
magazines and includes a list of them by name with historical
background.

*6 JONSSON, THORSTEN. Sidor ar Amerika (intryck och resonemang).
Stockholm: A. Bonnier.
Cited in 1963.8.

7   LEWIS, LLOYD. "Introduction." In Poems of the Midwest, by
Carl Sandburg. Cleveland and New York: World Publishing,
pp. 15-20.
    Quotes Carl Van Doren's belief that Sandburg's poetry is
"a direct answer to Whitman's hope of a democratic poetry that
would express a distinctively American speech" (see 1925.8;
1939.18). Discusses his association with Poetry and the impact
of his revolutionary style on American letters.

8   MORGAN, A[RTHUR] E[USTACE]. The Beginnings of Modern American
Poetry. London: Longmans, Green, pp. 14-21.
    Comments on Chicago Poems and Cornhuskers and gives atten-
tion to Sandburg's life, style, and chaotic temperament and form.

9   STRACHAN, PEARL. "The Language of Sandburg." Christian
Science Monitor Magazine, 30 November, p. 14.
    Review of Poems of the Midwest. Defends Sandburg against
his critics. Says his free verse "ranks among the best," that
he is both "realistic and fanciful," and that his compass is
"all-embracing." Notes the uproar caused by his "bold use of the
common speech of the American people and the defiance of conventional restrictions in form."

10 VAN GELDER, ROBERT. "An Interview with Carl Sandburg." In
Writers and Writing. New York: Scribner's, pp. 283-86.
    Sandburg discusses his work as poet and biographer as well
as his reactions to critics and his experiences as a reporter.

1947

1   CLEMENS, C. "Call upon Carl Sandburg." Hobbies 51
(February):126-28.
    Biographical background. Sandburg anticipated that
"Chicago" would stir up the critics, but he was pleased when

they admitted that he had struck a new path for poetry while using the right words for his themes.

2   FOSTER, I.W. "Carl Sandburg: Family Portrait." Christian Science Monitor Magazine, 19 July, p. 4.
     Biographical background.

3   GURKO, LEO. The Angry Decade. New York: Dodd, Mead, 360 pp., passim.
     Brief comments on Sandburg's "passion for the physical vastness" of America. For more than a generation he and others "monopolized the stage with as much finality as did the Victorians in an earlier day."

4   LEWIS, LLOYD. "Last of the Troubadours" and "The Big Shoulders Sag." In It Takes All Kinds. New York: Harcourt, Brace, pp. 73–81, 219–22.
     Recalls Sandburg's appearance at a 1925 dinner for Sinclair Lewis at which his singing made Lewis cry. Also discusses the significance of Sandburg's move from Chicago to Flat Rock, North Carolina.

5   MERRIAM, CHARLES E. "The People, Yes!" Radio Program, University of Chicago Round Table, no. 489 (3 August), pp. 1–13.
     Radio discussion with Merriam, Sandburg, and T.V. Smith.

6   MONTGOMERY, ELIZABETH RIDER. The Story behind Great Stories. New York: Robert M. McBride, pp. 88–91.
     Brief profile of Sandburg the writer.

7   SHANE, T. "The Week's Work: Biographical Note." Collier's 119 (15 February):8.
     Brief biographical background.

8   THOMAS, BENJAMIN PLATT. Portrait for Posterity: Lincoln and His Biographers. New Brunswick, N.J.: Rutgers University Press, pp. 285–301.
     Discusses Sandburg's work on the Lincoln biography--how he came to write it, what he focused on, how it was received by readers.

9   WITHAM, W. TASKER. Panorama of American Literature. New York: Stephen Daye Press, pp. 239–42.
     Brief survey of Sandburg's career along with biographical background.

1948

1   ALLEN, CHARLES. "Cadenced Free Verse." College English 9
     (January):195-99.
          Examines the devices Sandburg uses to establish his
     "cadenced verse." In "Nocturne in a Deserted Brickyard," the
     poet relies on natural, free rhythms, the cadence of ordinary
     speech. In "Chicago" the strophic rhythms work together to form
     the final rhythmic unity of a long poem.

2   ANON. "Books by Carl Sandburg." Southern Packet 4 (August):
     8.
          Lists Sandburg's publications from 1916 to 1946.

3   ANON. "Briefly Noted." New Yorker, 9 October, pp. 128-29.
          Review of Remembrance Rock. Says the thousand pages are
     "sonorous, right-minded, and passing dull."

4   ANON. "Fiction." Kirkus Reviews 16 (1 September):447.
          Review of Remembrance Rock. This book is written as "only
     Sandburg could write it." Calls it a book of "a poet, an his-
     torian, a biographer, a storyteller." Finds evidence in it of
     Sandburg's wisdom, understanding, and tolerance.

5   ANON. "Portions of Wisdom." Time 52 (11 October):108, 110,
     113.
          Review of Remembrance Rock. Finds this to be "an
     extraordinary mixture of learning and naïveté, of self-conscious
     poeticizing and shrewd observation, with dim characters wandering
     about in a grey, dreamlike fog." In broad outlines, the novel
     "seems the sort of book that U.S. critics have always asked for."
     But in its attempt to fulfill the "epic sweep" it fails because
     of its "grandiloquent language, the heroic characters, the poetic
     prose that on re-examination turns out to be well-nigh meaning-
     less."

6   BRADLEY, VAN ALLEN. "Sandburg's First Novel a Literary
     Treasure." Chicago Daily News, 13 December, p. 19.
          Review of Remembrance Rock. Calls this "the sum of every-
     thing" that Sandburg has "written, learned, done." Sees it as
     "an interpretation of the American Dream, . . . filled with the
     breath of life." Every page "sing[s] the influence of Lincoln."

7   BROOKS, CLEANTH. Modern Poetry and the Tradition. London:
     Poetry, pp. 77-80, 101-2, 119.
          Reprint of 1939.4.

8   BUTCHER, FANNY. "Sandburg Novel of American Dream." Chicago
     Sunday Tribune, 18 July, p. 4.
         Review of Remembrance Rock. The book transcends defini-
     tion. Calls it Sandburg's "evocation of the meaning of America."
     Could be called "a great sermon." Although it is "long, uneven
     reading," finds treasure here for "the reader with patience."

9   EMRICH, DUNCAN. "The Poet and the General: Carl Sandburg
     Meets General Eisenhower." Saturday Review of Literature 31
     (March):9-11, 45-47.
         Reports on Sandburg's meeting with General Eisenhower at
     the Pentagon, 25 July 1947. They discussed Eisenhower's role as
     general, the possibility of his becoming president, and his
     tenure as president of Columbia University. Sandburg called
     Eisenhower "the living embodiment of American tradition." In-
     cludes an interview with Luther Evans, librarian of Congress.

10   G[OODMAN], R[AY]. "The Author." Saturday Review of Litera-
     ture 31 (9 October):14.
         Brief biographical details with summary of the poet's
     attitude toward success and music.

11   H., P. Review of Remembrance Rock. Christian Century 65
     (13 October):1082.
         Comments on the "moving and unforgettable passages."
     Sandburg tries to reassure young Americans "of their country's
     greatness, and of the abiding worth of the contribution they
     have made to its future." Doubts that many will read all 1,067
     pages, but those that do will be "richly rewarded."

12   HART, H.W. "Fiction." Library Journal 73 (1 October):1385.
         Review of Remembrance Rock. Calls it "a prodigious effort
     to recover the past and . . . a monumental contribution to the
     literature of patriotism." The book is rich in "the local color,
     folk speech and folk wisdom of its times."

13   HORMEL, OLIVE D. "Highlights of the Book Week." Christian
     Science Monitor, 7 October, p. 11.
         Review of Remembrance Rock. Says this "rich and perceptive
     embodiment of the American dream" should take its place beside
     Tolstoy's War and Peace. It is both "a measured epic of the
     quest for individual freedom" and a contemporary appreciation for
     America.

14   JACKSON, J[OSEPH] H[ENRY]. Review of Remembrance Rock. San
     Francisco Chronicle, 10 October, p. 22.
         Comments on the concept ("noble"), the sweep ("broad and
     inclusive"), and the style ("Whitmanesque simplicity and scope").
     Unfortunately, the novel does not flow smoothly and severe edit-
     ing is needed. "The Civil War portion, most of all, is finely
     done."

15 LEWIS, LLOYD. "Sandburg's Fictional Epic of American Life."
New York Herald-Tribune Weekly Book Review, 10 October,
pp. 1-2.
    Review of Remembrance Rock. Says this is Sandburg's "ride
to an American Canterbury." As a personal expression, it is his
"fullest, ripest tribute to . . . the people who have remained
unswamped by fate and undulled by self-satisfaction." As a work
of art it stands beside the Lincoln biography. Excerpted:
1985.5.

16 LORIMER, S. "Carl Sandburg, His Influence on American Culture." In Will to Succeed. Stockholm: A. Bonniers,
pp. 277-84.
    Covers Sandburg's place in American letters and the re-
sponses he has received from both critics and general readers.

17 MILLER, PERRY. "Sandburg and the American Dream." New York
Times Book Review, 10 October, p. 1.
    Review of Remembrance Rock. Sees this as a script for a
Hollywood spectacular. All the ingredients are present: gory
battles, sexual encounters, and tender feeling. "There is no
more disheartening comment upon our era than to discover that at
this point in his career the author . . . has lent himself to
these maudlin devices."

18 MIMS, EDWIN. The Christ of the Poets. New York: Abingdon-
Cokesbury Press, p. 225.
    Finds the true spirit of Christ in Sandburg's "To a
Contemporary Bunkshooter."

19 POORE, CHARLES. "Books of the Times." New York Times,
7 October, p. 27.
    Review of Remembrance Rock. Finds here "the sprawling
power and warmth and humanity" of everything Sandburg has written. He writes "fiction like a historian." He is at his most
eloquent when he is writing about the people. Praises it for
"its rousing stories and its challenge to our day's fashionable
despair."

20 ROLO, CHARLES J. "Reader's Choice." Atlantic 183 (January):
85-86.
    Brief review of Remembrance Rock. Sandburg's patriotism
commands respect, but his language is "mushy with sentiment and
turgid with rhetoric." "The American past carries a more personal message, surely, than the lesson that 'life goes on.'"

21 SHAW, THOMAS SCULER, comp. "Carl Sandburg: A Bibliography."
Washington, D.C.: Library of Congress General Reference and
Bibliography Division, 62 pp.
    An unpublished listing of Sandburg holdings in the Library
of Congress.

22   SHOEMAKER, DON C. "Carl Sandburg at Flat Rock." Southern
     Packet 4 (August):1-4.
         Brief biographical essay that covers Sandburg's life-style
     at Flat Rock, North Carolina.

23   SKILLIN, E.S. "American Cavalcade." Commonweal 48
     (8 October):621.
         Review of Remembrance Rock. Sandburg's impulse in this
     "hulking new novel" is patriotic. Praises the Pilgrim period as
     his most successful reconstruction and Remember Spong as his most
     memorable heroine.

24   SOSKIN, WILLIAM. "The American Dream Panorama." Saturday
     Review of Literature 31 (9 October):14-15.
         Review of Remembrance Rock. Comments on Sandburg's detail,
     historical research, allegory, song, high romance, humor, lyri-
     cism, and folk-pattern of each period of American history. Con-
     cludes that his portrayals are "static," like looking at a mural.
     Sandburg's chief plea is for tolerance and avoidance of bigotry.
     Excerpted: 1985.5.

25   SPITZ, LEON. "Carl Sandburg's Bible Texts." American Hebrew
     158 (8 October):8, 13.
         Shows that Sandburg had a "lover's quarrel with God,
     religion, the Bible," and that he heard God's voice in the voice
     of the people. His verse "chants along a sort of scriptural
     pattern."

26   THOMPSON, RALPH. "In and Out of Books." New York Times Book
     Review, 10 October, p. 8.
         Gives details behind the writing and the selection of a
     title for Remembrance Rock.

27   THORP, WILLARD. "The 'New' Poetry." In Literary History of
     the United States. 3d ed., rev. Edited by Robert E. Spiller,
     Willard Thorp, Thomas H. Johnson, Henry Seidel Canby, and
     Richard M. Ludwig. New York: Macmillan, pp. 1181-84.
         Sees Sandburg in terms of the people. He knows America
     better than Whitman. He reports the people's dreams, their wis-
     dom, their metaphors, all in a completely original and American
     style that culminates in the great "strange and powerful book"
     The People, Yes. Also finds in Sandburg a lack of traditional
     or organic form, so that even this volume "defies classification."
     It is one of the great American books.

28   TRILLING, DIANA. "Fiction in Review." Nation 167
     (30 October):500.
         Review of Remembrance Rock. Expresses disappointment that
     Sandburg is too nationalistic without any humor to correct his
     mystic sentimentalism. Finds here the familiar elements from his
     verse: "the same soft affirmation and conscious optimism, the

same excessive impulse to social unity, the same love of the
rhythms of balladry and religion, the same massing of the people
and objects which compose our national strength." But somehow
all of this is "much more troubling" when we find it in
Remembrance Rock.

1949

1   ANGLE, P.M. Review of Lincoln Collector. Chicago Sunday
    Tribune, 6 November, p. 3.
       "If Sandburg had contented himself with mere description
    this would have been a book of limited interest. Fortunately, he
    has gone far beyond that, printing the full text of nearly
    200 letters."

2   DONALD, DAVID. "Lincoln Collector." New York Times Book
    Review, 6 November, p. 3.
       Review of Lincoln Collector. Calls this "a portrait gal-
    lery of mid-century Americans caught by the candid camera of
    contemporary letters." This is "Lincolniana at its best, Mr.
    Sandburg at his happiest."

3   FITZHUGH, HARRIET LLOYD, and P.K. FITZHUGH. "Carl Sandburg."
    In Concise Biographical Dictionary of Famous Men and Women.
    Rev. ed. New York: Grossett, pp. 815–16.
       Brief biographical background with survey of Sandburg's
    development as a writer.

4   HOPKINS, VIRGINIA A. "New Books." Catholic World 168
    (January):330–31.
       Review of Remembrance Rock. Says the book is "noble in
    intention" and developed with "a graciousness and a fine
    tolerance." But these strengths are diminished by "defects in
    form and pattern."

5   LADER, LAWRENCE. "Carl Sandburg: an American Legend."
    Coronet 25 (January):66–72.
       Biographical essay. Calls Sandburg "an American legend"
    and America's uncrowned poet laureate.

6   MEARNS, DAVID C. "Lincoln, Barrett and Sandburg: A Magnifi-
    cent Book!" New York Herald-Tribune Book Review, 4 December,
    p. 4.
       Review of Lincoln Collector. Examines it as a source book,
    a picture album, and "a rippling, billowing, flapping, visible
    standard of America." Praises it also as "a memorable represen-
    tation of a people and a time."

7   MONTGOMERY, ELIZABETH RIDER. The Story behind Modern Books.
     New York: Dodd, Mead, pp. 164–69.
         Discusses Sandburg's career, particularly as Lincoln's
     biographer.

8   OLDSEY, BERNARD S. "Sandburg's Broken-Face Gargoyles."
     Explicator 7 (May), item 50.
         Death in the poem is seen as a kind of "mystical evolution"
     and is part of his hope for a future state of perfection, when he
     "shall yet be footloose." Offers a stanza-by-stanza analysis.

9   RANDALL, J.G. "From Chain Letters to a Rich Cache."
     Saturday Review of Literature 32 (19 November):29–30.
         Review of Lincoln Collector. Classifies this as good
     reading, filled with "humor and playful nonsense, along with
     much that is portentous."

10   ROLLO, CHARLES J. "Reader's Choice." Atlantic Monthly 183
     (January):85.
         Review of Remembrance Rock. Calls the wisdom here "a
     troubled sort of uplift compounded of the rolling sonorities of
     populism and the naive solance of momentous clichés." Notes "the
     sincere and generous spirit of Sandburg's patriotism."

1950

1   ANON. "Books in Brief." Nation 170 (3 June):555.
         Brief review of Lincoln Collector. "Reading it is like
     going through the jumbled contents of an old desk; there is no
     great discovery but somehow the period comes quite magically to
     life."

2   ANON. "Complete Poems." Booklist 47 (15 December):154.
         Brief review of Complete Poems.

3   ANON. "Complete Poems." Bookmark 10 (December):57.
         Review of Complete Poems. Calls this the "definitive col-
     lection of the typically American poet's work."

4   ANON. "Of Thee I Sing." Time 56 (4 December):100.
         Review of Complete Poems. Sandburg is like a "true wander-
     ing minstrel, . . . short on intellectual penetration, long on
     sympathy and human curiosity."

5   ANON. "The Poetry of Carl Sandburg." English Journal 39
     (October):470.
         Review of Complete Poems. Summarizes Daniel Hoffman's
     review (see 1950.14).

6   BENÉT, LAURA. "Introduction." In Famous American Poets.
    New York: Dodd, Mead, pp. 135-42.
    Makes clear Sandburg's individual genius and contributions.

7   BRITTAIN, ROBERT. "Carl Sandburg and the People." San
    Francisco Chronicle ("This World"), 24 December, pp. 12, 14.
        Review of Complete Poems. Finds here the record of "forty
    years of the life of a great man in a great people." Most
    readers think of him as a "great affirmative voice of American
    democracy." But this collection shows "a strange tentativeness
    and uncertainty." Finds an increase in the questions he asks
    along with the affirmations he always states.

8   CARGILL, OSCAR. "Carl Sandburg: Crusader and Mystic."
    College English 11 (April):365-72.
        Offers a biographical background to account for the mild
    radicalism of "Chicago" and traces his development from his
    description of the city to his mystical faith in The People, Yes.
    Beginning here, notes a mellow optimism and faith in the future.
    This mellowing is a positive good, a sign of moral and intellec-
    tual growth, and a by-product of Sandburg's research and writing
    on Lincoln. In spite of a shift away from socialism, Sandburg
    has remained "the consistent friend of the workingman if not
    of . . . the proletariat." Includes a discussion of Chicago
    Poems, Cornhuskers, The People, Yes, and Abraham Lincoln: The
    War Years. Reprinted: 1950.9.

9   _____. "Carl Sandburg: Crusader and Mystic." English
    Journal 39 (April):177-84.
        Reprint of 1950.8.

10 COBLENTZ, STANTON A. New Poetic Lamps and Old. Mill Valley,
    Calif.: Wings Press.
        Responds to Amy Lowell (see 1917.2; 1921.5). In Sandburg
    and other vers librists "one can trace the very shadow of
    Whitman, the outlines of his manner, the reflections of his
    moods, the survival of his theory and the continuation of his
    practice." Examines "At the Gates of Tombs" and comments on his
    imitators.

11 COMMAGER, HENRY STEELE. "He Sings of America's Plain
    People." New York Times Book Review, 19 November, pp. 1, 40.
        Review of The People, Yes. Calls Sandburg "a symbol, a
    monument, almost an institution" who in thirty-eight years has
    remained unchanged in his interests, sympathies, and philosophy.
    He is the poet of the plain people and, like Whitman, "the
    Lincoln of our poetry." At a time when we are tempted into ir-
    rationality, superficiality, cynicism, Sandburg celebrates "what
    is best in us and recalls us to our heritage and to our human-
    ity." Sums up his achievement, and concludes that his technique

and philosophy are unchanged while his latest poems "show no
diminution of talents or slackening of spirit." Excerpted:
1985.5.

12   DENNY, MARGARET, and WILLIAM H. GILMAN, eds. The American
      Writer and the European Tradition. New York: McGraw-Hill,
      p. 76.
         Brief reference to Sandburg's "loose oratory."

13   G[OODMAN], R[AY]. "The Author." Saturday Review of Litera-
      ture 33 (18 November):14.
         Biographical sketch.

14   HOFFMAN, DAN[IEL] G. "Sandburg and 'The People': His
      Literary Populism Reappraised." Antioch Review 10 (June):
      265–78.
         Sandburg follows the aesthetic of literary populism as well
      as the spirit of Wordsworth's Lyrical Ballads. But he has lost
      modern poetry's serious readers because he has presented col-
      lective emotions divorced from the individual consciousness. His
      style has alienated those who see Eliot, Pound, and Wallace
      Stevens as chief poetic spokesmen. He only registers the senti-
      ments of the people and does nothing to enhance or change them.
      His form of verse is difficult to understand. Thus he has cut
      himself off from his own "deepest resources." Includes an
      examination of his method and themes in The People, Yes, and
      finds that his strength as a pioneer is that he denied himself
      "the experiences of the more introspective artist and the private
      diction of the individualistic poet." Summarized in 1950.5.
      Excerpted: 1952.19.

15   HUMPHRIES, ROLFE. "Verse Chronicle." Nation 171
      (9 December):536.
         Review of Complete Poems. Says the book is "more humorous
      and folksy in places than poetic," but then asks, "what's the
      matter with that?"

16   HUTCHENS, JOHN K. "On an Author." New York Herald-Tribune
      Book Review, 10 December, p. 3.
         Views Sandburg as "a great performer in the old tradition
      of the strolling player."

17   JENKINS, ALAN. "Portrait of a Poet at College." South
      Atlantic Quarterly 49 (October):478–82.
         Reviews Lombard Review and The Cannibal to answer the
      question, "What was Sandburg like as a student?" Finds vitality,
      a will-to-succeed, moral idealism, and ready humor.

18 _____. "Sandburg: A Poet Who Keeps on Learning and Growing."
Christian Science Monitor Magazine, 2 September, p. 18.
Three qualities make Sandburg exemplary: "a continuing
zest for learning, a continuing creativity, and a capacity to
keep old friends while making new ones." Refers to Sandburg's
kinship with the Japanese artist Hokusai and his own visits to
Connemara Farms.

19 JOHNSON, E. GUSTAVE. "Religion in the Poetry of Sandburg."
Prairie Schooner 24 (Winter):337–48.
Refers to Sandburg's early religious instruction and finds
in his poetry "the voice of one crying in the wilderness." He
asks the question for which no definite answer is expected. He
denies the existence of "authoritarian or divine revelation." He
has no use for the "fetishes of institutionalized religion, of
fanaticism and other religious shams." His God is "the immanent,
all-pervading spirit of the universe" and he identifies him with
humanity. Sandburg is in accord with the chief humanitarian
doctrines of Jesus and shares with Whitman "the doctrine of the
infinite worth of the human personality." He sees death as part
of "a beneficent, perfect divine order." Heaven and hell are
projections of the human mind. He expresses love for those
religious people who are honest, sincere, common, and he con-
demns the evils of war, oppression, social injustice, and
tyranny. Finds many biblical allusions in the poetry.

20 NIMS, JOHN F. "Vivid Panoramic Poetry of America by
Sandburg." Chicago Sunday Tribune, 17 December, pp. 1, 3.
Brief review of The People, Yes and Complete Poems.

21 NORVELL, GEORGE W. The Reading Interests of Young People.
Boston: D.C. Heath, p. 71.
Experts and anthologists recommend Sandburg's poems primarily for older children. Studies what interest boys and girls
find in his poetry.

22 RODMAN, SELDEN. "The Pulse of Common Activity." Saturday
Review of Literature 33 (18 November):14–15.
Review of Complete Poems. Considers the enduring values of
Sandburg's work and tries to discover why his generation has
remained indifferent to him. Examines Chicago Poems (Whitman
reborn "without the magnificent ego and the optimism," but with
his compassion and "knack of recording the pulse of common
activity"); Cornhuskers (has discovered the value of repetition,
foreshadows Jeffers, and is more conscious of his own style);
Smoke and Steel ("a casual rhythm and concreteness"); Slabs of
the Sunburn West (offers a new formulation, that it is wisdom to
think the people are the city), and Good Morning, America (his
style is more "self-conscious" and he often drags in folklore).
Sandburg's ultimate reputation, however, will rest on The People,

Yes--in which he expresses the "living paradox" of America. Concludes that one-quarter of his poems are, "along with the best of Emerson, Thoreau, Melville, Dickinson, Twain, Faulkner and Frost, the writing that has taught America the sound of its own voice." Excerpted: 1985.5.

23   SANDBURG, CARL. "Sandburg's Words at New Salem." Journal of the Illinois State Historical Society 17 (Spring):7-14.
      Provides a transcript of Sandburg's talk delivered at the golden anniversary meeting of the Illinois State Historical Society, 8 October 1949. Includes introductory remarks.

24   _____. "Trying to Write." Atlantic Monthly 186 (September): 31-33.
      Includes introductory remarks to Sandburg's preface for Complete Poems, and quotes him on writing.

25   SHERWOOD, ROBERT E. "Carl Sandburg's Ride on a Flimmering Floom." New York Herald-Tribune Books, 19 November, pp. 1, 26.
      Sums up Sandburg's accomplishments.

1951

1   ALLEN, GAY WILSON. "Complete Poems." Tomorrow 10 (March): 58-59.
     Review of Complete Poems. Sandburg is a positivist who lets facts speak for themselves. He has learned to be a better writer with the passing years, having outgrown his myth of the virile and provincial midwesterner. His poems are usable "in the tradition of the bardic singers of the heroic age who marched with their chieftains to battle."

2   ANON. "Pulitzer Prizes Awarded." Publishers Weekly 159 (12 May):1960.
     News of Sandburg's receipt of the Pulitzer Prize for Complete Poems.

3   ANON. "Verse." New Yorker (27 (10 March):123-24.
     Review of Complete Poems. Sandburg is "a popular minstrel of the American machine age" whose poetry is influenced by "Whitmanian optimism and Scandinavian mysticism" and often "pure moonshine." Finds evidence of a "shrewd common sense, fun, and music thrown in."

4   BEGAN, LOUISE. Achievement in American Poetry, 1900-1950. Chicago: Henry Regency, p. 45.
     Sandburg's chief fault is "his romantic insistence on the complete and all-embracing worth of folk material," so that he tends toward flattery or the sentimental.

5   BENNETT, JOSEPH. "Five Books, Four Poets." Hudson Review 4
    (Spring):133-34.
        Review of Complete Poems. Sandburg's preface is "a handy,
    and certainly an authoritative compendium of the dominant insti-
    tutionalized attitudes toward the art of poetry in America."

6   CARMER, CARL. "Carl Sandburg and Some Old Songs Made New
    Again." New York Herald-Tribune Book Review, 21 January,
    p. 7.
        Review of The New American Songbag. Says that Sandburg's
    "poetic and understanding mind has never been more intuitive and
    sure."

7   COFFIN, TRISTRAM P. "Folklore in the American Twentieth
    Century." American Quarterly 13 (Summer):526-32.
        Sandburg, among others, shares "the uncritical attitude of
    the public toward folklore."

8   GARRISON, WINIFRED E. "Hyacinths and Biscuits." Christian
    Century 68 (10 January):48.
        Review of Complete Poems. Change in Sandburg has been
    "very slight." He has no "'periods.'" At his best he is "a
    great imaginative artist with words." Recommends him for the
    Nobel Prize for literature.

9   HOFFMAN, DANIEL G. "Sandburg's Cool Tombs." Explicator 9
    (May), item 46.
        Comments on Sandburg's five subjects--power, treason, con-
    quest, corruption, material possessions--and his central theme,
    a celebration of love as the greatest joy in life. The repeat
    parallel structure is appropriate to Sandburg's purpose here.

10 McDONALD, GERALD [D.]. "Poetry." Library Journal 76
    (1 January):49.
        Review of Complete Poems. "Writing of ordinary people and
    things in a simple way, Sandburg [brings] the shape, sound and
    meaning of America into his work." Recommends this collection
    for all libraries.

11 MILLER, PHILIP L. "Music." Library Journal 76 (15 March):
    518.
        Review of The New American Songbag. Sandburg can make a
    song "come clearer by talking about, or around it." For the
    consumer, "it is so much velvet to find the material annotated
    with illuminating comment."

12 NILES, ABEE. "American Songs." Nation 173 (21 July):57.
        Review of The New American Songbag. "Sandburg is one of a
    very few writers who can make a song come clearer by talking
    about, or around, it." Praises the book as a superb addition to
    the 1927 Songbag.

13   RODMAN, SELDEN. "La storia, un secchio peino di centere.
     Carl Sandburg il poeta del paradossa americana." La fiera
     letteraria 3 (7 January):3.
        In Italian. Brief reference to Sandburg as a representa-
     tive American poet.

14   RUBIN, LOUIS D., Jr. "Chicago Revisited." Hopkins Review 4
     (Winter):63-69.
        Review of Complete Poems. Faults Sandburg for his senti-
     mentality but praises him for his "extraordinarily fine gift for
     language and feeling for lyric imagery." Like Eliot, his poetry
     was "created in revolt"; unlike Eliot, he "attempted to make the
     subject matter more immediate." Finds flaws, but also finds many
     pages of excellent poetry. Predicts that his eventual reputation
     will rest with The People, Yes.

15   STRAUMANN, HEINRICH. "The Realm of Imagination: Poetry."
     In American Literature in the Twentieth Century. London:
     Hutchinson's University Library, pp. 130-36.
        Sandburg gives eloquent expression to "the awareness of the
     power of reality and its social implications." Like Hart Crane,
     he is concerned with "a vision of the fundamentals of America,
     past and present," but his tone is different. Comments on
     Chicago Poems, Selected Poems, and American Songbag.

16   WILLIAMS, WILLIAM CARLOS. "Carl Sandburg's Complete Poems."
     Poetry 78 (September):345-51.
        Review of Complete Poems. Finds here no technical initia-
     tive other than their "formlessness," but his best is "touched
     with fire." As a poet he "petered out" ten years ago, and he
     sought no answers. "Chicago" is a deliberately successful poem
     and should have been his last. But facts overwhelmed him in
     much of his poetry. Had he followed the lead in Ashurnatsirpal
     III--man's natural love of violence-- he might have gone on to
     great distinction. But there is no development in thought or
     technique, only "a gradual inevitable slackening off to ultimate
     defeat." In effect, his work is "a monstrous kind of show." He
     is not an artist. His work is not memorable. Reprinted:
     1954.17. See 1960.18. Excerpted: 1980.7, 10 (with reply).

                                   1952

1   ANON. "Always the Young Strangers." Booklist 49
     (15 December):133.
        Brief review of Always the Young Strangers.

2   ANON. "A Birthday for 'Poetry.'" Life 33 (24 November):
    103, 116.
        Celebrates fortieth anniversary of Poetry magazine and
    refers to Sandburg's involvement with it. Includes brief bio-
    graphical information and a reprint of "Chicago."

3   ANON. "Carl Sandburg: Farmer." Coronet 32 (May):18B.
        Profile of Sandburg's life on the farm. Emphasizes his
    simplicity and desire for solitude.

4   ANON. "News of the Week: Birthday Dinner to Honor Carl
    Sandburg on January 6." Publishers Weekly 162 (20 December):
    2379.
        News of a banquet at the Blackstone Hotel to celebrate
    Sandburg's seventy-fifth birthday and the publication of Always
    the Young Strangers.

5   BABCOCK, FREDERIC. "Beginning of a Friendship." Journal of
    the Illinois State Historical Society 45 (Winter):326.
        Memoir of a friendship since 1942 between Sandburg and the
    editor of the Chicago Tribune Magazine of Books.

6   BREIT, HARVEY. "Talk with Carl Sandburg." New York Times
    Book Review, 1 June, p. 19.
        Interview with Sandburg on the occasion of his receiving
    the Gold Medal from the National Institute and American Academy
    of Arts and Letters. Covers his childhood and opinions of
    movies, radio, television, people, character, politics, poetry,
    newspapers, and work in progress. Reprinted: 1956.4.

7   BROOKS, VAN WYCK. The Confident Years: 1885-1915. New York:
    E.P. Dutton, pp. 185, 420.
        Sandburg is an incarnation of Whitman's "literatus." His
    belief in America is expressed in subject, form, and idiom. He
    is a symbol of his world, eminent not only for what he says but
    because it is he who says it.

8   BUTCHER, FANNY. "Bright Fellowships." Journal of the
    Illinois State Historical Society 45 (Winter):388-94.
        Memories of a forty-year friendship with the poet. In-
    cludes excerpts from his letters to her and a doggerel of his
    entitled "Improvisation." Describes a trip to their house in
    Maywood, Illinois.

9   CARRUTHERS, OLIVE. "Farewell to a Troubadour." Journal of
    the Illinois State Historical Society 45 (Winter):400.
        Poem bids farewell to Sandburg after he has left his home
    in Herbert, Michigan, for North Carolina.

10   DEUTSCH, BABETTE. <u>Poetry in Our Time</u>. New York: Henry Holt,
     p. 53.
        Views Sandburg's contribution to American poetry as the
     stimulation of appreciation of new people and a new poetic dic-
     tion based on the ordinary.

11   DILLIARD, IRVING. "Friends on the <u>Post-Dispatch</u>." <u>Journal of</u>
     <u>the Illinois State Historical Society</u> 45 (Winter):355–60.
        Recounts Sandburg's association with employees for the
     St. Louis Post-Dispatch: Bart Howard (editorial writer), Daniel
     E. Fitzpatrick (cartoonist), and Arthur Witman (photographer).

12   FELTS, DAVID V. "The Eloquent Drumstick." <u>Journal of the</u>
     <u>Illinois State Historical Society</u> 45 (Winter):354.
        Reminiscence by an editor of the <u>Decatur</u> (Illinois) <u>Herald</u>.

13   FINNEGAN, RICHARD J. "A Reporter, Yes." <u>Journal of the</u>
     <u>Illinois State Historical Society</u> 45 (Winter):373–78.
        Comments on Sandburg as reporter while writing <u>Abraham</u>
     <u>Lincoln: The Prairie Years</u> and how he was coaxed to join the
     <u>Chicago Times</u>.

14   GEORGE, ADDA. "The Galesburg Birthplace." <u>Journal of the</u>
     <u>Illinois State Historical Society</u> 45 (Winter):300–305.
        As the keeper of the Sandburg birthplace, comments on the
     formation of the Carl Sandburg Association and on the restoration
     of the house. Includes a description of its interior and the
     dedication of the Lincoln Room on 30 May 1949.

15   GERTZ, ELMER. "Birthday Snapshots." <u>Journal of the Illinois</u>
     <u>State Historical Society</u> 45 (Winter):379–83.
        Photograph of Sandburg as he appeared at his seventy-fifth
     birthday dinner at the Sherman Hotel, Chicago.

16   HANSEN, HARRY. "[Sandburg] and the <u>Chicago Daily News</u>."
     <u>Journal of the Illinois State Historical Society</u> 45 (Winter):
     321–35.
        "Industry, persistence and patience have played a large
     part in the flowering of Carl Sandburg's genius. No matter how
     hard he had to work there was always a singing inside him."
     Reviews the time when Sandburg worked for the <u>Chicago Daily News</u>
     and began to write about Lincoln.

17   HARCOURT, ALFRED. "Forty Years of Friendship." <u>Journal of</u>
     <u>the Illinois State Historical Society</u> 45 (Winter):395–99.
        Sandburg's publisher says that everything Sandburg writes
     is "music and full of wisdom."

18 HAVERLIN, CARL. "He Heard America Sing." Journal of the
Illinois State Historical Society 45 (Winter):385–87.
Comments on The New American Songbag. "To read [him], or
to be with him, is to be convinced that everything he has ever
written is part and parcel of one long continuing story about our
land and its people."

19 HOFFMAN, DANIEL [G.]. "Sandburg and 'The People'" and "What
Does the Symbol Symbolize?" In Paul Bunyan: Last of the
Frontier Demigods. New York and London: Temple University
Press, pp. 132–43, 162–63.
Discusses diction, lawless individualism, inappropriateness
of Paul Bunyan to Sandburg's theme, populist aesthetic, structure
(based on indirection), themes of recovery from the depression
and human dignity. Sandburg writes in the "populist tradition."
His chief concern is "to record the multitudinous voices of
America." The People, Yes is his "most ambitious and successful
effort" in this direction. Notes that the forty-seventh section
is devoted to Bunyan. Concludes that Sandburg has overlooked
many strands in American culture, thus seriously weakening the
validity of his achievement. Includes excerpt from 1950.14.

20 HOOK, J.N., ELLEN BURKHART, and LOUISE LANE. Illinois Authors
and a Literary Map of Illinois. Urbana: Illinois Assn. of
Teachers of English, 118 pp., passim.
References to Sandburg's life in Chicago and his depiction
of the city in his poems.

21 HORTON, ROD W., and HERBERT W. EDWARDS. Backgrounds of
American Literary Thought. Edited by Albert C. Baugh. New
York: Appleton-Century-Crofts, pp. 179, 359.
Sandburg, Steinbeck, and Saroyan "express a somewhat quali-
fied faith in the higher destiny of mankind." Imagism attracted
the poet in the 1920s. Reprinted: 1967.13.

22 JENKINS, ALAN. "Book Reviews." Journal of the Illinois State
Historical Society 45 (Winter):407.
Review of Always the Young Strangers. Sandburg's writing
is "mobile," "vivid," and convincing. His ear for colorful
American idiom is accurate. Through this book we learn more
about "the people, problems, and promises of America."

23 _____. "Mentor and First Publisher." Journal of the Illinois
State Historical Society 45 (Winter):311–15.
Sketch of Philip Green Wright, Sandburg's teacher at
Lombard College and publisher of his first early verse.

24 JORDAN-SMITH, PAUL. "A Folksy Friendly Fellow." Journal of
the Illinois State Historical Society 45 (Winter):319–20.
Memoir of the friendship between Sandburg and Wright. Men-
tions the poet's contribution to Tomorrow.

25 MESERVE, FREDERICK HILL. "Thoughts on a Friend." Journal of
    the Illinois State Historical Society 45 (Winter):337-38.
      Explains why Sandburg wrote about Lincoln and includes
    views of Sandburg by his collaborators on The Photographs of
    Abraham Lincoln.

26 NEVINS, ALLAN. "Sandburg as Historian." Journal of the
    Illinois State Historical Society 45 (Winter):361-72.
      Review of Abraham Lincoln: The War Years. Sandburg's pic-
    ture of Lincoln and the American people is convincing. Its most
    distinctive qualities are "pictorial vividness," "humanness,"
    and "cumulative force of its detail." Sandburg is both "a great
    historian" and "a finished artist."

27 NEWMAN, RALPH G. "A Selective Checklist of Sandburg's
    Writings." Journal of the Illinois State Historical Society
    45 (Winter):402-6.
      Covers the period 1904-53 and includes only his main
    writings and a few special printings.

28 PRATT, HARRY E[DWARD]. "A Tribute to Carl Sandburg at
    Seventy-Five." Journal of the Illinois State Historical
    Society 45 (Winter):295.
      Brief biographical details.

29 PRATT, HARRY EDWARD, ed. "Carl Sandburg Issue." Journal of
    the Illinois State Historical Society 45 (Winter):295-416.
      A tribute to Sandburg at seventy-five with articles by
    Frederic Babcock (1952.5), Fanny Butcher (1952.8), Irving
    Dilliard (1952.11), D.V. Felts (1952.12), R.J. Finnegan
    (1952.13), Adda George (1952.14), Elmer Gertz (1952.15), Harry
    Hansen (1952.16), Alfred Harcourt (1952.17), Carl Haverlin
    (1952.18), Alan Jenkins (1952.22), Paul Jordan-Smith (1952.24),
    F.H. Meserve (1952.25), Allan Nevins (1952.26), R.G. Newman
    (1952.27), Harry Edward Pratt (1952.28), J.G. Randall (1952.30),
    Robert E. Sherwood (1952.32), T.I. Starr (1952.33), Adlai E.
    Stevenson (1952.34), B.P. Thomas (1952.36), C.E. Van Norman
    (1952.37), Bruce Weirick (1952.38), Quincy Wright (1952.39).
    Reprinted: 1953.34.

30 RANDALL, J.G. "Carl." Journal of the Illinois State Histori-
    cal Society 45 (Winter):329-33.
      Finds in Rootabaga Stories and American Songbag "homely,
    friendly things expressed in jeweled language." His biography of
    Lincoln is "the richest, the most powerful, the most alive, and
    the most humanly interpretive of all Lincoln biographies." "One
    must put together the statements of men all over America to have
    even the beginning of an appraisal of what Sandburg means in
    poetry."

31   SHERMAN, DAVID EDWARD, and ROSEMARIE REDLICH. Literary
     America. New York: Dodd, Mead, pp. il, 136-37.
        Brief biographical background with photographs. "Critics
     saw a strong new voice, a disregard for poetic convention, a
     radical choice of subject, a slangy manner, and a lusty inde-
     pendence."

32   SHERWOOD, ROBERT E. "A Cold Walk with Carl." Journal of the
     Illinois State Historical Society 45 (Winter):327-38.
        Calls Sandburg one of America's "great natural resources."
     Reflects upon their thirty years of acquaintance all because of
     a common interest in Lincoln and motion pictures.

33   STARR, THOMAS I. Cattails." Journal of the Illinois State
     Historical Society 45 (Winter):334-35.
        Reflects on his friendship with Sandburg. With him a
     friendship is "a personal thing, you just enjoy it and appreciate
     it, and cherish the memories it calls up."

34   STEVENSON, ADLAI E. "A Friend and Admirer." Journal of the
     Illinois State Historical Society 45 (Winter):297-99.
        Offers a tribute to Sandburg and quotes from his speech at
     the 1949 inauguration.

35   TATE, ALLEN. "The State of Letters." Saturday Review 52
     (Autumn):608-14.
        Attacks Sandburg for saying in 1940 that T.S. Eliot was
     "close to the fascists" (see 1940.2).

36   THOMAS, BENJAMIN P[LATT]. "A Man of Faith in Man." Journal
     of the Illinois State Historical Society 45 (Winter):339-40.
        Calls Sandburg "a man of the common people," an artist with
     language.

37   VAN NORMAN, C.E. "A Pair of 'Dreamers.'" Journal of the
     Illinois State Historical Society 45 (Winter):316-18.
        Comments on Sandburg's foreword to Philip Green Wright's
     verses, The Dreamer.

38   WEIRICK, BRUCE. "Poetical Circuit Rider." Journal of the
     Illinois State Historical Society 45 (Winter):341-53.
        Comments on Sandburg's opinions about his contemporaries
     and attitudes toward the English classics. Says that he lacks
     "specific poetical judgments."

39   WRIGHT, QUINCY. "Lombard Memories." Journal of the Illinois
     State Historical Society 45 (Winter):307-10.
        Mentions Sandburg's attendance at Lombard College and his
     occasional visits to the University of Chicago in the late 1920s.
     Includes background material on the Asgard Press.

1953

1   ANON. "Briefly Noted." New Yorker 28 (14 February):116.
    Review of Always the Young Strangers. Says that Sandburg
"touches the surface in a thousand places and makes it give back
light, but the depths in which his passionate and endearing personality must have had its source are left concealed."

2   ANON. "Carl Sandburg Feted on His Seventy-Fifth Birthday."
    English Journal 42 (March):163.
    Reports that Sandburg received the Gold Medal from the
Poetry Society of America. "The note of affection for the man
was even stronger than that of admiration for the tireless, many-
sided author."

3   ANON. "Galesburg Nostalgia." Time 61 (12 January):98–99.
    Review of Always the Young Strangers. Notes "an artless
lack of point and discrimination that flirts perilously with
final boredom." The book is "almost always short on American
imagination."

4   ANON. "Honors to Carl Sandburg on His 75th Birthday."
    Publishers Weekly 163 (3 January):41.
    Brief biographical entry relating to Sandburg's long asso-
ciation with Alfred Harcourt, his publisher since 1916.

5   ANON. "Poetry Society to Award Medal to Carl Sandburg."
    Publishers Weekly 163 (10 January):131.
    Poetry Society of America honors Sandburg at a dinner in
the Ambassador Hotel, New York, on 13 January.

6   ANON. "Sandburg's 75th." Newsweek 41 (12 January):78–79.
    Review of Always the Young Strangers. His story is "almost
perfect background for [the] expressions of esteem from his fellow men." Much of the time the book evokes "that Swedish house-
hold with unfailing humor and unerring aptness of phrase."

7   ANON. "Sandburg's 75th Birthday Celebrated by the Nation."
    Publishers Weekly 163 (17 January):190–93.
    Reports on the celebration at the Blackstone Hotel,
Chicago, 6 January, and on the reception of Always the Young
Strangers.

8   BRADLEY, VAN ALLEN. "500 at Dinner for Sandburg." Chicago
    Daily News, 7 January, p. 6.
    Brief report of the birthday celebration.

9   BROGAN, D.W. "New Books." Spectator 190 (20 November):592.
    Review of Always the Young Strangers. Reprint of 1953.10
with minor revisions.

10   _____. "Prairie Years." Manchester Guardian, 23 October,
      p. 4.
         Review of Always the Young Strangers. Finds in this
      "admirable and diverting book" a familiar art form, but Sand-
      burg's story is different. He is not gloomy or pessimistic, his
      parents are not rich, his father is not "silent, unforthcoming
      and nearly illiterate." His story fully justifies telling it.
      Reprinted with revisions: 1953.9.

11   BROOKS, VAN WYCK. The Writer in America. New York: E.P.
      Dutton, p. 93.
         "Only unfashionable writers like Sandburg could see nobil-
      ity and dignity at home, as most of the writers had seen a
      century before."

12   BROWN, KARL. "Biography." Library Journal 78 (1 January):52.
         Review of Always the Young Strangers.

13   BUTCHER, FANNY. "Sandburg's Typically American Story."
      Chicago Sunday Tribune, 4 January, p. 3.
         Review of Always the Young Strangers. Calls the prose
      factual, "shot through with his personality." But he makes no
      attempt "to draw conclusions from his own life, to hint that in
      his boyhood and early manhood days there was anything that told
      him that one day he would be called a genius."

14   CALKINS, ERNEST E. "Education of an American Poet."
      Saturday Review of Literature 36 (17 January):9.
         Review of Always the Young Strangers. Comments on the
      frankness and honesty of this book. "This is authentic
      America, . . . a chapter in the history of this country."
      Finds here "everything that contributed to the shaping of
      [Sandburg's] life and mind."

15   CARRUTH, HAYDEN. "Sandburg's Middle West." Nation 176
      (24 January):82.
         Review of Always the Young Strangers. Notes the bad gram-
      mar, formlessness, "unfeeling use of language," and "appalling
      juxtapositions" in this "roundtable and sometimes vexatious
      memoir." Comments on the qualities we commonly associate with
      the Midwest.

16   CONRAD, WILL C. "Carl Sandburg's Milwaukee Days." Historical
      Messenger (Milwaukee) 9 (June):6–10.
         Reminisces about Sandburg's period in Milwaukee and com-
      ments on his development as a journalist and poet.

17 DODD, SUE. "This Swedish Family Grew up with America." Farm
    Journal 77 (June):110.
        Brief biographical background and review of Always the
    Young Strangers. Finds "inspiration for everybody in Sandburg's
    rich narrative." It is a "catalog of memories."

18 DUNN, LOUISE D. "Carl Sandburg." New York Herald-Tribune,
    10 October, p. 16.
        Poem in commemoration of Sandburg's achievement.

19 FREEMAN, DOUGLAS SOUTHALL, ed. Praise for Carl Sandburg
    (from Some of His Friends on the Occasion of His 75th Birth-
    day, January 6, 1953). San Francisco: Peregrine Press,
    24 pp.
        Friends write about the man who has become an American
    institution, combining the past and the present, art and
    instinct, "the wisdom of the head and the deeper reason of the
    heart."

20 HAMBURGER, PHILIP. "Television: Out of Galesburg." New
    Yorker 29 (21 February):7.
        Review of Sandburg's appearance on NBC television. His
    opening number was a bit "too pat and professional." But this
    "astonishing gentleman" improved when he told anecdotes of his
    years at Galesburg. He spoke with "genuine conviction and
    genuine passion."

21 HANSEN, HARRY. "This Is Carl Sandburg Week." Chicago Sunday
    Tribune Books, 4 January, p. 9.
        Details relating to celebrations on the occasion of
    Sandburg's seventy-fifth birthday.

22 HEINBERG, AGAGE. "Carl Sandburg--diktare och lantbrukare."
    Samtid och Framtid (Stockholm) 10 (Winter):21-23.
        In Swedish. Brief review of Sandburg's achievements as
    poet. Includes biographical information.

23 HUTCHENS, JOHN K. "The Prairie Town Boyhood That Shaped Carl
    Sandburg's Life and Art." New York Herald-Tribune Book
    Review, 4 January, p. 1.
        Review of Always the Young Strangers. Calls this "a big,
    fine, rich book, easy and colloquial like a poem in Good Morning,
    America, and alive with those myriad specific facts that have a
    music of their own when an artist puts them together."

24 JACKSON, JOSEPH HENRY. "Through Youth's Eyes." San Francisco
    Chronicle, 6 January, p. 11.
        Review of Always the Young Strangers. This book is written
    with "humanity and genuine affection." It is a book for every-
    one. Calls it "as thoroughly and individually American as any
    first-generation success-story ever told."

25   JENKINS, ALAN. "Sandburg's Private Printings." <u>Journal of</u>
     <u>the Illinois State Historical Society</u> 45 (Winter):401-6.
          Brief report on the private printing of some of Sandburg's
     books by Philip Green Wright of Galesburg.

26   JOHNSON, GERALD W. "The Grass Roots and the Artist." <u>New</u>
     <u>Republic</u> 128 (19 January):18.
          Review of <u>Always the Young Strangers</u>. This is not poetry
     but rather "mother-of-poetry." For that reason "it is better
     adapted to the common uses of life than are the gems too precious
     for everyday wear."

27   JOHNSTON, RICHARD J.H. "Chicago in Tribute to Sandburg at
     75." <u>New York Times</u>, 7 January, p. 29.
          Editorial calling Sandburg "a kind of literary Liberty Bell
     ringing across the prairies and the decades. . . . He has been
     honestly a seeker, never sure that what he sought he has found or
     ever will find."

28   JOOST, NICHOLAS. "The Poet of Galesburg." <u>Commonweal</u> 57
     (16 January):381-82.
          Review of <u>Always the Young Strangers</u>. Calls this "a
     thickly detailed portrait of a life and of a time, the background
     of a career and . . . at least the center of a nation." In con-
     trast, <u>Remembrance Rock</u> and <u>Home Front Memo</u> are "downright embar-
     rassing." His poetry is "ideologically, proletarian and tech-
     nically, insipid." But his weaknesses as a poet lend strength to
     his autobiography. Love informs and fills the book, and as an
     American document it is comparable to Wolfe's <u>Look Homeward,</u>
     <u>Angel</u>. Excerpted: 1985.5.

29   KIRKPATRICK, CLAYTON. "Hog Butcher for World Kills Fatted
     Calf for Carl Sandburg." <u>Chicago Daily Tribune</u>, 7 January,
     p. 20.
          Expression of Chicago's tribute on Sandburg's seventy-fifth
     birthday.

30   LERNER, LEO A. "From Abe Lincoln to Pogo and the Atomic Age."
     <u>North Side Sunday Side</u> (Chicago), 1 February, p. 3.
          Interview with Sandburg covering his interests and
     ambitions.

31   "Letters Honoring Carl Sandburg in Pack Memorial Public
     Library." Asheville, N.C., 1950-53.
          Unpublished collection of letters in which more than 140
     Americans, from Franklin P. Adams to Darryl F. Zanuck, express
     their personal feelings about the poet on his seventy-fifth
     birthday.

32   MEIGS, CORNELIA, ELIZABETH NESBITT, ANNE EATON, and RUTH HILL
     VIGNERS. A Critical History of Children's Literature. New
     York: Macmillan, pp. 433, 472.
          Rootabaga Stories established Sandburg as a fabulist on a
     par with other writers of the 1920s, who were writing modern
     fairy tales.

33   NICHOLS, LEWIS. "Talk with Carl Sandburg." New York Times
     Book Review, 4 January, p. 18.
          Sandburg calls Always the Young Strangers "a biography of a
     town as filtered through the life of a boy." Discusses his plans
     for future work and comments on hoboing and his brief experience
     as cadet at West Point. Includes description of Sandburg's
     appearance and manner.

34   PRATT, HARRY EDWARD, ed. A Tribute to Carl Sandburg at
     Seventy-Five. Being A Special Edition of the Journal of the
     Illinois State Historical Society. Issued to Commemorate the
     75th Birthday of a Great American, January 6th, 1953.
     Chicago: Abraham Lincoln Book Shop, 416 pp.
          Reprint of 1952.29.

35   PRESCOTT, ORVILLE. "Books of the Times." New York Times,
     6 January, p. 27.
          Review of Always the Young Strangers. Marvels at
     Sandburg's "réclame" in this era of mass popularity for non-
     literary personages.

36   SHERWOOD, ROBERT E. "The Boy Grew up in Galesburg." New
     York Times Book Review, 4 January, pp. 1, 24.
          Review of Always the Young Strangers. Calls this "the best
     autobiography ever written by an American." It is utterly honest
     and hence has an universal appeal remindful of Pilgrim's
     Progress. Excerpted: 1985.5.

37   STROUD, PARRY. "Sandburg the Young Stranger." Prairie
     Schooner 27 (Fall):320-28.
          Review of Always the Young Strangers. Examines the main
     currents in Sandburg's earliest work, in which his "genuine
     modesty" prevents him from fully exploiting his early self. In
     the earliest poems are found seeds of some of the major ideas
     and attitudes that appear in his later work. They reveal
     Sandburg to have been "a wild young rebel and idealist," a man
     of honesty, courage, humor, and sensitivity. In Reckless Ecstasy
     represents a "modest advance" in his poetry. Incidentals is
     philosophical. Notes a recurrence of the word silence (or
     silences) here, akin to meditation. All this suggests that
     Sandburg was already consciously formulating "a theory of great-
     ness, linking experience, meditation, creativeness, and action."

38   THOMPSON, BLANCHE JENNINGS. "Other New Books." Catholic
      World 177 (April):77-78.
          Review of Always the Young Strangers. Comments on the
      "humor and wisdom and . . . abiding faith in the greatness of
      America" found in this volume. Reviews briefly his life.

39   TYLER, ALICE FELT. "United States History." American His-
      torical Review 58 (July):1003-4.
          Review of Always the Young Strangers. This is an "exact
      and careful picture" of a midwestern town covering twenty years
      of its history. "Every place, every person, even every collo-
      quialism, and every event which can be checked is true in fact
      and in spirit." Sandburg's vision is clear.

40   WEEKS, EDWARD. "What Makes an American." Atlantic Monthly
      191 (February):76, 78.
          Review of Always the Young Strangers. Sandburg is never
      obtrusive in a book which is "happy in tone, eager, full of
      character, and domestic in its interests."

                                1954

1   ANON. "Current Books." American Heritage 6 (December):115.
          Review of Abraham Lincoln: The Prairie Years and The War
      Years. "Very little has been lost in the condensation. The book
      is still Sandburg, and Sandburg at his best."

2   BAKER, RUSSELL. "Sandburg Muses on Goats, Guitars; Poet,
      Here to Accept Honor, Thinks a Strong President Is 'Diaboli-
      cally Cunning.'" New York Times, 15 December, p. 38.
          Interview on the occasion of receiving from the Civil War
      Round Table of New York a scroll hailing Sandburg as "'the
      Lincoln of our literature'" and "'the voice of America singing.'"

3   BOLTON, SARAH KNOWLES. Famous American Authors. Revised by
      William A. Fahey. New York: T.Y. Crowell, pp. 191-208.
          Introduces Sandburg, the man and the writer, with attention
      given to the development of his verse and life.

4   CAHOON, HERBERT. "General." Library Journal 79 (15 Septem-
      ber):1587.
          Review of Abraham Lincoln: The Prairie Years and The War
      Years. Finds everywhere Sandburg's "lyrical styles and absolute
      absorption in his subject." His Lincoln "stands by itself."

5   COURNOS, JOHN. "The Mind and Heart of a Hero." Commonweal 61
      (15 October):43-44.
          Review of Abraham Lincoln: The Prairie Years and The War
      Years. Calls the book "loose, rambling, diffuse," but because
      Sandburg was possessed by Lincoln "he has created not so much a

                                 85

book as a man." Sandburg has "wrought a heroic figure which none
should neglect, a figure of integrity, of wholeness."

6   COWLEY, MALCOLM. The Literary Situation. New York: Viking
    Press, 219 pp., passim.
        Brief references to Sandburg and his writings on Chicago.
    Includes discussion of his work habits.

7   DUFFEY, BERNARD. "The Struggle for Affirmation--Anderson,
    Sandburg, Lindsay." In The Chicago Renaissance in American
    Letters: A Critical History. East Lansing: Michigan State
    University Press, pp. 209-22.
        Develops the thesis that as Sandburg departs from facts,
    his ideas are lost in romantic vaporizings. His great theme is
    "the character of American life." Includes biographical back-
    ground. Reprinted: 1972.3.

8   HECHT, BEN. A Child of the Century. New York: Simon &
    Schuster, pp. 245-49, 252-55, 331-32, 339, 341.
        As a reporter for the Day Book and Chicago Daily News,
    Sandburg spoke with "the finest voice I have ever heard, reading
    or talking." In his voice lives all his poetry. "He always
    spoke like a man slowly revealing something." Found thrilling
    the way the commonplace was his center of focus. Includes an
    anecdote pertaining to the time that Sandburg sat for a portrait.

9   HEINEY, DONALD W. Essentials of Contemporary Literature.
    Great Neck, N.Y.: Barron's Educational Services, p. 141.
        Classifies Sandburg with E.A. Robinson, Frost, John
    Masefield of England, and Richard Dehmel of Germany as "verse
    naturalists."

10 McGILL, RALPH. "The Most Unforgettable Character I've Met."
    Reader's Digest 64 (May):109-13.
        Recalls visiting Sandburg at age seventy-six. "He is, him-
    self, so much the story of what America is supposed to mean:
    opportunity and life." Finds it easier to listen to him than to
    write about him. Covers his views on mountain life, loneliness,
    time, work habits, his mother's advice shortly before her death,
    and Lincoln.

11 MURROW, EDWARD ROSCOE. This I Believe: 2. New York: Simon
    & Schuster, pp. 128-29.
        Brief tribute to Sandburg, the man and the writer.

12 SHERWOOD, ROBERT E. "A Lincoln Portrait--and Monument." New
    York Times Book Review, 10 October, p. 10.
        Review of Abraham Lincoln: The Prairie Years and The War
    Years. This volume contains much but not all of "the grandeur of
    the originals." Calls it "a fine and incalculably valuable book"
    and those who never read the full work should be grateful for

"the labor and the pain" that Sandburg must have endured to prepare it.

13   STEINBERG, S.H.   "Carl (August) Sandburg."   In Cassell's Encyclopedia of World Literature.   2 vols.   New York: Funk & Wagnalls, pp. 202-5.
        Brief discussion of Sandburg's life and work with primary bibliography to date.

14   VAN DOREN, MARK.   "Sandburg's Great 'Abraham Lincoln,' Condensed and Still Masterly."   New York Herald-Tribune Book Review, 10 October, p. 3.
        Review of Abraham Lincoln: The Prairie Years and The War Years.   Sandburg gives us the figure of Lincoln: "unique and vast, and by some means we cannot measure, clear."   In either book, the original or this condensation, "we have a Lincoln whom no other man than Carl Sandburg could have given us."

15   WEST, REBECCA.   "Introduction."   In Selected Poems, by Carl Sandburg.   New York: Harcourt, pp. 15-28.
        The main determinant of Sandburg's art is "the power of his native idiom to deal with the inner life of man."   Comments on his technical virtuosity, propaganda, and similarities to Robert Burns.   Says that his vast image requires a thousand poems.   Includes biographical background.

16   WILLIAMS, T. HARRY.   "Lincoln in 500,000 Words."   Saturday Review of Literature 37 (13 November):16-17.
        Review of Abraham Lincoln: The Prairie Years and The War Years.   As a whole this biography is "superior" to the longer life.   It has "a form which the six [volumes] lacked."   Calls it "a tighter and tidier" book.   "It retains the superb qualities of the original work without the faults of the latter."

17   WILLIAMS, WILLIAM CARLOS.   "Carl Sandburg's 'Complete Poems.'"   In Selected Essays of William Carlos Williams.   New York: Random House, pp. 272-79.
        Reprint of 1951.17.

1955

1   ANON.   "Lincoln's Man Sandburg."   Newsweek 45 (14 February): 49-53.
        Biographical overview of Sandburg's contributions in poetry, folk songs, children's stories, and Lincoln biography. "Behind the public figure, the many roles of a long, busy life, he is an 'old man, mad about writing.'"

2   BECHTEL, LOUISE SEAMAN. "A Review of 'Prairie-Town Boy.'"
    New York Herald-Tribune Book Review, 15 May, p. 12.
        "In a book lacking climax or much drama, thoughtful older
    boys will feel the special spirit of a special person, of a boy
    unsure of any 'calling' or direction in his life, but growing in
    mental eagerness and in his judgments of people and of his
    world." Excerpted: 1985.5.

3   BENÉT, WILLIAM R[OSE]. "Carl Sandburg." In The Reader's
    Encyclopedia. New York: Thomas Y. Crowell, pp. 883–84, 987.
        Compares Sandburg to Whitman. Views him as part of the
    "proletarian literature" movement in England and America.

4   BUELL, ELLEN LEWIS. "Sandburg's Youth." New York Times Book
    Review, 10 April, p. 16.
        Review of Prairie-Town Boy. This volume lacks the "breadth
    and the depth" of the original (Always the Young Strangers) and
    also something of its "gusto." But it is still an "illuminating
    re-creation" of boyhood. Excerpted: 1985.5.

5   CIMINO, MARIA. "New Books." Saturday Review of Literature 38
    (14 May):52.
        Review of Prairie-Town Boy. Finds interesting the inci-
    dents and observations, for they are presented with "never-
    failing sparkle" in Sandburg's "inimitable storytelling style."
    Describes that style as "a sensitive and vigorous speech that has
    the ring of a living voice in it, full of warmth and sympathy."

6   DONLON, R.E. "Widening Horizons in Junior Reading."
    Christian Science Monitor, 7 April, p. 11.
        Review of Prairie-Town Boy. Notes Sandburg's "sympathetic
    awareness of people," his clarity of thought, his "staccato
    freshness." He seems to be "presenting pictures of his youth in
    the light of today."

7   EMERSON, WILLIAM A., Jr. "At Home: All Brightness and
    Whiteness." Newsweek 45 (14 February):53.
        Interview with Sandburg's wife and others and a description
    of their home. For her, "married life with a genius has been
    most rewarding. . . . The time a man is difficult is before he's
    found himself."

8   GREEN, A.B. "Trade Winds: Boston Arts Festival Award."
    Saturday Review of Literature 28 (30 July):5.
        In June Sandburg received a poetry prize at the Boston Arts
    Festival. Archibald MacLeish praised him as the "poet of the
    American affirmation." Includes a reproduction of the citation
    on the plaque.

9   HOFFMAN, FREDERICK J. The Twenties. New York: Viking Press,
    pp. 259, 262.
        Discusses Sandburg's poetry in terms of "mechanomorphism"--
    the worship or distorted viewing of the machine. But shows that
    with Sandburg it is always in terms of the human relationship
    with which all machines are intertwined.

10 KRIM, SEYMOUR. "Voice of America." Commonweal 62 (17 June):
    283-84.
        Review of Prairie-Town Boy. In a "lean, hard prose"
    Sandburg drives home everything he intends, and yet remains
    "quite boyishly fresh and engaging in spite of its obvious
    mastery."

11 L., J.D. "Biography and History." Horn Book 31 (June):
    189-90.
        Review of Prairie-Town Boy. Calls this a "genuine biog-
    raphy, often moving, often full of fun."

12 MEARS, LOUISE WILHELMINA. They Come and Go: Short
    Biographies. Boston: Christopher Publishing House, pp. 96-97.
        Brief information about Sandburg's life and his travels as
    an entertainer.

13 REID, MARGARET WALRAVEN. "Junior High." Library Journal 80
    (15 June):1514.
        Review of Prairie-Town Boy. Sandburg tells his story "un-
    emotionally, with restraint and modesty, but with sincerity and
    straightforwardness, in his own eloquent, moving style."

14 SCOGGIN, MARGARET C. "Interesting People." Horn Book 31
    (August):277.
        Review of Prairie-Town Boy. Calls this "an introduction
    not only to Sandburg but also to America." Its manner is
    "poetic but clear and vigorous."

15 SWANSON, JAMES A. A History of Lombard College, 1851-1930.
    Macomb: Western Illinois State College, 194 pp., passim.
        Includes discussion of Sandburg's years as a student at
    Lombard College and of how he grew to distinction among his
    colleagues.

16 WALDORP, EVELYN BROCK. "Carl Sandburg, the Musician." Étude
    73 (September):11, 41-43.
        Finds in Sandburg the qualities that account for his suc-
    cess as a writer the same as for a musician: his vision, passion
    for humanity, "deep probing for beauty," and Lincolnesque sense
    of humor. Includes a memoir of seeing him in 1936 and an inter-
    view in which he explains how his love for music grew. Sandburg
    can "sell" a song.

1   ANON. "News of the Week: Broadcast Music Honors Carl
    Sandburg." Publishers Weekly 169 (3 March):1250.
        Reports on a dinner held in honor of Lincoln (and there-
    fore of Sandburg) at the Netherlands Club, New York, on
    26 January.

2   ANON. "Visit with Carl Sandburg." Look 20 (10 July):95–100.
        Offers an appreciation of the Sandburgs' life in Flat Rock,
    North Carolina; includes photographs.

3   BREIT, HARVEY. Writers Observed. Cleveland: World
    Publishing, pp. 251–53.
        Reprint of 1952.6.

4   HART, JAMES D. "Carl Sandburg." In The Oxford Companion to
    American Literature. 3d ed. New York and London: Oxford
    University Press, p. 667.
        Characteristics of Sandburg's poetry come not only from his
    experience with America, but from what "Whitman had taught him to
    recognize as symbolic of a free, untrammeled, democratic promised
    life."

5   HAVIGHURST, WALTER. "The Prairie Poets." In The Heartland:
    Ohio, Indiana, Illinois. New York: Harper & Row, pp. 320–24.
        Of the poet, says he could be "cryptic and sardonic like
    Masters, expansive like Lindsay, and pure Sandburg," as in
    "Chicago." All of his landscapes are for people. His language
    is "the language of life, the strong, plain, common language of
    the people." For Sandburg, language "never could grow stale."

6   LENHART, CHARMENY. Musical Influences on American Poetry.
    Athens: University of Georgia Press, p. 289.
        Refers to Sandburg and Lindsay as troubadour poets. Both
    are "vibrant examples of the influence of music upon modern
    verse." Mentions American Songbag.

7   SCHERMAN, DAVID EDWARD, and ROSEMARIE REDLICH. America: The
    Land and Its Writers. New York: Dodd, Mead, p. 73.
        Brief reference to Sandburg. Includes photograph and brief
    biography.

8   SCHLAUCH, MARGARET. Modern English and American Poetry.
    London: A.C. Watts, p. 116.
        The People, Yes is the outstanding example of Sandburg's
    democratic statement in poetry. But finds there a "flatness of
    effect [which] is in turn traceable to his passive conception of
    the very people he glorifies. They listen, they suffer, but
    their revolt is indefinitely postponed."

9   STROUD, PARRY. "Carl Sandburg: A Biographical and Critical
     Study of His Major Works." Ph.D. diss., Northwestern Univer-
     sity, 491 pp.
        Discusses the influence of time and place of Sandburg's
     birth on his literary career, including his themes, intellectual
     heritage, and style. Examines The Chicago Race Riots, poetry
     books for children, fiction, and biography, which he calls "an
     act of devotion to America."

10   TAYLOR, WALTER F[ULLER]. The Story of American Letters.
     Chicago: Henry Regnery, p. 374.
        Sandburg is the poet of industry. He fulfills the creed of
     the Imagists without being one. He writes cadenced poetic prose.
     He is reminiscent of Whitman. "His worst fault is his uneven-
     ness."

                                1957

1   ANON. "Poet in Chicago." New York Times Magazine,
     15 September, p. 40.
        Photographs of Sandburg touring Chicago railway and Lake
     Michigan, U.S. Steel's Gary works, and construction site.

2   ANON. "Wright, Sandburg Steal Chicago Dynamic Show."
     Architectural Forum 107 (December):12-14, 71.
        Brief account of Sandburg's speaking engagement at the
     "Chicago Dynamic Week" conference sponsored by U.S. Steel. In-
     cludes excerpts from his speech. Describes Sandburg and Frank
     Lloyd Wright as "Chicago's--and the nation's--leading profes-
     sional personalities."

3   DEMPSEY, DAVID. "Auditing the Treasury." New York Times Book
     Review, 1 December, p. 7.
        Review of The Sandburg Range. An excellent beginning for
     the reader coming to Sandburg for the first time. For the expe-
     rienced reader, this selection is not generous enough.

4   DRINKWATER, JOHN, ed. The Outline of Literature. London:
     George Newnes, p. 989.
        Brief survey of Sandburg's life and career.

5   GANNETT, LEWIS. "A Carl Sandburg Gathering, Wide as His
     Prairie Sky." New York Herald-Tribune Book Review,
     8 December, p. 1.
        Review of The Sandburg Range. Calls the book "magnifi-
     cent." Finds it hard to quarrel with "a prairie sky, and that
     is what this book is."

6   KREYMBORG, ALFRED. "Chicago." In Troubadour: An Auto-
     biography. New York: Hill & Wang, pp. 279–85.
     Reprint of 1925.7.

7   McDONALD, GERALD D. "General." Library Journal 82
     (1 October):2450.
          Review of The Sandburg Range. Whatever form Sandburg uses,
     "he has been the poet . . . of America's past, present and
     future." The results are "impressive."

*8   MAURIN, MARIO. "Carl Sandburg y el mito de América."
     Cuadernos del Congreso por la libertad de la cultura 26
     (Spring):35–40.
          In Spanish. Cited in 1963.8.

9   NEWMAN, RALPH G. "The Essence of the Many Carl Sandburgs."
     Chicago Sunday Tribune Magazine of Books, 3 November, p. 3.
          Review of The Sandburg Range. Calls this "an amazing feat
     of selection and editing." It is a book to fit "any mood, a
     volume you can live with--and most profitably."

10   _____. "A Shelf of New Anthologies and Other Books that Are
     Made Not Born." Christian Science Monitor, 21 November,
     p. 15.
          Review of The Sandburg Range. This collection reaches into
     "every phase of Carl Sandburg's prodigious creative activity."

11   SPENCER, BENJAMIN T. The Quest for Nationality. Syracuse:
     Syracuse University Press, pp. 288, 337.
          Refers to Sandburg's "vigor" and "raciness." Neither was
     "wholly fused into a Western mind and idiom." Sandburg and
     others depicted the immigrant not merely as "picturesque mate-
     rial" but as "an imaginative worker."

12   WALSER, RICHARD GAITHER. Picturebook of Tar Heel Authors.
     Raleigh, N.C.: State Department of Archives and History,
     p. 12.
          Photograph of Sandburg.

13   YATRON, MICHAEL. "The Influence of Populism on Edgar Lee
     Masters, Vachel Lindsay, and Carl Sandburg." Ph.D. diss.,
     Temple University, 297 pp.
          Calls Sandburg both "Populistic and nostalgic." He wrote
     in "a distinctively American idiom." Finds that nostalgia is a
     consistent theme throughout his writings. Examines the influence
     on his work of populism and friendship with Masters and Lindsay.

1958

1   ANON. "Sandburg, Nearing 80, Looks to Future." New York Times, 5 January, p. 16.
    Brief interview in which Sandburg discusses plans for another book of verse.

2   BREIT, HARVEY. "Sandburg at 80: To Life Itself, Yes." New York Times Magazine, 5 January, p. 14.
    Sandburg has stood out against the need to be "fashionable, to be expedient, to compromise." His verse is "independent, honest, direct, lyric, and it endures." He has never deflected from the poems.

3   COOKE, ALISTAIR. "Chicago Dynamic." AIA Journal 29 (January):18–23.
    Excerpts from a conversation between Frank Lloyd Wright and Sandburg, guided by Cooke.

4   COURNOS, JOHN. "Sandburgiana." Commonweal 67 (14 March): 622–23.
    Sandburg's literary reputation probably will rest on his Lincoln biography. In The Sandburg Range, some of his poems are serious, others are "mild postscripts" to Whitman, others are not poems at all. But he never fails as a poet when he comes to the theme of Lincoln. The Rootabaga Stories are "extremely fanciful, and have a peculiar charm." His biographical material is forthright, modest, matter-of-fact. Remembrance Rock communicates a message to America, but the author "seems scarcely interested in Americans as individuals." Excerpted: 1985.5.

5   DUFFEY, BERNARD. "Progressivism and Personal Revolt." Centennial Review 2 (Spring):125–38.
    Discusses Garland, Masters, and Sandburg and the western populist movement.

6   FLANAGAN, JOHN T. "Carl Sandburg at Eighty." Journal of the Illinois State Historical Society 51 (Summer):191–98.
    Tribute on the occasion of his eightieth birthday visit to to the University of Illinois, Urbana. "Surely no writer better represents today the idealism of the American folk and the conviction that the people will triumph in the future than this rugged, prairie-born poet of Swedish descent." Recommends him for the Nobel Prize. Includes brief biographical background.

7   FLANAGAN, JOHN T., ed. "Introduction." In The Sandburg Range: An Exhibit of Materials from Carl Sandburg's Library Placed on Display in the University of Illinois Library on January 6, 1958. The Adah Patton Memorial Fund Publication no. 6. Urbana: University of Illinois, 47 pp.

Seeks "to show the versatility and vitality of a great
writer and a rich personality." Arranged in ten headings:
Apprenticeship, "Juvenilia," Journalist, Poet, Teller of Tales,
Troubadour, Essayist, Biographer, Collector, Celebrity. Comments
on Sandburg's "awareness of nature, his appreciation of nuance
and tone and an equal awareness of man." Includes tributes from
Nelson Algren, Norman Corwin, Christopher Morley, William
Saroyan, and John Steinbeck.

8   GLAUBER, ROBERT H. "Right Word." Christian Century 75
     (12 February):199.
        Review of The Sandburg Range. This collection demonstrates
"the scope of his mind, the fluidity of his pen and the remarkable grasp he has of the unique genius of this country." His
poetic vision of America is "uniquely vital."

9   HEINEY, DONALD. "Carl Sandburg (born 1878)." In Recent
     American Literature. Woodbury, N.Y.: Barron's Educational
     Series, pp. 449–53, 592.
        Biographical overview. Traces Sandburg's literary reputa-
tion and influences on him and his work. His early writings are
"vigorous, often emotional lyrics of urban and proletarian life
in the manner of Whitman's Leaves of Grass." His later works are
"the small carefully-polished word-pictures resembling the work
of Amy Lowell and the other Imagists."

10   MAGILL, FRANK N. "Sandburg, Carl." In Cyclopedia of World
     Authors. New York: Harper, pp. 388–41.
        Covers Sandburg's career and significant milestones in his
life.

11   NELSON, JAMES, ed. "Introduction." In Wisdom: Conversations
     with the Elder Wise Men of Our Day. New York: W.W. Norton,
     pp. 141–50.
        Conversation between Sandburg and Edward Stanley, director
of public affairs for NBC. Sandburg talks about his favorite
poems.

12   REXROTH, KENNETH. "Search for Sandburg." Nation 186
     (22 February):171–72.
        Review of The Sandburg Range. Praises this as "magnifi-
cent," even though it "may be argued that there are, or aren't,
greater contemporary poets," that Sandburg is not the greatest
biographer, or that Remembrance Rock is not a novel. Prefers the
early Sandburg to the later. After 1925 his verse ceases to con-
tain anything of interest. His reputation will rest upon the
poetry that is "absolutely right" because it is "rooted in real
speech, in folksongs and lore, in real people, with never the
slip of literature showing."

13   SANDBURG, HELGA. "Life with Father and Our Books." Saturday
      Review of Literature 41 (29 November):10–13.
         Memoir of Sandburg and family by his daughter. Comments on
      the poet as monologist, on how she was raised to believe that her
      father was a "genius and his faculties uncommon," on how she
      typed Abraham Lincoln: The War Years for him, and her own grow-
      ing desire to write, leading to the publication of The Wheel of
      Earth. "He spoke the truth, the divine word."

                                    1959

1   ANON. "Carl Sandburg Visits Swedish Kinfolk." Life 47
      (21 September):169–71.
         Accompanies Sandburg on his first visit to his Swedish
      homeland to visit the village where his mother was born. In-
      cludes photographs.

2   ANON. "Poet in Flight." Newsweek 54 (3 August):44.
         Describes Sandburg's trip across the United States on the
      first jet passenger flight.

3   CLEMENS, C. "Carl Sandberg [sic] at Galesburg." Hobbies 63
      (February):121.
         Brief biographical insights into Sandburg's life at
      Galesburg.

4   CORWIN, NORMAN [LEWIS]. "The Magic of Sandburg." In The
      World of Carl Sandburg (souvenir magazine). Los Angeles:
      Gilbert Rich.
         The results of a 1958 UCLA program called "The Sandburg
      Tribute." (See also 1961.3.)

5   DE JOUVENAL, BERTRAND. "Carl Sandburg: Éléments d'une bio-
      graphie." Europe 37 (February–March):70–78.
         In French. Overview of Sandburg's life with references to
      his poetry and prose.

*6   DE POLI, FRANCO, ed. and trans. "Gente d'America." Il Ponte
      15 (July–August):965–72.
         Cited in 1963.8.

7   DODD, LORING HOLMES. Celebrities at Our Hearthside. Boston:
      Dresser, Chapman & Grimes, pp. 116–20.
         Biographical details with photographs of Sandburg relaxing.

8   GARCIA BLANCO, MANUEL. "Unanumo y tres poeta Sandburg norte-
      americanos." Asomante 15 (April–June):39–44.
         In Spanish. Finds in Unanumo's Cancionero echoes of
      Sandburg's Selected Poems, among others. Poem 1347 shows the
      strong impression resulting from Sandburg's "Haze."

9   No entry

10   HARKNESS, DAVID J., and R. GERALD McMURTRY. Lincoln's Favorite Poets. Knoxville: University of Tennessee Press, p. 88.
      Calls attention to Sandburg's Lincoln poems, his being called "poet of the people," and the widespread recognition given him as "the most Lincolnian of our modern poets." Those who have heard him read have "felt the spirit of the Great Emancipator speaking again."

11   JONES, HOWARD M[UMFORD]. Guide to American Literature and Its Background since 1890. Cambridge: Harvard University Press, pp. 176, 231, 233.
      Lists Sandburg's publications to date and refers to secondary sources.

12   KARSH, YOUSUF. Portraits of Greatness. New York: Nelson, p. 174.
      Photograph of Sandburg with description of how it was taken. (See also 1961.9)

13   KOLBE, HENRY E. "Religion and the Arts: Christ and Carl Sandburg." Religion in Life 28 (Spring):248-61.
      Finds a strong religious feeling and expression running through his poetry. Comments on his sensitivity to God and Christ, his hatred of injustice, and his interest in the meaning of human history and destiny. Includes a discussion of "Sandburg's Picture of Jesus," "Poems of Wrath and Indignation," and "The Eternal Christ."

14   RUGGLES, ELEANOR. The West-Going Heart: A Life of Vachel Lindsay. New York: Norton, p. 261.
      Quotes Lindsay's comment to Harriet Monroe that although he doesn't approve of free verse, he does approve of Sandburg and Masters: "I am certainly glad they are alive."

15   UNTERMEYER, LOUIS. Lives of the Poets: The Story of One Thousand Years of English and American Poetry. New York: Simon & Schuster, pp. 636-38, 707.
      Brief biographical background, discussion of the critical reception given to Complete Poems, and comment on the importance of The People, Yes. "More volubly than any poet since Whitman, Sandburg ranged over the United States." He is the "laureate of industrial America" and his poetry is "the slow, rambling transcriptions of the skald who made himself a national bard."

16   YATRON, MICHAEL. "Carl Sandburg: The Poet as Nonconformist." English Journal 48 (December):524-27, 539.
      Sandburg has always been "the voice of the free man." His popular appeal is due to both diction and content. He communicates with the masses. His sounds are recognizable, and he is

"a model of nonconformity and humanitarianism." Comments on
Sandburg's attitude toward war, big business, prejudice, class
stratifiction, honest toil. Recommends that the secondary
teacher introduce the subject of poetry to students who have an
aversion to it by beginning with the work of Sandburg. From him,
the teacher can lead his pupils on to more complex and rewarding
poetry. Excerpted: 1985.5.

17   _____. "Carl Sandburg" and "The Spirit of the Rustic." In
      America's Literary Revolt. New York: Philosophical Library,
      pp. 123-64, 165-69.
          Discusses the influence of populism on Sandburg. Where the
      people are concerned, Sandburg has the faith and irrationality of
      a mystic. He is a literary populist, agrarian and nostalgic in
      outlook, hostile to modern technology.

                                1960

1   ALLEN, GAY WILSON. "Carl Sandburg: Fire and Smoke." South
     Atlantic Quarterly 59 (Summer):315-31.
         Examines Sandburg's acceptance of the Midwest myth, the
     creation of his own private myth, and reevaluates him to discover
     "exactly what as a poet he is or is not." He is not a thinker
     (like Robinson or Eliot) or a philosopher (like Frost), but a
     seeker and wanderer. His philosophy is "pluralistic, empirical,
     positivistic." His faults: often false logic, simplified view
     of people, sentimentality, slang and colloquialisms. But he is
     a master of the enigmatic metaphor characteristic of metaphysical
     poetry. And like that in the haiku manner, his poetry is dis-
     tinguished by "his oblique approach (and paradox) of deeply
     etched implication." Calls him "one of the most formal of all
     free verse poets, with a greater sense of form than many poets
     who use rhythm and meter." Excerpted: 1974.1.

2   ANON. "Carl Sandburg's Day." New York Times, 14 September,
     p. 42.
         Mayor Robert Wagner declares 14 September to be "Carl
     Sandburg Day." The World of Carl Sandburg debuts at the Henry
     Miller Theatre on Broadway.

3   BARON, JEAN. Review of Wind Song. Chicago Sunday Tribune,
     6 November, p. 18.
         Calls these "gentle poems about familiar things." Finds
     none of Sandburg's "tense, harsh city poems."

4   BISHOP, CLAIRE HERBERT. "A Selective List of Children's
     Books." Commonweal 73 (18 November):210.
         Review of Wind Song. Refers to Sandburg as "the beloved
     poet." Recommends these poems to all ages.

*5　COMBECHER, HANS. "Bemerkungen und Interpretationsvorschläege zur Behandlung der War Poetry." Die Neueren Sprachen 9 (January):24–38.
　　　Cited in 1963.8.

6　EWING, RUBY. "Grades 3–6." Library Journal 85 (15 December): 4570.
　　　Review of Wind Song. "This is modern verse about people, places, and things with strong nature themes." It is of special appeal to young people.

7　GIBSON, WALKER. "Second Harvest." New York Times Book Review, 25 December, p. 13.
　　　Review of Wind Song. Young readers should have little difficulty with these poems. Sandburg is not "particularly profound" but gives "much pleasure with these vigorous, if sometimes bombastic, lines of poetry."

8　GOLDEN, HARRY [LEWIS]. "Only in America." New York World Telegram and Sun, 6 January, p. 13.
　　　Overview of Sandburg's career. He made "the best of the time he lived in." Despite all the cruelty he witnessed and reported, "the message of his books was that Americans are really nice guys."

9　HOWARD, LEON. Literature and the American Tradition. New York: Doubleday, p. 315.
　　　Compares Sandburg and Whitman. Sandburg is a "professed" follower of the "Good Gray Poet."

10　KERR, WALTER. "World of Carl Sandburg." New York Herald-Tribune, 15 September, p. 14.
　　　Review of The World of Carl Sandburg. Devotes most of the review to the performers. "The poet requires no vote from me. And the people, yes."

11　LIBBY, MARGARET SHERWOOD. "Imaginative Riches in Song, Story, Poetry and Myths for All Ages." New York Herald-Tribune Book Review, 13 November, sec. 12, p. 2.
　　　Review of Wind Song. Expresses gratitude for Sandburg's gift to young readers.

12　LOVEJOY, ARTHUR O. The Great Chain of Being: A Study of the History of an Idea. New York: Harper, p. 317.
　　　Reprint of 1936.14.

13　ROBIN, AL. "Living Legends." Today's Health 38 (February): 6, 79.
　　　Brief portrait of Sandburg.

14   ROSENFELD, M.L. The Modern Poets. New York and London:
      Oxford University Press, pp. 155–56.
            Calls Sandburg a minimal stylist who learned much from the
      imagists. He is most effective as a "poetic socialist." His
      popular poetry enchants us as "not too savage, not too committed,
      not too unpleasant or 'difficult' for contemplation." Calls it
      "half poetry" few of us would want to do without.

15   SCHEER, JULIAN. "Carl Sandburg Tells Parade Readers What Made
      Lincoln Laugh." Parade, 7 February, pp. 20–21.
            Interview in which Sandburg discusses Lincoln's sense of
      humor.

16   SCHUMACH, MURRAY. "Hollywood Feat: Carl Sandburg Scores Hit
      in Funny, Iconoclastic Press Conference." New York Times,
      31 July, sec. 2, p. 5.
            Interview news conference to announce Sandburg's work as
      consultant for The Greatest Story Ever Told. Comments on
      religious movies, casting, Remembrance Rock (as a possible
      film), and his hotel room.

17   _____. "Sandburg's World." New York Times, 11 September,
      sec. 2, pp. 1, 7.
            Reveals that Sandburg was literary consultant to Hollywood
      director George Stevens in the latter's production of a motion
      picture biography of Jesus, worked with Twentieth Century–Fox
      studio, and met with Marilyn Monroe, Elvis Presley, and others.

18   SHAPIRO, KARL. In Defense of Ignorance. New York: Random
      House, pp. 265–66.
            Refers to his solicitation of William Carlos Williams to
      write a review of Collected Poems for Poetry (see 1951.17;
      1954.17). "Sandburg never forgave this essay."

19   TAUBMAN, HOWARD. "Soul of a Poet." New York Times,
      15 September, p. 44.
            Review of The World of Carl Sandburg. Says that Sandburg
      was a man of many roles, but had the "soul of a poet."

20   THORP, WILLIAM. "New Voices." In American Writing in the
      Twentieth Century. Cambridge: Harvard University Press,
      pp. 26, 33–35.
            Says the realism of Chicago Poems "delighted some
      Chicagoans and disgusted others." His themes and style in
      subsequent volumes changed little. At best, he writes "short,
      vivid impressions of persons or places" in formal, free-verse
      mode. "Though Sandburg made little technical progress as a
      poet, his faith in the people, in their ability to endure and
      come through, remained strong through the years." His best
      testament to the American people is in The People, Yes. In

Lincoln, however, he found the subject "best suited to his talents and his democratic faith."

21   V., R.H. "Poetry and Rhymes." Horn Books 36 (December): 518-19.
     Review of Wind Song. These poems "all are the kind young people will keep in their hearts and minds."

22   VAN DOREN, MARK. "Introduction." In Harvest Poems 1910-1960, by Carl Sandburg. New York: Harcourt, Brace, pp. 5-10.
     Stresses Sandburg's view of the world, not his style, as "the chief thing about his poetry." He has a sense of humor and questions the meaning of life.

1961

1   ANON. "An Afternoon with Carl Sandburg." Telefilm Magazine 5 (July-August):28-31.
     Brief interview with Sandburg covering his poetry and plans for new work.

2   BAKER, RUSSELL. "Sandburg Is Critical of Eisenhower on the Peace Corps." New York Times, 26 October, pp. 37, 39.
     Press conference held on the occasion of the opening of the Civil War Centennial exhibition at the Library of Congress, and Sandburg's visit with President Kennedy.

3   CORWIN, NORMAN LEWIS. The World of Carl Sandburg: A Stage Presentation. New York: Harcourt, Brace & World, 113 pp.
     State presentation composed of excerpts from Sandburg's writings, illustrating the varied aspects of his career and life, joined by a commentary written by Corwin (see 1959.4).

4   CREMASCHI, INISERO. "Chicago di Sandburg." La fiera letteraria 16 (9 July):5.
     In Italian. Mentions Sandburg's treatment of Chicago in verse.

5   GOLDEN, HARRY LEWIS. Carl Sandburg. Cleveland: World Publishing, 287 pp.
     Anecdotal recounting of Sandburg's success as poet, historian, biographer, novelist, musician, journalist, and man of his country. Drawn from letters, journals, anecdotes, and other unpublished documents. Says that Sandburg's deep knowledge of America became distinctively his--"the America of the working Midwesterner, the laborer, the union man, the scab, the Wobbly." Includes background on the Lincoln books and Sandburg's work in behalf of the Socialist party. Lists primary works to 1960. Includes excerpt from 1920.15.

6   HARRIS, MARK. "Pride and Wisdom of Two Great Old Poets:
    Sandburg and Frost." Life 51 (1 December):101.
    Comparative commentary on the two poets.

7   HAVERLIN, CARL. "Introduction." In Address, Upon the Occa-
    sion of Abraham Lincoln's One Hundredth Inaugural Anniversary,
    East Front of the Capitol, March 4, 1961, by Carl Sandburg.
    Chicago: Black Cat Press, pp. v–vii.
    Discusses Sandburg's interest in Lincoln.

8   JENKINS, ALAN. "Portraits of Carl Sandburg." Lincoln Herald
    63 (Summer):77–84.
    Penned pictures of Sandburg from the data on his Spanish-
    American War discharge form (1898) to a thumbnail portrait (1953)
    by Adlai E. Stevenson. Characterizations involving the voice,
    features, and dress of Sandburg as student, reporter, folk
    singer, and poet are included. Given also are testimonies by
    Harry Hansen, Ben Hecht, Lloyd Lewis, Edgar Lee Masters, Burton
    Rascoe, Don C. Shoemaker, Henry Justin Smith, and Philip Green
    Wright.

9   KARSH, YOUSUF. Portraits of Greatness. London and
    Edinburgh: Thomas Nelson, p. 175.
    Says that Sandburg must "delight any photographer." He is
    and looks "a self-made man." Includes photograph taken in
    Karsh's New York studio-apartment and the poet's remarks on
    public readings and Winston Churchill. (See also 1959.12)

10 LAWSON, EVALD BENJAMIN. "Carl Sandburg: Notes from a Friend-
    ship." Swedish Pioneer Historical Quarterly 12 (July):89–99.
    Finds in Sandburg's writings an influence from his early
    experiences with manual labor and his acquaintance with common
    people. His work habits owe much to the traits inherited from
    his Swedish immigrant parents. Includes several anecdotes
    illustrating Sandburg's admiration for Lincoln.

11 LEE, RANDY. "Hear Your Heroes: Carl Sandburg." Seventeen 20
    (January):92–93, 100.
    Appreciation of Sandburg as a man and writer.

12 PEARCE, ROY HARVEY. "The Old Poetry and the New." In The
    Continuity of American Poetry. Princeton: Princeton Univer-
    sity Press, pp. 269–71.
    Sandburg's optimistic faith in the people is noted, but he
    fails to fulfill his social role. Regrets that Sandburg only
    registers the sentiments of the people and does nothing to
    enhance or change them.

13   PEARSON, NORMAN HOLMES. "Kaleidoscope of the Poet." Saturday Review of Literature 44 (16 December):19.
        Mentions Sandburg's comment about Harry Golden: "Whatever is human interests [him]." Refers to Sandburg's "perpetual vitality and kindness."

14   REXROTH, KENNETH. "Poets Old and New." In Assays [sic]. New York: New Directions, pp. 223–25.
        Sandburg's poetry is "rooted in real speech, in folksongs and lore, in real people." At the start of his career he had "sound ideas and fine intentions." But then he "fell for the American Way of Life, and gave up 'real people.'" Excerpted: 1973.9.

15   SCHORER, MARK. Sinclair Lewis: An American Way of Life. New York: McGraw-Hill, pp. 305, 337, 339, 399, 423.
        Brief mention of Lewis's contacts with Sandburg in Chicago, at his home at Elmhurst, at a coffeehouse, as dinner guest of Dr. Fishbein. Includes memoir of Sandburg's singing "The Buffalo Skinners."

1962

*1   BRADLEY, PRESTON. Along the Way. New York: David McKay. Cited in 1963.8.

2   BRADLEY, SCULLEY. "The Renaissance in Poetry." In A Time of Harvest: American Literature 1910-1960. Edited by Robert E. Spiller. New York: Hill & Wang, p. 22.
        Sandburg, Frost, and Robinson wanted to express the immediate condition of twentieth-century humanity in appropriate poetry. Their best work "approaches greatness."

3   BROWNING, D.C., comp. "Sandburg, Carl." In Everyman's Dictionary of Literary Biographies: English and American. New York: E.P. Dutton, pp. 133–34.
        Biographical essay with brief mention of his major works.

4   ELMEN, PAUL. "The Fame of Jeremy Taylor." Anglican Theological Review 34 (October):389–403.
        Discusses Sandburg's use of Jeremy Taylor as a source for his own work.

5   GARLAND, H.B. "Carl Sandburg, poeta del pueblo norteamericano." Salon 13 (Summer):17–23.
        In Spanish. Tribute to Sandburg as poet.

6   GERTZ, ELMER. "Birthday Snapshots." Journal of the Illinois State Historical Society 45 (Winter):379–83.
        Describes Sandburg's seventy-fifth birthday celebration; includes photographs.

7   HELMSTADTER, FRANCES. Picture Book of American Authors. New
    York: Sterling, pp. 41-43.
    Photographs of Sandburg.

8   KORGES, JAMES. "James Dickey and Other Good Poets."
    Minnesota Review 3 (Winter):481-82.
        Review of Honey and Salt. Calls this volume "negligible,"
    the achievement, slight. Says that respect for Sandburg has
    tempered much criticism of his later work. Regrets that pub-
    blicity is given to a "minor talent"--"easy irony, easy postur-
    ing, easy nihilism, and easy yea-saying."

9   PRATT, JOHN CLARK. The Meaning of Modern Poetry. New York:
    Doubleday, pp. 178, 181, 184.
        Analyzes Sandburg's verse line by line with questions and
    answers for purposes of self-study and self-teaching. Covers
    language, form, style, theme, and meaning.

10 WHITRIDGE, ARNOLD. "Robert Frost and Carl Sandburg: The Two
    Elder Statesmen of American Poetry." Bulletin of the New York
    Public Library 66 (March):164, 171-77.
        Frost and Sandburg complement each other. Both are worthy
    successors of the great Victorian poets. Frost is independent, a
    lover of nature, restrained, isolated from urban society, and
    consciously artistic. Sandburg is democratic, noisy, exuberant,
    a lover of cities and machines, and in revolt against the re-
    straints of traditional poetic form. Each poet reveals "a new
    vision of the nature of things."

11 WILSON, EDMUND. Patriotic Gore: Studies in the Literature of
    the American War. New York and London: Oxford University
    Press, pp. 115-17.
        Sandburg's biography of Lincoln, although useless as a
    source for reported incidents, is of value as "an album of
    Lincoln clippings." Unfortunately, Sandburg has contributed to
    the folklore himself. In writing the biography he was out of his
    depth, and the result was "a long sprawling book that eventually
    had Lincoln sprawling.

1963

1   ANON. "Carl Sandburg at 85." Publishers Weekly 183
    (28 January):228.
        Covers a party given on 6 January at the Waldorf-Astoria by
    Harcourt, Brace and World to honor Sandburg's birthday and the
    publication of Honey and Salt. Quotes from Sandburg's tribute
    and remarks. "Being a poet is a damned dangerous business."

2   ANON. "Notes on Current Books: Poetry." Virginia Quarterly
    Review 39 (Summer):95.
        Review of Honey and Salt. Behind Sandburg's favorite sub-
    jects "one can hear the voice of their maker, the affirmer, the
    accepter, the man of age and wisdom." Doubts that the book will
    become a real success. These new poems lack "just what almost
    the whole of Sandburg's poetry lacks--a particular life of its
    own." Calls the poems "really clichés."

3   ANON. "Sandburg, Carl (August)." In Contemporary Authors.
    Vols. 5-8. Edited by Barbara Harte and Carolyn Riley.
    Detroit: Gale Press, pp. 1001-1003.
        Biographical background with listing of primary and
    secondary writings. Includes sidelights and brief critical
    history.

4   ANTHONY, MOTHER MARY. "New Books." Best Sellers 22
    (15 January):401.
        Review of Honey and Salt. Says that these poems combine
    "mellow lyricism and the tang of wisdom, the seeming ease and
    unrelenting mastery of the craftsman who knows and loves his
    material and whose fire is still burning." Each poem is struc-
    tured according to "its own inner specifications."

5   DEUTSCH, BABETTE. Poetry in Our Time. Rev. ed. New York:
    Doubleday, p. 53.
        Like Whitman, Sandburg shows an interest and delight in the
    American scene and speaks out against a "repressive respectabil-
    ity." His "affirmative character" reminds one of Allen Ginsburg
    as Sandburg tries to deify "the people." Excerpted: 1975.7.

6   FLANAGAN, JOHN T. "Presentation Copies in the Sandburg
    Library." College and Research Libraries 24 (January):47-52.
        Reports on books sent to Sandburg as gifts and now held in
    the University of Illinois Library collection. "In the second
    decade of this century Sandburg's own verse was often deemed
    lusty, reckless, and perhaps unaccountable. Today, in the
    1960's, Sandburg is a revered man of letters. Time has made
    him, too, respected."

7   FUCHS, DANIEL. "Sandburg." Chicago Review 16 (Summer):
    119-22.
        Review of Honey and Salt. Comments on the current critical
    judgments of Sandburg. Finds him to be "the too apparent para-
    digm of Tocqueville's democratic poet, the recorder of the
    minute and clear on the one hand, and the extremely vague and
    general on the other." At his best, the two are integrated.
    Notes the allusions to death.

8   GREEN, JEROME. "Carl Sandburg as Poet: A Study of the Criti-
    cism and Other Factors Contributing to His Reputation as a
    Poet through 1960." Ph.D. diss., New York University, 293 pp.
        Focuses on Sandburg's subjects, his bias for common people,
    his language and free verse, and the development of his critical
    reputation. Includes a primary and secondary bibliography.

9   JARRELL, RANDALL. "Fifty Years of American Poetry."
     Prairie Schooner 37 (Spring):3.
       Calls Sandburg's poems "improvisations whose wording is
     approximate." He is a very American writer who "sings more
     stylishly than he writes" and recites his poems better than they
     are written. Reprinted: 1969.5. Excerpted: 1975.7.

10   KLAUSER, ALFRED P. "Let Us Praise Poets." Christian Century
     80 (20 March):369.
       Review of Honey and Salt. Sandburg is at his "homespun
     best" in this collection, but also at times at his "banal worst."

11   KODOLIN, IRVING. "Philharmonic." Saturday Review of Litera-
     ture 46 (15 June):51.
       Reports on Aaron Copeland's A Lincoln Portrait with
     Sandburg as speaker at the New York Philharmonic Hall. Calls
     Sandburg "the least affected, the most eloquent, the closest in
     identity" with Lincoln. His presence was "towering."

12   MORRISON LILLIAN. "Poetry and Young People." Horn Book 39
     (October):522.
       Review of Honey and Salt. Finds here "a dreamy, whimsical,
     soft quality." Sandburg is "unpretentiously romantic" but lacks
     the "really deep, dark colors."

13   NITTA, HIRAOKI. "Carl Sandburg as a Poet for Children." Kobe
     Gaidai Ronso 13 (February):52-64.
       Discusses Sandburg's verse for children with attention
     given to theme and form.

14   QUIGLEY, MIKE. "Carl Sandburg: Noted Poet, Historian and
     Lincoln Scholar." Ebony 18 (September):158-59.
       Interview in which Sandburg speculates about how he thinks
     Lincoln would have reacted to today's race problems.

15   REXROTH, KENNETH. "The Institutionalization of Revolt, the
     Domestication of Dissent." Arts in Society 2 (Spring-Summer):
     114-23.
       Includes Sandburg in a discussion of why American poetry is
     culturally deprived.

16   ROBIE, BURTON A. "Poetry." Library Journal 88 (1 February):
     566.
       Review of Honey and Salt. This is a "great, grand book"
     filled with "beauty and meaning." Says that this "intensely
     lyrical and human volume should be a part of all collections."

17 SANDBURG, HELGA. <u>Sweet Music: A Book of Family Reminiscence</u>
    <u>and Song</u>. New York: Dial Press, 180 pp.
        Tells the inner story of events as they affected herself,
    her sisters, her mother, and the "towering, vague figure . . .
    humming, singing," as the head of the household. Includes a
    preface by Carl Sandburg (in which he calls this "a sweet book,"
    but not sentimental) and guitar arrangements by Richard
    Harrison.

18 SANDOZ, MARI. "Outpost in New York." <u>Prairie Schooner</u> 37
    (Spring):95–106.
        Examines Sandburg's relationship with his publisher, Alfred
    Harcourt.

19 SPENDER, STEPHEN, and DONALD HALL. "Sandburg, Carl." In <u>The</u>
    <u>Concise Encyclopedia of English and American Poets and Poetry</u>.
    New York: Hawthorn Books, pp. 27, 28–29, 280, 293, 386.
        Divides Sandburg's work between the "personal lyrical
    episode" and the "vigorous commentary on the industrial and
    agrarian scene." Discusses how Sandburg fits into the develop-
    ment of American poetry. Includes biography.

20 STAFFORD, WILLIAM. "Comment: In the Sandburg Tradition."
    <u>Poetry</u> 102 (September):388–89.
        Review of <u>Honey and Salt</u>. In his early poems, Sandburg
    confronted his readers with abrupt realizations about themselves.
    In his new book he gives himself over to an aspect begun in <u>The</u>
    <u>People, Yes</u>: he "[cozies] up to large groups not differentiated
    by troublesome particularities." Finds here "an alertness, a
    readiness to capture what is implicit in the material."

21 THORP, WILLARD. "The 'New' Poetry." In <u>Literary History of</u>
    <u>the United States</u>. 3d ed., rev. Edited by Robert E. Spiller,
    Willard Thorp, Thomas H. Johnson, Henry Seidel Canby, and
    Richard M. Ludwig. New York: Macmillan; London: Collier-
    McMillan, pp. 1181–84 and passim.
        Offers an overview of Sandburg's career. Says that "not
    even Whitman . . . knew America as he knew it." Sandburg laid
    his ear to "the heart of America." Discusses <u>Chicago Poems</u>,
    <u>Good Morning, America</u>, <u>Abraham Lincoln</u>, and <u>The People, Yes</u>.

22 WESTERFIELD, HARGIS. "<u>Harvest of Youth</u>: Jesse Stuart's First
    Published Book." <u>American Book Collector</u> 13 (February):23–24.
        Jesse Stuart's <u>Harvest of Youth</u> (1930) contains eighty
    poems in which he exorcised Sandburg's influence and developed a
    modified sonnet form.

23 WHIPPLE, T.K. "Carl Sandburg." In <u>Spokesmen</u>. Berkeley and
    Los Angeles: University of California Press, pp. 161–83.
        Reprint of 1928.27 with a foreword by Mark Schorer.
    Reprinted: 1978.21.

24   ZEHNPFENNIG, GLADYS.   Carl Sandburg, Poet and Patriot.
     Denison's Men of Achievement Series. Minneapolis: T.S.
     Denison, 265 pp.
       Biographical study of Sandburg appealing to the juvenile
reader.

                              1964

1   BENÉT, LAURA. "Carl Sandburg." In Famous Poets for Young
     People. New York: Dodd, pp. 148–51.
       Brief portrait of Sandburg with attention given to his life
and career.

2   CROWDER, RICHARD [H]. Carl Sandburg. Twayne United States
     Authors Series. Edited by Sylvia E. Bowman. New York:
     Twayne, 176 pp.
       Covers works, career, and life of Sandburg along with a
survey of his critical reputation. Admits flaws and diffuseness,
cataloging, excessive use of anecdotes. Finds color, suggestions, melodic variety in the poetry, and calls his work a
permanent contribution to American literature. Sees some justice
in criticizing his uncritical optimism. "To have read Sandburg
is to have been in the company of a profoundly sincere American
and of a craftsman of communicating pity, scorn, brawl, beauty,
and an abiding love." Excerpted: 1973.9.

3   DUNCAN, HUGH DALZIEL. The Rise of Chicago as a Literary
     Center from 1885 to 1930. Totowa, N.J.: Bedminster, p. 347.
       Brief reference to Sandburg's treatment of Chicago in
Chicago Poems.

4   FROST, ROBERT. Selected Letters of Robert Frost. Edited by
     Lawrence Thompson. New York: Holt, Rinehart & Winston,
     pp. 276, 277, 286, 499.
       Account of Frost bringing Sandburg to the University of
Michigan in 1922. Calls him "probably the most artificial and
studied ruffian the world has had." Also says that "his works
prove you can play tennis more imaginatively with the net down."

5   HILBERT, ROBERT. "Carl Sandburg." In Michigan Poets; with
     Supplement to Michigan Authors, 1960. Ann Arbor: Association
     of School Librarians, pp. 41–47.
       General survey of Sandburg's life and career including time
spent in Michigan.

6   INGALLS, JEREMY. "The Epic Tradition: A Commentary, II."
     East-West Review 1 (Autumn):173–211.
       Sandburg, among others, has a body of poems in which he
defines, by his own "completed" publications, his representative
past-and-present sequence of immersion, emergence, and return.

7   McGILL, R[ALPH].   "Prophet in Poetry: Great Lives, Great
     Deeds."   Reader's Digest 79 (June):65–68.
          Celebrates Sandburg's talent as a poet and points to his
     prophetic spirit as he promotes love of country.

8   MUNSON, GORHAM [B.].   "The Classicism of Robert Frost."
     Modern Age 8 (Summer):295.
          Contrasts Frost's classical nature with Sandburg.   Says
     that in time, Sandburg will become "a sentimental humanitarian
     poet."

9   RUBIN, LOUIS D., Jr.   "The Search for Lost Innocence: Karl
     Shapiro's The Bourgeois Poet."   Hollins Critic 1 (December):
     1–16.
          Comments that one of Shapiro's models was Sandburg.

10   SANDBURG, HELGA.   "A Visit with Sandburg at Sunset."
     Saturday Evening Post 237 (6 June):62.
          Brief reminiscence by Sandburg's daughter.   Now eighty-six,
     he is "a curious blend of irreverence and wisdom."   Includes
     photographs of Connemara and of Sandburg at home with his
     wife.

11   WELLS, HENRY W.   "New America."   In The American Way of
     Poetry.   New York: Russell & Russell, pp. 135–47 and passim.
     Reprint of 1943.12.

                                   1965

1   DURNELL, HAZEL.   The America of Carl Sandburg.   Foreword by
     Gordden Link.   Washington, D.C.:   University Press of
     Washington, D.C., 253 pp.
          In this study written for a European audience, Durnell
     probes a biographical-critical, literary history and cultural
     analysis of Sandburg's career.   Her task: An American studies
     investigation of how "in many and varied ways the life and writ-
     ings of Carl Sandburg reflect a long period in American social
     history."   Traces the influence of his Scandinavian heritage
     upon his writings.   Depicts him as a social conscience and a
     voice of national awareness.   Compares him to other American
     writers.   The poet's "revolutionary style" is the principal
     reason for the disparity between the conclusions of many of his
     critics.   Until his viewpoint finds some acceptance among the New
     Critics, they will continue to see his work as "an assault on the
     English language."   Includes primary and secondary bibliography.

2   GERTZ, ELMER.   A Handful of Clients.   Chicago: Follett,
     pp. 50, 71, 122, 197, 219, 222.
          Recalls Sandburg's speaking in behalf of Nathan Leopold,
     and his own debate with Sandburg about The Diary of a Public Man.
     Calls him "the authentic voice of America."

3   HART, JAMES ALFRED. "American Poetry of the First World War
     (1914-1920): A Survey and Checklist." Ph.D. diss., Duke
     University, 526 pp., passim.
          Suggests the literary merit and ascertains the importance
     of Sandburg's verse. Discusses the value of the world conflict
     for civilian authors, including Sandburg, Lindsay, Masters,
     Frost, and others.

4   LINK, GORDDEN. "Foreword." In The America of Carl Sandburg,
     by Hazel Durnell. Washington, D.C.: University Press of
     Washington, D.C.
          Recounts his first meeting with Sandburg.

5   SØRENSON, SOMNER. "Poets New and Old: Reviews of Ammons and
     Sandburg." Discourse: A Review of the Liberal Arts 8
     (Spring):143-52.
          Review of Honey and Salt. About half of the poems "do not
     merit any serious consideration." Although Sandburg shows
     moments of greatness, the total effect is marred by many inferior
     poems. Excerpted: 1985.5.

                              1966

1   ANON. "Penny Parade for Carl Sandburg Day." Instructor 76
     (November):45.
          Brief biographical background and information on the Carl
     Sandburg Association's work to restore his homestead as a his-
     torical point of interest.

2   BOROUGH, REUBEN W. "The Sandburg I Remember." Journal of the
     Illinois State Historical Society 59 (Autumn):229-51.
          Anecdotal reminiscences of his friendship with Sandburg,
     one-time reporter for the Chicago Daily Socialist, 1907 to 1908.
     Emphasizes Sandburg's interest in the working class.

3   DOBIE, J[AMES] FRANK. "Introduction." In Carl Sandburg and
     Saint Peter at the Gate, by Bertha Dobie. Austin: Encino
     Press, pp. i-vi.
          Frank Dobie and Sandburg met in 1921. By 1935 they were
     swapping "Saint Peter at the Gate" stories and decided to collect
     them. They never completed the book, but shortly after 1935
     Dobie wrote out "the conversations, the tale-telling, and his own
     impressions" of the poet. "Three things I shall never forget
     about Carl Sandburg: his voice, his laughter, his fecundity of
     anecdote."

4   GERBER, PHILIP L. "'My Rising Contemporaries': Robert Frost
     amid His Peers." Western Humanities Review 20 (Spring):
     135-41.
          In his later years Frost spoke of Sandburg as a rival.
     Reprinted: 1966.5.

                              109

5   ____.' Robert Frost. Twayne United States Authors Series.
       Edited by Sylvia A. Bowman. Boston: Twayne, pp. 32–33, 59,
       63–65, 76–78, 138.
           Refers to Sandburg as one among several of Frost's rivals.
       Discusses the literary establishment at the time. Includes
       reprint of 1966.4.

6   GIROUX, ROBERT. "A Personal Memoir." In T.S. Eliot: The Man
       and His Work. Edited by Allen Tate. New York: Delacorte
       Press, pp. 339–40.
           Description of Eliot's famous encounter with Sandburg and,
       later, Eliot's presence at Sandburg's speech given before the
       American Academy of Arts and Letters.

7   JENKINS, ALAN. "Anecdotes about Carl Sandburg." Lincoln
       Herald 68 (Winter):70–74.
           Humorous stories about Sandburg's activities as a public
       figure.

8   KRAMER, DALE. "Six Poor Boys in Search of Themeselves:
       5. Carl Sandburg" and "Burst of Trumpets: 20. For Sandburg,
       a Taste of Glory." In Chicago Renaissance: The Literary Life
       in the Midwest: 1900–1930. New York: Appleton–Century,
       pp. 52–65, 278–87.
           Emphasizes Sandburg's early artistic development as a
       struggling writer in Chicago and discusses the genesis of Chicago
       Poems as well as his personal relationship with the Chicagoans.
       Says that Chicago Poems is padded out with "oddments."

9   MITGANG, HERBERT. "Speaking of Books: Carl Sandburg." New
       York Times Book Review, 2 January, pp. 24–25.
           Discusses Sandburg's life and work on the occasion of his
       eighty-eighth birthday. Includes a portrait.

10   SANDBURG, HELGA. "Carl Sandburg, My Father." Redbook 126
       (February):60–61, 111–15.
           Brief memoir by Sandburg's daughter. Remembers him as a
       "towering figure" and a man who always "found time for continual
       praise of my mother." Comments on their "romantic and realistic
       marriage"; "his quizzical ways and his courtesy and . . . his
       ability to stir all of us to belief in ourselves"; and his being
       hospitalized with peritonitis. Calls him "the Poet Patriarch of
       our country."

11   STEICHEN, EDWARD. "Introduction." In Sandburg: Photog-
       raphers View Carl Sandburg. New York: Harcourt, Brace &
       World, 113 pp.
           Includes short quotes from his poetry, the text of his
       address on Lincoln given before Congress in 1959, and a three-
       page sketch of him by Steichen. Photographs, taken by more than

seven photographers, attempt to create Sandburg's life integrated
with his environment and pride of heritage.

12   WREDE, JOHAN. "'Det nya havet': En havyssymbol, mörne och
     modernism." Finsk-Tidskrift 179-80 (Spring):354-66.
        In Finnish. Offers the possibility that Mörne's poem is a
     commentary on Diktonius's "Ungt hau," which is based in turn on
     Sandburg's "Young Sea."

                              1967

1   ANDERSON, JAMES BRUCE. "Frost and Sandburg: A Theological
     Criticism." Renascence 19 (Summer):171-83.
        Sandburg's anti-intellectualism apparently leads to "an
     ignorance of theology" and thus there is "no 'Christian intel-
     lect' that governs all his seeing."

2   ANON. "American Troubadour." Time 90 (28 July):17.
        Obituary in which Sandburg is called essentially "an Ameri-
     can troubadour." He solidly established himself as "a poet and
     historian . . . [and] minstrel."

3   ANON. "Carl Sandburg, Poet and Biographer of Lincoln, Dies in
     South at 89." New York Times, 23 July, p. 62.
        Editorial in which Sandburg is called one of the nation's
     "truly significant writers." Calls him "the American bard. The
     sense of being American informed everything he wrote." President
     Lyndon Johnson called him "the bard of democracy [who] gave us
     the truest and most enduring vision of our greatness."

4   ANON. "Newsmakers: Remembrances." Newsweek 70
     (16 October):52.
        Details of a memorial service for Sandburg and his burial.

5   ANON. "Obituary Notes." Publishers Weekly 192 (31 July):
     36-37.
        Obituary with review of Sandburg's life and achievements.

6   ANON. "Transition: Poet of the People." Newsweek 70
     (31 July):49.
        Obituary in which Sandburg is called "the kind of poet
     laureate that could only happen in America." He was a poet of
     "the American present and an interpreter of its past."

7   ANON. "The Voice of Carl Sandburg Lives Forever." Saturday
     Review of Literature 50 (19 August):11.
        Advertisement and brief note for recordings of Sandburg's
     work in his own voice. Each recording reveals "a distinctive
     facet of Sandburg's art."

8　　ANON. "Years of a Poet Who Sang of America." Life 63
　　　　(4 August):44-52.
　　　　　　Obituary with photographs. Calls Sandburg "the finder,
　　absorber, celebrator, chronicler, conveyer of facts [who] could
　　build, inspire and affirm." He became a "legend that made both
　　him and his America dance a little bit." Includes biographical
　　background.

9　　CHRISTIAN, HENRY A. "Ten Letters to Louis Adamic."
　　　　Princeton University Library Chronicle 28 (Winter):85-86.
　　　　　　Sandburg admired Adamic. Recounts how Adamic wrote to him
　　for a Guggenheim recommendation. In his reply Sandburg refers to
　　the theme of "class violence" he shares with Dynamite and that
　　runs through Sandburg's first four volumes of verse.

10　　CORWIN, NORMAN [LEWIS]. "The Poet and the Gangster." Los
　　　　Angeles Times West Magazine, 24 September, pp. 10-15.
　　　　　　Sandburg, Corwin, and Hal Kanter discuss a script for
　　Sandburg's guest appearance on a Milton Berle television show.

11　　GRAVES, ELIZABETH MINOT. "Picture Books." Commonweal 86
　　　　(26 May):294.
　　　　　　Review of The Wedding Procession of the Rag Doll and the
　　Broom Handle and Who Was in It. Calls this "a memorable edition
　　of Carl Sandburg's lively, rhythmical tale."

12　　HAAS, JOSEPH, and GENE LOVITZ. Carl Sandburg: A Pictorial
　　　　Biography. New York: Putnam, 222 pp.
　　　　　　Survey of Sandburg's life in pictures, showing the ele-
　　vated tracks under which he walked, department stores he visited,
　　the train station where he entered a city. Includes selective
　　secondary bibliography.

13　　HORTON, ROD W., and HERBERT W. EDWARDS. Backgrounds of
　　　　American Thought. New York: Appleton-Century-Crofts,
　　　　pp. 179, 359.
　　　　　　Reprint of 1952.21.

14　　JENKINS, ALAN. "Carl Sandburg, 1878-1967." Lincoln Herald
　　　　69 (April):162-64.
　　　　　　An appreciation of Sandburg emphasizing the achievements
　　that brought him public recognition and the personalities most
　　responsible for shaping his life and thought.

15　　MARSH, PAMELA. "Scaled for Lilliput." Christian Science
　　　　Monitor, 4 May, p. B2.
　　　　　　Review of The Wedding Procession of the Rag Doll and the
　　Broom Handle and Who Was in It. Finds here a mixture of in-
　　fluences, "some Maurice Sendak, a touch of the surrealists,
　　atmosphere from the Wizard of Oz." But the result is original.

16   MITGANG, HERBERT. "Carl Sandburg, 1878-1967." Saturday
      Review of Literature 50 (12 August):18-19.
         Reminiscence of his walks and talks with the Poet. In-
      cludes Sandburg's comments on television commercials, language of
      advertising, politicians, Frost, and visit to his birthplace. He
      is delighted that some high schools have been named for him.
      Says that in his books Sandburg wrote his life.

17   SENDAK, MAURICE. Review of The Wedding Procession of the Rag
      Doll and the Broom Handle and Who Was in It. Book Week,
      7 May, p. 24.
         Praises Harriet Pincus's illustrations. Says that the book
      is "an example of the flexibility, depth, and originality a new
      artist can bring to . . . a form that nowadays is so often merely
      commercial, worn-out, and vulgar." Pincus has served "the author
      and herself beautifully."

*18   SØRENSON, POUL. "To amerikanske prosalyrikere." In Fremmede
      digtere i det 20. århundrede. Edited by Sorn M. Kristensen.
      Copenhagen: G.C. Gad, pp. 425-38.
         Cited in 1963.8.

19   SUTHERLAND, ZENA. "For Younger Children." Saturday Review of
      Literature 50 (13 May):48, 50.
         Review of The Wedding Procession of the Rag Doll and the
      Broom Handle and Who Was in It. Calls the style "distinctively
      Sandburg." Finds the book "most engaging."

20   THOMAS, DELLA. "Preschool and Primary Grades." Library
      Journal 92 (15 March):1312.
         Review of The Wedding Procession of the Rag Doll and the
      Broom Handle and Who Was in It. Finds the book to be "eminently
      suitable for primary grades."

21   TURNBULL, ANDREW. Thoms Wolfe. New York: Charles
      Scribner's, p. 126.
         Refers to the American renaissance heralded by such
      "realists" as Sandburg and others.

22   VANCE, ELEANOR G. "Glimpses of Carl Sandburg." North
      American Review, n.s. 4 (March):9-10.
         Recalls Sandburg's appearance in 1931 in a public recital
      (reading, singing, guitar playing) at Northwestern University.

23   VAUGHAN, FRANKLIN H. "Smog: The Old Possum's Insidious Cat."
      Lock Haven Review, no. 9, pp. 37-41.
         Speculates that if T.S. Eliot borrowed Sandburg's "fog-cat"
      for the image in "Prufrock," he changed it to "an enemy of man,
      his selfmade, suffocating milieu."

24   WARD, MARTHA E., and D.W. MARQUARDT. Authors of Books for
      Young People. Metuchen, N.J.: Scarecrow, p. 232.
         Brief reference to Sandburg and his writings for children.

25 WEST, THOMAS REED. Flesh of Steel: Literature and the
    Machine in American Culture. Nashville, Tenn.: Vanderbilt
    University Press, p. 7.
        Examines Sandburg briefly to show "the discipline of the
    machine as that discipline works its way into the souls of the
    servants of industry."

26 WOODS, GEORGE A. "New Books for Young Readers." New York
    Times Book Review, 9 April, p. 26.
        Review of The Wedding Procession of the Rag Doll and the
    Broom Handle and Who Was in It. This is "truly the social
    event--old-fashioned, country style--of the season." Praises
    the illustrations.

                                1968

1   ADERMAN, RALPH M. "Carl Sandburg, trubadur al Americii."
    Luceafărul (Bucharest) 24 (February):6.
        In Romanian. Appreciation of Sandburg as an American
    troubadour.

2   AIKEN, CONRAD. Skepticisms: Notes on Contemporary Poetry.
    New York and London: Johnson Reprint, pp. 143-48.
        Reprint of 1919.1.

3   ANON. "Carl Sandburg: Get to Know Him during his Birthday
    Month." Instructor 77 (9 January):66-69.
        Includes schedule of activities to honor Sandburg and a
    listing of books, tapes, and films on him. "His courage, vigor,
    and genius paved the way for freedom of expression, individuality
    of style, and an awareness that real life has its own beauty."

4   ANON. "A Collection of Jake Falstaffiana." Ohioana 5
    (Spring):17-18.
        In reviewing Herman Fetzer's Pippins and Cheese
    (pseudonym, Jake Falstaff), mentions that Sandburg praised his
    work in Akron and Cleveland newspapers.

5   BRODERICK, JOHN C., et al. "Recent Acquisitions of the
    Manuscript Division of the Library of Congress." Quarterly
    Journal of the Library of Congress 25 (Spring):328-49.
        Reviews Sandburg's papers acquired by the library.

6   CORWIN, NORMAN [LEWIS]. "Sandburg in Glendora." Lincoln
    Herald 70 (Spring):20-26.
        Includes dedicatory program for naming the Sandburg Junior
    High School in Glendora, California. Includes his speech about
    his twenty-seven years of friendship with Sandburg and letters
    to Paula Steichen.

7   DICKEY, JAMES. "Barnstorming for Poetry." Babel to
    Byzantium: Poets and Poetry Now. New York: Farrar, Straus &
    Giroux, p. 250.
        Brief reference to Sandburg as Dickey considers his own
    identity as poet. "He has acquired a guitar, which he carries
    about with him as though he was Carl Sandburg."

8   FERRILL, THOMAS HORNSBY. "Recollections of Carl Sandburg."
    Lincoln Herald 70 (Spring):27-28.
        Discusses the impediments to Sandburg's fame (his "univer-
    sality, the variety of his genius, his radiant vulgarity").
    Includes anecdotes.

9   FUSON, BEN W. "Literature." Library Journal 93 (August):
    2872.
        Review of The Letters of Carl Sandburg. Says this could be
    cut in half "with little loss of vigor, variety, and topical
    interest." Many of the letters are "superb." With few excep-
    tions, however, they do not provide insights into Sandburg or his
    poems.

10 GATES, ARNOLD. "Sandburg as I Knew Him." Lincoln Herald 70
    (Spring):57-58.
        Describes three meetings with Sandburg. Comments on his
    "boundless warmth and generous spirit" and his "spiritual big-
    ness."

11 GILBERT, JAMES BURKHART. Writers and Partisans: A History of
    Literary Radicalism in America. American Cultural History
    Series. New York and London: John Wiley & Sons, pp. 82, 192.
        Refers to Sandburg as one of the contributing editors for
    the first issue of the New Masses and to the Partisan Review's
    preferences for poetry excluding Steinbeck, Frost, and Sandburg.

12 GRAEBEL, RICHARD PAUL. "'Talk about Good Times.' We Had
    'Um!'" Lincoln Herald 70 (Spring):44-46.
        Recalls Sandburg's seventy-fifth birthday party at the
    Blackstone in Chicago, the inaugural of Governor Stevenson
    (10 January 1949), and Sandburg's visit to Springfield, Illinois
    (8 October 1961), to dedicate a new school named after him.
    Sandburg loved life.

13 HANSEN, HARRY. "The Best of America." Lincoln Herald 70
    (Spring):31.
        Sandburg is "like a mighty oak." On television he communi-
    cates his "seriousness and evident sincerity." Behind what he
    said there is "conviction and emotion." He never lost "the
    common touch." Notes his confidence in mankind.

14   JENKINS, ALAN. "Fraternal Night Owl." Lincoln Herald 70
      (Spring):59-62.
         Sandburg visited the Jenkins' home three times--1946, 1951,
      1960. Reminisces about the second visit, when the poet discussed
      his boyhood, happiness, love for walking, and opinions of the
      modern media, politics, and American writers.

15   _____. "Memorial Lines to Carl Sandburg Suggested by His Poem
      'Finish.'" Lincoln Herald 70 (Spring):1.
         Poem addressed to Sandburg.

16   JENKINS, ALAN, ed. "Sandburg Memorial Issue." Lincoln Herald
      70 (Spring):1-69.
         Features articles by Norman Corwin (1968.6), Thomas Hornsby
      Ferrill (1968.8), Arnold Gates (1968.10), Richard Paul Graebel
      (1968.12), Harry Hansen (1968.13), Alan Jenkins (1968.14), Otto
      Kerner (1968.19), Catherine McCarthy (1968.24), Herbert Mitgang
      (1968.30), Allan Nevins (1968.32), Ralph G. Newman (1968.33),
      Ruth Painter Randall (1968.34), Helga Sandburg (1968.35), Don
      Shoemaker (1968.38), Edward Steichen (1968.40), Jesse Stuart
      (1968.41), Wayne C. Temple (1968.43), and George C.B. Tolleson
      (1968.44).

17   JUERGENSEN, HANS. "The American Scene: Our Heritage, Carl
      Sandburg, 1878-1967." Discourses on Poetry 3 (Autumn):18-20.
         Discusses Sandburg's contributions to Americana and surveys
      his accomplishments.

18   KAUL, A.N. "Folkways and Frontiers." Yale Review 58
      (December):304-7.
         Review of The Letters of Carl Sandburg. Says the letters
      lack excitement. Although they reveal little that is new about
      Sandburg's life and work, his public will find them welcome
      reading. His primary problem here is his "self-conscious
      repetition."

19   KERNER, OTTO. "Illinois' Sandburg." Lincoln Herald 70
      (Spring):4-6.
         Quotes from Governor Adlai E. Stevenson's proclamation on
      Sandburg's seventy-fifth birthday and a House Joint Resolution.
      Kerner named him poet laureate of Illinois for 1962. Mourns his
      passing.

20   LUBBERS, KLAUS. Emily Dickinson: The Critical Revolution.
      Ann Arbor: University of Michigan Press, pp. 117, 282.
         Sandburg imitated Dickinson. Comments on Sandburg's con-
      cern with her legacy and refers to a poem dedicated to her.

21   LYNN, KENNETH. "A Correspondence with Friends." Virginia
     Quarterly Review 44 (Autumn):682.
         Review of The Letters of Carl Sandburg. "For all his self-
     centeredness, Sandburg had the gift of friendship." What
     attracted so many people to him? Speculates it was his kindness,
     his commitment to writing.

22   LYON, ZOË. "Harris Merton Lyon: Early American Realist."
     Studies in Short Fiction 5 (Summer):368–69.
         Sums up Sandburg's assessment of Lyon as "a brave searcher
     after new methods for getting an art record for the thoughts and
     viewpoints of a modern man."

23   McALEER, JOHN J. "Book Reviews." America 119 (19 October):
     358.
         Review of The Letters of Carl Sandburg. Seems that
     Sandburg took as much care with his letters as with his poems.
     Finds them dominated by "the force of spirit made always to
     answer to enlightened discipline." Regrets there are no letters
     after 1962.

24   McCARTHY, CATHERINE. "Carl Sandburg: The Lincoln Years."
     Lincoln Herald 70 (Spring):33–39.
         Discusses Sandburg's relationship with his publisher,
     Alfred Harcourt, and the printing of the Lincoln biography.

25   MACKSEY, R.A. "The Old Poets." Johns Hopkins Magazine 16
     (Fall):42–48.
         Includes Sandburg in a discussion of American poets who
     contributed to an apparent revolution in the genre. Contrasts
     him to the previous generation's poets.

26   MacLEISH, ARCHIBALD. "A Memorial Tribute to Carl Sandburg."
     Massachusetts Review 9 (Winter):41–44.
         Praises Sandburg for his belief in humanity and for saying
     what Americans have always known. Excerpted: 1985.5.

27   MALOFF, SAUL. "The Swede Bard." Newsweek 72 (7 October):107.
         Review of The Letters of Carl Sandburg. The best letters
     cover politics and society, poetry and literature, hatred of in-
     justice and devotion to the "people." Always he is his own man,
     "speaking from his own soul, heart and self."

28   MARTYNOVA, ANNA. "Carl Sandburg and the Soviet Reader (On the
     Occasion of the 90th Anniversary of Sandburg's Birth)."
     Soviet Literature 1 (Fall):192–93.
         The common Russian people love Sandburg as representative
     of "the best humanitarian traditions in American literature."
     Discusses various Russian translations of Sandburg's publica-
     tions.

29   MICHELSON, PETER. "The Private Sandburg." <u>New Republic</u> 159
      (7 December):27–28, 30.
          Review of <u>The Letters of Carl Sandburg</u>. Sandburg emerges
      "compassionate, sentimental, large–souled, reverent." He is, at
      best, an "authentic humanist." His sentiments have become so
      subsumed in sentimental rhetoric that the reality of his values
      is dissipated.

30   MITGANG, HERBERT. "Carl Sandburg, Newspaper Man." <u>Lincoln</u>
      <u>Herald</u> 70 (Spring):29–30.
          Offers an overview of Sandburg's work as a reporter.

31   MITGANG, HERBERT, ed. "Introduction." In <u>The Letters of Carl</u>
      <u>Sandburg</u>. New York: Harcourt, Brace & World, pp. v–xiv.
          Letters are arranged chronologically, 1 May 1898 through
      1 July 1962. Occasional explanatory notes identify persons and
      situations. Says that "writing letters too is writing" is the
      theme of the book. "At the core is Sandburg's writing; within
      that core, Carl Sandburg himself."

32   NEVINS, ALLAN. "A Tribute to Carl Sandburg." <u>Lincoln Herald</u>
      70 (Spring):8.
          Praises Sandburg's "strong sense of the values of democ-
      racy." Comments on his deep humanity, interest in people,
      religious feelings, and contributions as reporter, poet, and
      prose writer.

33   NEWMAN, RALPH G. "Sandburg Memorial Tribute." <u>Lincoln</u>
      <u>Herald</u> 70 (Spring):53–56.
          Sandburg is "very nearly all things to all men." Offers an
      overview of his career, and quotes Sandburg's 250–word capsule
      biography of Lincoln.

34   RANDALL, RUTH PAINTER. "Our Friendship with Carl Sandburg."
      <u>Lincoln Herald</u> 70 (Spring):14–19.
          Writes of the friendship between Sandburg and James G.
      Randall.

35   SANDBURG, HELGA. "Addressed to a Father." <u>Lincoln Herald</u> 70
      (Spring):9.
          Poem addressed to Sandburg.

36   SAWYER, ROLAND. "Carl Sandburg's Letters." <u>Christian Science</u>
      <u>Monitor</u>, 5 December, p. 23.
          Review of <u>The Letters of Carl Sandburg</u>. These letters dis-
      close Sandburg's "politics and social views as well as his love."
      They prove that his radicalism was "held to constitutional
      bounds." Finds many "quotable quotes" here. What he wrote of
      Edward R. Murrow would apply to himself: "sanity, love of man-
      kind and a sense of history."

37 SHAPIRO, KARL. Review of The Letters of Carl Sandburg. Book
    World, 8 September, p. 1.
        Review of The Letters of Carl Sandburg. As a kind of
    "epistolary biography," the book is "highly successful and in-
    formative." Recommends reading these letters and reconsidering
    Sandburg's "assent to American greatness."

38 SHOEMAKER, DON [C.]. "Flat Rock Friend." Lincoln Herald 70
    (Spring):23–26.
        Recounts his many visits with Sandburg, who spoke of
    children, diets, and clothing. Includes numerous anecdotes.

39 STALLMAN, R.W. Stephen Crane: A Biography. New York:
    George Braziller, p. 159.
        Brief reference to Chicago Poems and Sandburg's acknowl-
    edgement of Crane's influence as a contemporary.

40 STEICHEN, EDWARD. "My Poet Brother-in-Law." Lincoln Herald
    70 (Spring):11–13.
        Recounts their first meeting (1907) at which they shared
    each other's dreams and aspirations.

41 STUART, JESSE. "Sandburg, My Hero." Lincoln Herald 70
    (Spring):40–43.
        "He taught me much; I loved the man as much or more than
    I loved the work." After 1943 he appeared with Sandburg on
    various programs, and "each time my faith in his immortality
    increased."

42 SUTTON, WILLIAM A. "Personal Liberty across Wide Horizons:
    Sandburg and the Negro." Negro American Literature Forum
    2 (Summer):19–21.
        Explores Sandburg's consciousness of and attitude toward
    blacks.

43 TEMPLE, WAYNE C. "Once upon a Time." Lincoln Herald 70
    (Spring):63–69.
        Recounts Sandburg's visit to Springfield, Illinois, and his
    friendship with James G. Randall.

44 TOLLESON, GEORGE C.B. "A Sandburg Serendipity." Lincoln
    Herald 70 (Spring):47–52.
        Reviews the program at Sandburg's funeral and in his eulogy
    mentions his own enjoyment of the writings.

45 WAGGONER, HYATT. "Carl Sandburg." In American Poets from the
    Puritans to the Present. New York: Houghton Mifflin,
    pp. 452–57.
        Calls Sandburg's early work, with few exceptions, "sub-
    literary." Honey and Salt is his best volume of verse. In it
    finds a "mellowness and wisdom of age" that reminds one of the

development of William Carlos Williams in his last decade, both
in "sound and sense." In place of ideology and sentimentality,
finds "a mature romantic imagination." Excerpted: 1975.7.
Reprinted: 1984.10.

46   WEIGEL, JOHN C. Letter to Carl Sandburg after Reading His
     Autobiography Always the Young Strangers: Published on His
     75th Birthday, January 6, 1953. New York: Joseph Halle
     Schaffner, 44 pp.
         Sandburg evoked "the spirit of a generation." Praises his
     tribute to his parents and shares reminiscences. Sandburg
     brought to life for Weigel the "modest wants, the strict Lutheran
     self-discipline, and the unimpeachable integrity" of his own
     parents.

47   WEINTRAUB, STANLEY. "A Mountain of a Man Seen Close-Up."
     Saturday Review of Literature 51 (7 December):46.
         Review of The Letters of Carl Sandburg. Finds most inter-
     esting the letters marking the transition from private citizen to
     "pre-legendary" poet, reflecting vanishing populist America.
     Praises the editing.

48   WINTERICH, JOHN T. "Bard with a Guitar: Carl Sandburg." In
     Writers in America: 1842-1967. Jersey City: Davey,
     pp. 60-62.
         Sandburg's death closed one of "the largest and most
     varied careers in American letters." Includes an anecdote of
     Sandburg's appearance at a spaghetti roast in New York's
     Greenwich Village. "If any man's life was an open book, his was,
     and he opened the book himself." Offers brief biographical back-
     ground.

                                   1969

1   BASLER, ROY P[RENTICE]. "Your Friend the Poet: Carl
     Sandburg." Midway 10 (Autumn):3-15.
         Analyzes the poetry and critical opinion of it. Despite a
     prevalent opinion among many to the contrary, Sandburg's poetry
     is valid and significant. He reverted to the primary poetic task
     of trying to apprehend by naming. There is no need to apologize
     for him. Because he did not suffer from "psychoemotional
     dyspepsia," English professors have virtually ignored him.
     Calls him a "pagan mystic."

2   COBLENTZ, STANTON A. "The Repudiation of the Beautiful."
     In The Literary Revolution. New York: Johnson Reprint,
     pp. 91-92.
         Reprint of 1927.4.

3   DEKLE, BERNARD. "Carl Sandburg (1878-1967): Poet and Lincoln
    Biographer." In Profiles of Modern American Authors.
    Rutland, Vt.: C.E. Tuttle, pp. 51-56.
       Sandburg had "great faith in the wisdom and goodness of the
    human race." Includes biographical details and primary
    bibliography.

4   DEUTSCH, BABETTE. This Modern Poetry. New York: Kraus
    Reprint, pp. 53-56, 212-14, and passim.
       Reprint of 1935.3.

5   HARTE, BARBARA, and CAROLYN RILEY, eds. "Carl Sandburg." In
    200 Contemporary Authors. Detroit: Gale, pp. 238-40.
       Examines Sandburg's career and includes primary bibliog-
    raphy. Notes his themes, style, and varied interests as writer
    and entertainer.

6   JOYNER, NANCY. "Robinson's 'Pamela' and Sandburg's 'Agatha.'"
    American Literature 40 (January):548-49.
       Explores the similarities between Sandburg's "Plaster" and
    Edwin Arlington Robinson's "The Tree in Pamela's Garden."
    Robinson changed the name from Agatha to Pamela after having
    discovered that Sandburg had used Agatha in "a somewhat similar
    connection." Nevertheless, the resemblances remain superficial.

7   McGILL, RALPH. "Preface." In The Chicago Race Riots, by Carl
    Sandburg. Introductory note by Walter Lippmann. New York:
    Harcourt, Brace & World, p. v.
       Reprint of 1919.8 with added preface.

8   MEARNS, DAVID C. "Ever and Ever, Carl." Manuscripts 21
    (Summer):169-73.
       Reminisces about the poet and biographer beginning with
    the days when Sandburg was collecting materials for Abraham
    Lincoln: The War Years. Includes events surrounding the publi-
    cation of Always the Young Strangers and Sandburg's reactions to
    one brutally unkind review. Includes obituary.

9   MITGANG, HERBERT. "A Life in Letters." Manuscripts 21
    (Summer):54-56.
       Reflects on his editing of the Sandburg letters. The view
    that emerges is that of "a frequent artist in language; a per-
    former who occasionally served beyond the call of his writing
    talents; a fairly consistent believer in progressive causes and
    human betterment."

10 MONAGHAN, JAY. "The Carl Sandburg I Knew." Soundings:
    Collections of the University Library, University of
    California, Santa Barbara 1 (May):20-28.
       Character portrait of Sandburg. Covers his award for
    Chicago Poems (from Poetry) in 1914, his move from poet to

biographer, his reactions to unkind criticism of others and
praise by Edgar Lee Masters, his absentmindedness, his meeting
in 1920 with Eugene V. Debs, and his lecture tours, along with
the history of the printing of Abraham Lincoln: The Prairie
Years. "Carl Sandburg had eccentricities, and for him, life itself was a stage performance in his later years, but his literary
stature cannot be denied." He was a rare writer, for he made
readers "see things as they never saw them before and the way
they would always see them in the future."

11   P[ARKES], D[AVID] L. "Sandburg, Carl (1878-1967), American
      Poet." In Twentieth Century Writing: A Reader's Guide to
      Contemporary Literature. Edited by Kenneth Richardson.
      London and New York: Newnes Books, pp. 541-42.
          Sandburg is "a poet of the people," like Whitman. As a
      poet, he is "perhaps the most representative spokesman of the
      emerging America of the twenties and thirties." Includes brief
      biographical details.

12   STEICHEN, PAULA. My Connemara. New York: Harcourt, 178 pp.
          Memoir of Sandburg on the Connemara Farms. Covers the
      period from their arrival to their departure. Describes it as an
      idyllic life. "My grandfather always had this knack of trans-
      forming the ordinary into the delightful."

13   SUTTON, WILLIAM [A.]. "On the Sandburg Trail." Indiana
      English Journal 3 (Winter):8-11.
          Traces the places Sandburg lived, beginning in Illinois and
      ending in North Carolina.

14   VAN DOREN, MARK. Carl Sandburg--With a Bibliography of
      Sandburg Materials in the Collections of the Library of
      Congress. Washington, D.C.: Printed for the Library
      of Congress by the Gertrude Clarke Whittall Poetry and
      Literary Fund, 83 pp.
          Praises Sandburg's poetry as "powerful, . . . dis-
      tinct, . . . unmistakably poetry." The short ones are best.
      The long ones are accumulations of brief sections. Finds a
      "thread of softness" in his later work. Sandburg was always
      able to find something of interest, something moving, in even
      the most obscure human being. Includes Archibald MacLeish's
      "Where a Poet's From." Lists all holdings, both primary and
      secondary, of Sandburg materials in the Library of Congress.

15   WAGNER, SELMA. "Sandburg's 'A Fence.'" Explicator 27
      (February), item 42.
          The words death, rain, and tomorrow in the last line
      symbolize three facets of nature--biological, physical, abstract.
      Finds here the optimism of Sandburg. The poem ends on a hopeful
      note, "when possibly the unfeeling dwellers in the stone house
      may yet develop full maturity and transcend the self."

1970

1 CALLAHAN, NORTH. Carl Sandburg, Lincoln of Our Literature:
    A Biography. New York: New York University Press, 253 pp.
       Draws from anecdotes, conversations and correspondence with
    family members, reviews, other essays, and works. Includes
    summaries of the Lincoln biography, the novel, and the children's
    books. Chapter on verse surveys reviewers' comments. Compares
    Sandburg with Lindsay, Masters, Robinson. Treats highlights of
    his career, notably as a biographer. Arranged chronologically.
    Includes primary and secondary bibliography. Excerpted:
    1981.5. Reprinted with revisions and additional material:
    1987.1.

2 CLARE, WARREN L. "'Posers, Parasites and Pismires':
    'Status Rerum,' by James Stevens and H.L. Davis." Pacific
    Northwest Quarterly 61 (January):22-24.
       In the fall of 1927 Sandburg came to Willamette University
    in Salem and spent the night at Dick Wetjen's home. After his
    lecture, there was an open house. H.L. Davis, coauthor of the
    "manifesto" entitled Status Rerum (1927), won the admiration of
    Sandburg.

3 FORD, THOMAS W. "The American Rhythm: Mary Austin's Poetic
    Principle." Western American Literature 5 (Spring):6, 7-8.
       Sandburg was influenced by the American Indian in the
    rhythm of his verse. Occasionally he succeeded in restoring in
    his verse the American heritage of natural rhythms.

4 FRANCHERE, RUTH. Carl Sandburg, Voice of the People. New
    York: Garrard, 144 pp.
       Biography with much fictionalized dialogue.

5 GRAVES, ELIZABETH MINOT. "Children's Books: Poetry and
    Humor." Commonweal 93 (20 November):206.
       Review of The Sandburg Treasury. Brief comments with
    summary.

6 GURKO, MIRIAM. "For Young Readers." New York Times Book
    Review, 15 November, p. 42.
       Review of The Sandburg Treasury. Although Sandburg's
    verse lacks complexity, it remains "great poetry for the young."
    His most appealing songs are about prairie and city life,
    children, animals, and nature. The Lincoln selection is
    "densely sentimental" and marred by artificially "poetic lan-
    guage." Prairie-Town Boy is one of the best pieces here. Calls
    this "an attractive storehouse of his prose and poetry."
    Excerpted: 1985.5.

7   PAVESE, CESARE. American Literature: Essays and Opinions.
    Translated by Edwin Fussell. Berkeley and Los Angeles:
    University of California Press, pp. 103-4, 107, 177.
       Says that Sandburg is the bridge between Whitman and Dos
    Passos. "Carl Sandburg has substituted the social problems of
    his own years for the apocalyptic 'democracy' of Whitman, but in
    other respects, through sensibility, he clearly descends from
    Whitman." Rarely has he attempted in poetry "the refined
    ingenuities of sensation to which the content of this poetry is
    usually reduced in Europe."

8   POPESCU, PETRU. "Carl Sandburg: Povesti din tara Rutabaga."
    Romania literara 3 (January):19.
       In Romanian. Brief reference to Sandburg's short fiction.

9   QUIGLEY, MICHAEL J. "A Study of Carl Sandburg: A Major
    Writer for the Secondary School of Today." Ph.D. diss., Ohio
    State University, 251 pp.
       Points out the value of a number of Sandburg's works in the
    teaching of English in today's high school. Offers overview of
    his critical reputation, surveys and discusses ten of his works,
    and offers a variety of testing methods for study and discus-
    sion. Says that his poetry and prose communicates with today's
    students in such important areas as nature of beauty, justice,
    racial prejudice, personal stress, war, patriotism, empathy, and
    optimism.

10 REED, K.T. "Carl Sandburg and T.S. Eliot: Some Poetical
    Exchanges." Poet and Critic 6 (Fall):45-46.
       Notes the similarities between the cat-fog images in
    Eliot's "Prufrock" and Sandburg's "Fog." Concludes that Eliot
    borrowed from Sandburg and that Sandburg, in turn, borrowed from
    Eliot when writing "Prairie."

11 ROGERS, W.G. Carl Sandburg, Yes: Poet, Historian, Novelist,
    Songster. New York: Harcourt Brace Jovanovich, 212 pp.
       Biography of Sandburg, strong on social history of environ-
    ment that produced the singer. Shows him as an organizer for the
    Social-Democrat party, as a journalist, singer, and collector of
    American ballads. Emphasizes his early years, before he emerged
    as a writer. Quotes generously from many of his works. Includes
    primary and secondary bibliography.

12 ROTHWELL, KENNETH S. "In Search of a Western Epic: Neihardt,
    Sandburg, and Jaffe as Regionalists and 'Aristocrats.'"
    Kansas Quarterly 2 (Summer):53-67.
       The People, Yes has more popular than literary appeal. It
    fits the category of an Astoriad--a work that turns history,
    saga, and tale into epic, dealing with "themes of settlement and
    conquest."

13   SANDBURG, HELGA. <u>To a New Husband</u>. New York: World, 79 pp.,
      passim.
      Brief references to Sandburg.

14   SUTTON, WILLIAM A. "A Frost-Sandburg Rivalry?" <u>Ball State</u>
      <u>University Forum</u> 11 (Winter):59–61.
      Surveys many people who should know how to examine the
      potential rivalry between the two poets. Says that the two men
      were friendly, although given to "razzing and kidding" each
      other.

15   THOMPSON, LAWRENCE. <u>Robert Frost: The Years of Triumph 1915–</u>
      <u>1938</u>. New York: Holt, Rinehart & Winston, pp. 179, 180, 209,
      577.
      Quotes Frost on his meetings with Sandburg.

16   WELSCH, ROGER L. "A 'Buffalo Skinner's' Family Tree."
      <u>Journal of Popular Culture</u> 4 (Summer):107–29.
      Includes Sandburg in tracing the tangled history of the old
      American ballad, "Caledonia." Establishes a genealogy for it.

17   ZHURALEV, IGOR. "The Relationship between Socialist Poetry in
      the U.S.A. at the Beginning of the Twentieth Century and the
      Graphic Arts of the Socialist Press." <u>Zeitschrift für</u>
      <u>Anglistik und Amerikanistik</u> 18 (Fall):168–82.
      Points to a connection between "The Walking Man of Rodin"
      and the statue of John the Baptist.

                              <u>1971</u>

1   ANON. "Sandburg, Carl (August)." In <u>Contemporary Authors</u>.
      Vols. 25–28. Edited by Christine Nasso. Detroit, Gale
      Research, p. 626.
      Brief biographical entry with list of obituary notices.

2   B[URNS], M[ARY] M. <u>"The Sandburg Treasury: Prose and Poetry</u>
      <u>for Young People."</u> <u>Horn Book</u> 47 (February):59–60.
      Sandburg depicts the American character as "sometimes
      heroic, sometimes wistful, sometimes obnoxious, yet never full."
      Says that time has not yet "diminished the appeal of Sandburg's
      vigorous, vital style." Excerpted: 1985.5.

3   FEENEY, JOSEPH JOHN, S.J. "American Anti-War Writers of
      World War I: A Literary Study of Randolph Bourne, Harriet
      Monroe, Carl Sandburg, John Dos Passos, E.E. Cummings, and
      Ernest Hemingway." Ph.D. diss., University of Pennsylvania,
      149 pp., passim.
      All six writers opposed the war at different times in dif-
      ferent genres. In his poems and essays, Sandburg criticized it
      until 1917, supported it through 1918, and then changed his

opinions early in the 1920s. Describes his attitudes toward war and charts his change of opinion or emphasis. Includes how he changes. Sandburg was "characteristically imagistic."

4 HINDUS, MILTON, ed. "Introduction: Criticism after 1914." In Walt Whitman: The Critical Heritage. London: Routledge & Kegan Paul; New York: Barnes & Noble, p. 19.
  Comments on Whitman's influence on Sandburg. Says that he "claimed the whole Whitmanian inheritance--aesthetic, social and political--as his own." But Sandburg's claim can be granted only in part.

5 JONES, ALFRED HAWORTH. "The Search for a Usable American Past in the New Deal Era." American Quarterly 23 (December): 723-24.
  Studies the way an image of Lincoln was created by Sandburg and used as an analogy for Franklin Delano Roosevelt's New Deal and foreign policies. In Abraham Lincoln: The Prairie Years, Sandburg "humanized" Lincoln. The War Years won him recognition and firmly established him as the "contemporary popular writer" on Lincoln. "This joining of two democratic humanitarians . . . in the public imagination further reinforced the continuity between present and past." Reprinted: 1974.4.

6 LONGO, LUCAS. Carl Sandburg: Poet and Historian. Outstanding Personalities Series. Charlottesville, N.Y.: Sam-Har Press, 32 pp.
  Overview of his life and career, including bibliography of primary works.

7 McCONNELL, LYNDA L. "Brief Mention." Library Journal 96 (15 May):1828.
  Review of The Sandburg Treasury. The introduction and illustrations "add to the attractiveness of this collection." Finds it especially useful for junior high school students.

8 MIEDER, WOLFGANG. "'Behold the Proverbs of a People': A Florilegium of Proverbs in Carl Sandburg's Poem, 'Good Morning, America.'" Southern Folklore Quarterly 35 (June): 160-68.
  In section II of Good Morning, America, Sandburg describes the American people through the characteristic aphorisms common to all of them. Includes a list of proverbs with authorities for sources.

9 REXROTH, KENNETH. American Poetry in the Twentieth Century. New York: Seabury Press, p. 48.
  Comments on Sandburg's empathy (for "the poor, frustrated, heroic, and ordinary"), his prosody and "perfect ear" for the potentials of common speech. Excerpted 1975.7.

10 SUTHERLAND, DONALD. "Alice and Gertrude and Others." Prairie
    Schooner 45 (Spring):289.
        Recalls helping Sandburg keep warm prior to going onstage
    at Ogontz to lecture and sing. Bundled in ermine, Sandburg "was
    a great showman and knew very much what the effect was."

                            1972

1 ALLEN, GAY WILSON. Carl Sandburg. Pamphlets on American
    Writers, no. 101. Minneapolis: University of Minnesota
    Press, 48 pp.
        Summarizes Sandburg's life and work. Outlines the major
    themes and influences, evaluates the success of his career as
    "the voice and conscience of his time and generation." Also
    assesses academe's dubious response to him. Feels that Sandburg
    suffered from too much recognition (the "curse of success") and
    that critics found his "love affair with the people" a source of
    irritation. Includes bibliography of all major primary sources
    and limited secondary sources. Excerpted: 1979.2.

2 CANANT, RAY M. "A Catalogue of the Carl Sandburg Collection
    at the University of Texas at Austin." Ph.D. diss., Univer-
    sity of Texas at Austin, 251 pp.
        Covers description of books by Sandburg according to genre
    (chapters 1–8), his contributions to other books (chapter 9) and
    to periodicals (chapter 10), his manuscripts (chapter 11), and
    translations of his works (chapter 12).

3 DUFFEY, BERNARD. "The Struggle for Affirmation." In The
    Chicago Renaissance in American Letters: A Critical History.
    East Lansing: Michigan State University Press, pp. 209–22
    and passim.
        Reprint of 1954.7.

4 FLANAGAN, JOHN T. "Three Illinois Poets." Centennial Review
    16 (Fall):313–27.
        Surveys Sandburg's career. Compares him to Edgar Lee
    Masters and Vachel Lindsay. Since their peak of recognition,
    "the reputations of all three poets have seriously shrunk."
    Sandburg's decline may be owing to objections to his optimism.

*5 KOROTYČ, V. "Karl Sendberg: Ja narod . . ." Žoutem (Soviet
    Union) 23, no. 2:4–11.
        Cited in 1963.8.

6 SUTTON, WILLIAM A. "The Swedishness of Carl Sandburg."
    American-Scandinavian Review 60 (Summer):144–47.
        Account of Sandburg's family background and his trip to
    Sweden.

1   ALEXANDER, WILLIAM. "The Limited American, the Great Loneli-
    ness, and the Singing Fire: Carl Sandburg's 'Chicago Poems.'"
    American Literature 45 (March):67-83.
        Comments on individual poems and finds in them the major
    themes of American writing of the first thirty years of this
    century. These include "human existence is limited; material
    progress has its limitations; your average American, compared
    with the poet, has a limited perspective upon life." The con-
    temporary American is thus shown to have lost touch with the
    eternal verities and with his own deeper national traditions.
    Excerpted: 1975.7.

2   BASLER, ROY [PRENTICE]. A Touchstone for Greatness: Essays,
    Addresses, and Occasional Pieces about Abraham Lincoln.
    Westport, Conn.: Greenwood Press, pp. 10, 13-52.
        Sandburg depended far too much upon hearsay in his writings
    on Lincoln and upon that well-meaning but sometimes undependable
    source, William Herndon. Covers his friendship with Sandburg and
    explains how the poet helped him find a publisher for this
    collection.

3   CHU, JAMES C.Y. "Carl Sandburg: His Association with Henry
    Justin Smith." Journalism Quarterly 50 (Spring):43-47, 133.
        Comments on Sandburg's work as journalist with the Chicago
    Daily News. Smith recalled Sandburg as a "leisurely, genial,
    enigmatic" man.

4   CORNING, HOWARD M. "A.R. Wetjen: British Seaman in the
    Western Sunrise." Oregon Historical Quarterly 74 (Summer):
    145-78.
        Discusses Wetjen's relationship with Sandburg, who resided
    in Salem, Albany, and Portland.

5   FINK, GUIDO. "Le bugie colorate di Carnevali." Paragone 290
    (Winter):88.
        In Italian. Traces poet Carnevali's inspiration to
    Sandburg and others.

6   HENDERSON, BILL. "Do-It-Yourself Publishing." Publishers
    Weekly 204 (13 August):31.
        Gives the history of printing In Reckless Ecstasy with
    Philip Green Wright.

7   MELIN, GRACE HATHAWAY. Carl Sandburg: Young Singing Poet.
    Childhood of Famous Americans Series. New York: Bobbs-
    Merrill, 200 pp.
        A fictionalized account of Sandburg's youth in the last
    quarter of the nineteenth century. Includes a chronology of

world events that occurred during his lifetime as well as research suggestions, project ideas, and vocabulary lists.

8   MIEDER, WOLFGANG. "Proverbs in Carl Sandburg's Poem 'The
    People, Yes.'" Southern Folklore Quarterly 37 (March):15-36.
       Identifies and discusses 322 proverbs in Sandburg's verse
    and lists them alphabetically by key words.

9   RILEY, CAROLYN, ed. "Sandburg, Carl, 1878-1967." In
    Contemporary Literary Criticism 1. Detroit: Gale Research,
    p. 300.
       Excerpts of 1961.14; 1964.2.

10 WEIGEL, JOHN C. Letter to Carl Sandburg, after Reading His
    Autobiography, "Always the Young Strangers," Published on His
    75th Birthday, January 6, 1973. New York: Joseph Halle
    Schaffner, 43 pp.
       Says Always the Young Strangers has "the unmistakable
    stamp of living." Praises his tribute to his parents and de-
    scribes memories evoked by the volume. Distributed privately
    were 450 copies of this Letter.

11 WELLS, HENRY W. "Carl Sandburg and Asian Culture." Literary
    Half-Yearly (India) 14, no. 173:31-54.
       Lengthy essay offering an examination of Sandburg's recep-
    tion by Asians and the development of his career.

                              1974

1   ALLEN, GAY WILSON. "Carl Sandburg 1878-1967." In American
    Writers: A Collection of Literary Biographies. Vol. 3.
    Edited by Leonard Unger. New York: Scribner's. pp. 575-98.
       Gives an overview of Sandburg's life and career. Sees him
    as a great celebrity and superb entertainer, but asks, "Was he a
    great poet?" Acknowledges the critical debate about him and con-
    cludes: "God created Sandburg as a writer, but by his own ef-
    forts he became a poet." Offers primary and secondary bibliog-
    raphy. Includes excerpt from 1960.1.

2   BLACK, ANTHONY J. "Carl Sandburg's 'Limited': The Quality of
    Response." English in Education 8 (Spring):44-48.
       Outlines how Sandburg's poem "Limited" is used as the
    focus of a sixth-form critical appreciation lesson and as a work
    of art to be responded to in its own right.

3   FERLAZZO, PAUL J. "The Urban-Rural Vision of Carl Sandburg."
    In MidAmerica 1. Edited by David D. Anderson. East Lansing,
    Mich.: Midwestern Press, pp. 52-57.
       Explores how Sandburg's midwestern experience shaped his
    imagination. Examines Chicago Poems and Cornhuskers. Sandburg

lived with and took from the city "intellectual stimulation, culture, fame" and from the prairie, "refreshment, identity, the good life." City and countryside are not only settings but "truly sources of particular states of mind and sets of value."

4 JONES, ALFRED HAWORTH. Roosevelt's Image Brokers: Poets, Playwrights, and the Use of the Lincoln Symbol. Port Washington, N.Y.: Kennikat Press, 134 pp., passim.
    Examines how the depression-era work of "three liberal middlebrow writers"--Sandburg, Robert E. Sherwood, Stephen Vincent Benét--helped fortify Roosevelt and a people during the Great Depression and the war years that followed. Includes reprint of 1971.5.

5 STAUFFER, DONALD BARLOW. "The New Poets: Regionalism and the Renewal of Language." In A Short History of American Poetry. New York: E.P. Dutton, pp. 236-41 and passim.
    Gives insights into the range of Sandburg's work, what makes it unique, and how it relates to the work of other poets and other times.

1975

1 BROER, LAWRENCE. "Stanley Kimmel--He Knew Them All." Lost Generation Journal 3 (Fall):11-13, 16.
    Offers photograph, excerpts from letters, and a note from Sandburg dated 23 December 1926. From 1946 until his death, he stayed with the Kimmels whenever he came to Washington, D.C. "They protected him, kept him organized, even loaned him clothes." Comments on the personal tensions between Sandburg and Frost.

2 CRANE, JOAN ST. C., comp. and ed. Carl Sandburg, Philip Green Wright, and the Asgard Press, 1900-1910. A Descriptive Catalogue of Early Books, Manuscripts, and Letters in the Clifton Waller Barrett Library. Charlottesville: University Press of Virginia, 132 pp.
    A descriptive catalog of the early books, manuscripts, and letters in the Clifton Waller Barrett Library.

3 GREASLEY, PHILIP ALAN. "American Vernacular Poetry: Studies in Whitman, Sandburg, Anderson, Masters, and Lindsay." Ph.D. diss., Michigan State University, 284 pp.
    Sandburg adopted Whitman's "oral vernacular techniques" and adapted the mode to "changing American conditions and literary values." Sandburg's poetry is "the full embodiment of the Whitmanic poetic synthesis."

4   HENDERSON, BILL. "Independent Publishing: Today and Yester-
    day." Annals of the American Academy of Political and Social
    Science 421 (September):100.
        Brief entry describing the circumstances that led to the
    publication of Sandburg's first collection of poems, In Reckless
    Ecstasy. Refers to the Poor Writers' Club, where Sandburg and
    others met weekly to read to one another.

5   KNOX, GEORGE. "Idealism, Vagabondage, Socialism: Charles A.
    Sandburg in To-Morrow and the FRA." Huntington Library
    Quarterly 38 (February):161–88.
        Discusses Sandburg's early poetry and prose contributions
    to the FRA and To-Morrow. Between 1901 and 1910, he was a mere
    "poetaster." Includes quotations from his letters about Elbert
    Hubbard and the Roycrofters.

6   RAGAN, SAM. "The Day North Carolina Honored Carl Sandburg."
    Pembroke Magazine 6:167–70.
        Describes the activities devoted to a day of celebration
    for Sandburg, his life and work.

7   RILEY, CAROLYN, ed. "Sandburg, Carl: 1878–1967." In
    Contemporary Literary Criticism. Vol. 4. Detroit: Gale
    Research, pp. 462–64.
        Excerpts from 1963.5, 9; 1968.45; 1971.9; 1973.1.

8   SANDBURG, MARGARET. "Foreword." In Carl Sandburg, Philip
    Green Wright, and the Asgard Press, 1900–1910: A Descriptive
    Catalogue of Early Books, Manuscripts, and Letters in the
    Clifton Waller Barrett Library. Compiled and edited by
    Joan St. C. Crane. Charlottesville: University Press of
    Virginia, 132 pp.
        Explores Sandburg's work with Wright and the Asgard Press.
    Includes primary bibliography.

9   TARG, WILLIAM. "Sandburg." In Indecent Pleasures: The Life
    and Colorful Times of William Targ. New York: Macmillan,
    pp. 57–59.
        Recalls knowing Sandburg in the early Chicago days. His
    biography of Lincoln is "the best American biography ever
    written." His poetry is "underrated beyond belief." When he
    died, America lost an irreplaceable "treasure."

                                1976

1   ALTENBERND, [A.] LYNN, and GEORGE HENDRICK. The Sandburg
    Roots: An Essay and Exhibit of the Sandburg Collection.
    Urbana: University of Illinois Library Friends, 26 pp.
        Includes descriptive bibliography of Sandburg holdings and
    narrative describing his career.

2   ANON. "Viewpoints: A Lot of Nerve." Time 107 (15 March):86.
     Brief reference to Sandburg's "singsong" voice.

3   BATES, J. LEONARD. "Progressivism: Its Growth and Diversity."
     In The United States: 1898-1928--Progressivism and a Society
     in Transition. Modern America Series. Edited by Dewey W.
     Grantham. New York: McGraw Hill, p. 51.
          Calls Sandburg a "proponent of efficiency" as well as a
     poet and "a passionate believer" in human rights. Sandburg
     believes that "the movement for efficiency could be reconciled
     with traditional virtues of justice and democracy."

4   BRUMM, ANNE-MARIE LOUISE. "The Poet Visits the City: A Study
     of Carl Sandburg, Rainer Maria Rilke and Federico Garcia
     Lorca." Ph.D. diss., University of Michigan, 319 pp., passim.
          Explores Sandburg's encounter with the metropolis and the
     effect on his poetry. Finds similarities in themes, motifs, and
     sources among the three poets. The city experience was a turning
     point in Sandburg's life and work.

5   CARRINGER, ROBERT, and SCOTT BENNETT. "Dreiser to Sandburg:
     Three Unpublished Letters." Library Chronicle 40 (Winter):
     252-56.
          Dreiser championed Sandburg, among others as seen in these
     three letters dated 6 August and 19 October 1915, and 20 August
     1927.

6   COMMIRE, ANNE. "Sandburg, Carl (August)." In Something about
     the Author: Facts and Pictures about Contemporary Authors.
     Vol. 8. Detroit: Gale Research, pp. 177-80.
          Sketch of Sandburg including comments on his personal life,
     career, writing, sidelights, and other sources. Career and per-
     sonal data, bibliography and list of criticism also included.

7   CROWDER, RICHARD [H.]. "Sandburg's Chromatic Vision in Honey
     and Salt." In The Vision of This Land: Studies of Vachel
     Lindsay, Edgar Lee Masters, and Carl Sandburg. An Essays in
     Literature Book. Edited by John E. Hallwas and Dennis J.
     Reader. Macomb: Western Illinois University Press,
     pp. 92-104.
          Sandburg's abundant use of vivid color in Chicago Poems
     and in Honey and Salt is a testimony to his vigorous interest in
     the objective world, normally found in a much younger man.
     Excerpted: 1980.4.

8   HALLWAS, JOHN E., and DENNIS J. READER, eds. "Introduction."
     In The Vision of This Land: Studies of Vachel Lindsay, Edgar
     Lee Masters, and Carl Sandburg. An Essays in Literature Book.
     Macomb: Western Illinois University Press, pp. 7-10.
          Reviews the growth of Sandburg's reputation. Along with his
     first volume he, along with Lindsay and Masters, "formed the

peak of what later came to be called the Chicago Renaissance."
But the early volumes overshadowed Sandburg's achievement in
later volumes. All three writers became important influences
because they were raised on the prairies. Discusses why they
have failed to become figures of lasting prominence in twentieth-
century literature.

9 HICKEN, VICTOR. "Sandburg and the Lincoln Biography: A
   Personal View." In The Vision of This Land: Studies of
   Vachel Lindsay, Edgar Lee Masters, and Carl Sandburg. An
   Essays in Literature Book. Edited by John E. Hallwas and
   Dennis J. Reader. Macomb: Western Illinois University Press,
   pp. 105-13.
      Recalls his impressions of Sandburg's personal appearances
   and juxtaposes his story of Lincoln with the "facts."

10 HILL, ARCHIBALD A. "Poetry and Stylistics." In Constituent
   and Pattern in Poetry. Austin and London: University of
   Texas Press, pp. 49-50.
      Examines the analogies around which the poem "Lost" is
   brilliant, thereby increasing our understanding of the poem.

11 HUNTER, WILLIAM B., Jr. "An Evening with Robert Frost and
   Carl Sandburg." Forum 13 (Winter):51-55.
      Describes the meeting between Frost and Sandburg at Wofford
   College (14 March 1950). Focuses on Frost's jealousy of Sandburg
   and includes stories illustrating the rivalry between the two
   men.

12 MAYER, CHARLES W. "The People, Yes: Sandburg's Dreambook for
   Today." In The Vision of This Land: Studies of Vachel
   Lindsay, Edgar Lee Masters, and Carl Sandburg. An Essays in
   Literature Book. Edited by John E. Hallwas and Dennis J.
   Reader. Macomb: Western Illinois University Press,
   pp. 82-91.
      Sandburg is two poems--of democracy and of evanescence--
   dominated by thoughts of "loss and death, uncertain of life's
   purpose, and yearning for some release from the lonely prison of
   the senses." He had difficulty in being consistent in an
   affirmative view.

13 PERKINS, DAVID. "Carl Sandburg." In A History of Modern
   Poetry from the 1890's to the High Modernist Mode. Cambridge:
   Harvard University Press, pp. 356-61 and passim.
      Discusses Sandburg's poetry as being "popular." Notes his
   approach ("whole, direct and accessible"), intentness in life,
   faith in American democracy ("huge, unfocused"), setting
   ("agreeable" or "interesting"), and personality (attractive).
   Sandburg sought to start afresh, "with new forms and idioms
   appropriate to the present age." Says that he represents better
   than any other poet "the new style of the 1910's." Finds most

striking about his early poems their "flexibility and inventive-
ness, [their] freedom to use whatever means or methods seem
appropriate." Says that his legacy is his "report of the
people" (according to William Carlos Williams) and his methods
of presentation. Includes a survey of critical reactions to
Chicago Poems, Cornhuskers, and the Lincoln biography.
Excerpted: 1979.2.

14   THOMPSON, LAWRENCE, and R.H. WINNICK. Robert Frost: The
     Later Years 1938-1963. New York: Holt, Rinehart & Winston,
     pp. 89-91, 98-99, 195, 273-74, 286-87, 303.
        Refers to Sandburg's defense of free verse in the Atlantic
     Monthly and Frost's response, his encounter with Frost in
     Washington in 1960, Frost's anger at being compared to him, and
     Frost's reaction to Sandburg's criticism of Eisenhower.
     Excerpted: 1981.5.

15   WHITE, WILLIAM. "Lindsay/Masters/Sandburg: Criticism from
     1950-1975." In The Vision of This Land: Studies of Vachel
     Lindsay, Edgar Lee Masters, and Carl Sandburg. An Essays in
     Literature Book. Edited by John E. Hallwas and Dennis J.
     Reader. Macomb: Western Illinois University Press,
     pp. 114-28.
        A working bibliography arranged under each poet's name by
     year.

16   WHITNEY, BLAIR. "The Garden of Illinois." In The Vision of
     This Land: Studies of Vachel Lindsay, Edgar Lee Masters, and
     Carl Sandburg. An Essays in Literature Book. Edited by
     John E. Hallwas and Dennis J. Reader. Macomb: Western
     Illinois University Press, pp. 17-28.
        Neither as optimistic as Lindsay nor as pessimistic as
     Masters, Sandburg's poems provide "glimpses of the good life in
     the present." They share a knowledge of the beauty of central
     Illinois. Their vision is agrarian. All three poets were
     active in a variety of liberal, even radical causes. They
     imagined "the garden of Illinois as a place where America's
     promises might be fulfilled."

1977

1   ANON. "Carl Sandburg 13 Cent Commemorative to be Issued
     6th January 1978." Stamps 181 (17 December):788-89.
     Biographical essay.

2   CALLOW, JAMES T., and ROBERT J. REILLY. Guide to American
     Literature from Emily Dickinson to the Present. New York:
     Barnes & Noble, pp. 70-71.
     Brief survey of Sandburg's career.

3   DJIVA, SANDRA. "'A New Soil and a Sharp Sun': The Landscape
    of a Modern Canadian Poetry." Modernist Studies: Literary
    and Cultural 1920-1940 2 (Fall):3-17.
        Brief references to Sandburg's poetry from a Canadian point
    of view.

4   FLANAGAN, JOHN T. "Carl Sandburg, Lyric Poet." Mid America 4
    (Winter):89-100.
        Although Sandburg may have written too much and failed to
    explore the depths possible in imagery, he did maintain his
    lyricism to the end of his career. All along, he was true to
    "the spirit and idiom of the American people."

5   HALLWAS, JOHN E. "'Fire Flowers': An Uncollected Poem by
    Carl Sandburg." Notes on Modern American Literature 1
    (Summer), item 16.
        Uncollected poem by Sandburg with brief commentary.

6   MARSHALL, JON ELDER. "The Whitman Tradition in Twentieth-
    Century American Poetry." Ph.D. diss., Ohio State University,
    212 pp., passim.
        Sandburg, Masters, and Lindsay "celebrated Whitman's ideas
    and shared many of his beliefs," but their poetry has become
    "dated because of their inattention to the formal problems of
    their craft."

7   RUBIN, LOUIS D., Jr. "Not to Forget Carl Sandburg . . ."
    Sewanee Review 85 (Winter):181-89.
        Wonders what has happened to Sandburg, Masters, and
    Lindsay. Sandburg was the best of the Chicago poets. After
    Chicago Poems, his poetry shows an increasing tendency to
    "substitute rhetoric about experience for evocation of his
    experience." By the early 1920s he had lost interest in writing
    poems and turned to prose. The Prairie Years may well be un-
    reliable and impressionistic, but The War Years is "solidly
    anchored in abundantly recorded facts." In Always the Young
    Strangers he leaves behind all the "hokum, pretense, and self-
    serving rhetoric" and writes with "freshness, candor, without
    pose or glibness." Suggests that there is in Sandburg two
    people: "one of them the private, sensitive artist, the other
    the public performer, self-important and pompous, willing to
    debase the language for gain." Predicts an eventual restoration
    of Sandburg as an excellent poet and a long life for his work.
    Excerpted: 1979.2.

8   STEIN, FREDERICK C. "Carl Sandburg as Poet--an Evaluation."
    Midwestern Miscellany 5:1-11.
        Disagrees that "When Death Came April Twelve, 1945" is one
    of Sandburg's best later works. Views his poetry as a good
    introduction to poetry for teenagers, but of little challenge to
    serious readers.

9 WEST, JERRY, LARRY KRUPKA, and ERIC LUNDE. "Three Poems +
   Three Professors = Third Culture?" University College
   Quarterly 23 (Spring):13-16, 19-20.
      Examination of Sandburg's "The Hammer" in the context of
   C.P. Snow's essay on the split between two cultures—sciences and
   humanities.

10 WILLIAMS, ELLEN. Harriet Monroe and the Poetry Renaissance:
    The First Ten Years of "Poetry," 1912-22. Urbana: University
    of Illinois Press, 312 pp., passim.
       Discusses Sandburg's early years as a published poet and
    his contributions to Poetry, attacks by Dial, and reactions of
    others. Includes excerpt from 1914.2.

11 WILSON, EDMUND. Letters on Literature and Politics 1912-1972.
    Edited by Elena Wilson. New York: Farrar, Straus & Giroux,
    p. 610.
       In a letter to John Dos Passos, Wilson writes that Sandburg
    is "the worst thing that has happened to Lincoln since Booth shot
    him" (see 1978.15).

                              1978

1 ANON. "Notes on Current Fiction." Virginia Quarterly Review
   54 (Summer):100.
      Review of Breathing Tokens. Calls this a "treasure trove"
   and looks forward to more of the same.

2 BROOKS, GWENDOLYN. "Carl Sandburg, 1878-1967." Chicago
   Tribune, 1 January, sec. 7, p. 1.
      In all his writing, Sandburg composed "a direct cool line"
   born of passionate fire. He faced the world's problems with
   "mighty faith," "strange courage," and "beautiful doggedness."
   Reviews the shocked reception given to Chicago Poems.

3 CROWDER, RICHARD H. "The Influence of Carl Sandburg on Modern
   Poetry." Western Illinois Regional Studies 1 (Spring):45-64.
      Examines the poetry published from 1916 to 1963. Sandburg
   was the first poet to depart from the genteel tradition. Con-
   trasts tone and technique in Eliot's The Wasteland and Sandburg's
   "The Windy City." Finds a debt to Sandburg in the poems of John
   Ashberry, Kenneth Koch, Galway Kinnell, and Robert Penn Warren.

4 DUFFEY, BERNARD. Poetry in America: Expression and Its
   Values in the Times of Bryant, Whitman, and Pound. Durham,
   N.C.: Duke University Press, pp. 248-49.
      Unlike Pound, Sandburg worked from "a strong idealism."
   He departed from the Imagists in trusting "more to the possibil-
   ities of subject for its expression than to new technique." He

invoked a "populistic faith." His early poems had a "quick impact" on Masters.

5   FINCH, ROBERT. "The Carl Sandburg Memorial in Galesburg." Stamps 182 (14 January):1.
      Biographical essay with details on various ceremonies cele-brating the memory of Sandburg.

6   FLANAGAN, JOHN T. "Book Reviews." American Literature 50 (November):502.
      Review of Breathing Tokens. Finds here Sandburg's earmarks: "loose, rough lines, colloquial speech mixed with literary dic-tion, occasional vivid images mostly from nature, a persistent interest in the working man and a hatred of capitalist wars." Detects few departures from his earlier style and themes.

7   GOLD, DORIS. "Carl Sandburg--American Poet, Historian." Stamps 182 (14 January):104-5.
      Reviews Sandburg's achievements and awards.

8   GUILLORY, DANIEL L. "Poetry." Library Journal 103 (1 January):96.
      Review of Breathing Tokens. Says that the bulk of this collection is of "historical rather than aesthetic value, and one suspects that Sandburg would have suppressed most of these verses had he lived." Finds a few "genuine" pleasures in the collection.

9   HALL, DONALD. Remembering Poets: Reminiscences and Opinions. New York: Harper & Row, p. 62.
      Reports a story Frost had told on Sandburg when invited to read his poems at the University of Michigan, Ann Arbor.

10 HALLWAS, JOHN E. "Sandburg's 'Ashes and Dreams': An Uncollected Poem." Notes on Modern American Literature 2 (Summer), item 24.
      Uncollected poem by Sandburg with commentary.

11 HENDRICK, GEORGE, and A. LYNN ALTENBERND. "Carl Sandburg, 1878-1978: A Century of America." Non Solus (University of Illinois Library), p. 5.
      Special issue on the Exposition of the Sandburg collection.

12 _____. "Wallace Stevens' Manuscripts at the University of Illinois." Wall Street Journal, 11 November, pp. 17-20.
      Texts of previously unpublished letters to Sandburg.

13 HOFFMAN, DANIEL [G.]. "'Moonlight Dries No Mittens': Carl Sandburg Reconsidered." Georgia Review 32 (Summer):390-407.
      Reprint of his lecture at the Library of Congress on Sandburg's one hundredth birthday, 6 January 1978. Examines his works, explores his style, and defends it against the criticism

of William Carlos Williams. Considers the poems depicting
American life, his gentle stories for children, his autobiography,
and his masterful biography of Lincoln. Excerpted: 1980.4.
Reprinted: 1979.6.

14   HUBBELL, JAY B., Sr. "My Friend Carl Sandburg." Library
      Notes (Duke University) 48 (Fall):5-17.
         Recalls his contacts with Sandburg at Southern Methodist
      and Duke, in Flat Rock and Raleigh. Quotes from their corre-
      spondence. Sandburg was blessed with the virtue of "magnanimity."

15   MITGANG, HERBERT. "Carl Sandburg." New Republic 178
      (14 January):24-26.
         Surveys Sandburg's career with biographical background.
      His life and times can be found in his poetry, biographies, and
      history. In the literary establishment, he occupied a standing
      similar to John Steinbeck's. He helped free poetry of old
      strictures. He opened up new regions of America to literature.
      He "dignified" the most ordinary people and subjects. He was an
      original. Refers to Edmund Wilson as his severest critic in
      Patriotic Gore (see 1977.11). Excerpted: 1980.4.

16   PETTINGELL, PHOEBE. "On Poetry: The People's Poet." New
      Leader 61 (27 February):19-20.
         Review of Breathing Tokens. Summarizes Sandburg's career
      and says that this collection fairly represents his techniques
      and themes but lacks the "gusto" of his best-known work. His
      strength lies in the vernacular. His "oversized enthusiasm" kept
      him out of sympathy with the major poetic influences. He does
      not overdo his "deep belief in human dignity." Excerpted:
      1985.5.

17   RUBIN, LOUIS D., Jr. "Books Considered." New Republic 178
      (28 January):35-36.
         Review of Breathing Tokens. Finds this collection superior
      to Honey and Salt because there is none of "the rhetorical
      expansiveness and attitude-striking that makes so much of his
      later verse empty and sentimental."

18   SANDBURG, HELGA. A Great and Glorious Romance: The Story of
      Carl Sandburg and Lilian Steichen. New York and London:
      Harcourt Brace Jovanovich, 319 pp.
         Sandburg's youngest daughter traces the family roots back
      to Sweden and Luxembourg and, basing her account on letters
      exchanged between the couple, relates the developing love
      between Sandburg and Steichen after their first meeting as two
      Social-Democrat party workers. Account ends in 1926 when
      Sandburg published Abraham Lincoln: The Prairie Years. Sheds
      additional light on his home life and development as a writer as
      well as his role as husband and father.

19   SANDBURG, MARGARET, ed. "Introductory Note." In <u>Breathing</u>
     <u>Tokens</u>, by Carl Sandburg. New York and London: Harcourt
     Brace Jovanovich, pp. xiii-xiv.
         Discusses how she decided which poems to publish. Refers
     to Sandburg as "the old idealist, fighter, philosopher, dreamer,
     and poet, still with something to say."

20   SHAPIRO, KARL. "<u>Breathing Tokens</u>, by Carl Sandburg." <u>Chicago</u>
     <u>Tribune</u>, 1 January, sec. 7, pp. 1-2.
         Sandburg is truly an American poet, along with Poe,
     Whitman, Frost, and perhaps Dickinson. Suggests that he is now
     "America's most official poet." His influence on contemporary
     poetry is equal to that of Pound and Williams.

21   WHIPPLE, T.K. "Carl Sandburg." In <u>Spokesmen: Modern Writers</u>
     <u>and American Life</u>. New York: Arno, pp. 161-83.
         Reprint of 1928.27 and 1963.23.

                                1979

1   BABIC, LJILJANA. "Karl Sandburg: Pesnik puka i istine."
     <u>Letopis Matice Srpske</u> (Yugoslavia) 424 (Spring):343-49.
         In Serbo-Croatian. Discusses Sandburg as poet of the
     people and of the truth.

2   BRYFONSKI, DEDRIA, ed. "Carl (August) Sandburg 1878-1967."
     In <u>Contemporary Literary Criticism</u>. Vol. 10. Detroit:
     Gale Research, pp. 447-52.
         Excerpts of 1972.1; 1976.13; 1977.7.

3   DOWDING, NANCY E. "Sandburg the Biographer." <u>Lincoln Herald</u>
     81 (March):159-62.
         Discusses Sandburg's successful biography of Lincoln, which
     accurately captures Lincoln's personality and the times in which
     he lived.

4   DUFFEY, BERNARD. "Carl Sandburg and the Undetermined Land."
     <u>Centennial Review</u> 23 (Summer):295-303.
         Reevaluates Sandburg and says that he "located a poetically
     constructed imagination" of America, unlike Masters or Lindsay.
     Excerpted: 1985.5.

5   FERLAZZO, PAUL. "The Popular Writer, Professors, and the
     Making of a Reputation: The Case of Carl Sandburg." In
     <u>Mid America IV</u>. Edited by David D. Anderson. East Lansing:
     Mich.: Midwestern Press, pp. 72-78.
         Although taught in high schools, Sandburg is ignored in
     colleges. The problem is that professors and literary critics
     have not conceded greatness to him because of his popularity,
     his social philosophy, and "the long reign . . . of the New

Critics." These conditions seem to have worked against his
reputation as poet.

6   HOFFMAN, DANIEL [G.] "'Moonlight Dries No Mittens': Carl
    Sandburg Reconsidered." Journal of the Library of Congress 36
    (Winter):4-17.
        Reprint of 1978.13.

7   KISHI, KUNIZO. "An Anthology of Contemporary American
    Poetry." Eigo Seinen: The Rising Generation (Tokyo) 125
    (Fall):211.
        Recalls his first translation of Sandburg.

8   LYNN, JOANNE L. "Hyacinths and Biscuits in the Village of
    Liver and Onions: Sandburg's Rootabaga Stories." Children's
    Literature 8 (Fall):118-32.
        Offers a lengthy appreciation of Sandburg's stories for
    children. Explores themes and style and includes summaries of
    most of them.

9   McJUNKIN, PENELOPE NIVEN. "Steichen and Sandburg: Two Ameri-
    can Giants Shared Artistic Inspiration and a Rare Friendship."
    Horizon 22 (August):46-53.
        Describes the friendship between artist and photographer
    Edward Steichen and writer Sandburg, who met during the courtship
    of Steichen's sister Lilian Anna Maria Elizabeth Steichen and
    Sandburg in 1908. This friendship lasted until the poet's death.

10 MILLER, JAMES E., Jr. The American Quest for a Supreme Fic-
    tion: Whitman's Legacy in the Personal Epic. Chicago:
    University of Chicago Press, pp. 22, 292.
        Comments on Sandburg's "expansiveness." The People, Yes
    is "a long poem that seems to out-Whitman Whitman in its embrace
    of Americans 'En-Masse.'"

11 NAMIKI, SETSUKO. "Nature Poems of Carl Sandburg." Chu-
    Shikoku Studies in American Literature, Sendamachi (Hiroshima
    City) 15 (January):47-58.
        Analyzes Sandburg's treatment of nature in his poetry.

12 READ, ALLEN WALKER. "The Evocative Power of Place Names in
    the Poetry of Carl Sandburg." Literary Onomastics Studies 6
    (January):1-14.
        Surveys Sandburg's poetry to find the function of place
    names. Relates these to his themes and philosophy.

13 STANFORD, DEREK. "The Scholar-Poet." Books and Bookmen 25
    (November):34.
        Review of Breathing Tokens. Finds here aspects unfamiliar
    to most British readers. The amatory imagist, for example, is

one of many "attractive surprises" in this handsome collection.
Excerpted: 1980.4.

14   STEIN, RITA. "Chicago" and "Galesburg." In A Literary Tour
     Guide of the United States: West and Midwest. Americans-
     Discover-America Series. New York: William Morrow, pp. 78,
     81-83, and passim.
        Offers details on Sandburg's birthplace and its restora-
     tion. Refers to his involvement in the "Chicago Renaissance."
     Includes biographical details.

15   SUTTON, WILLIAM A., ed. Carl Sandburg Remembered. Metuchen,
     N.J., and London: Scarecrow Press, 340 pp.
        Collection of biographical material about Sandburg: diary
     entries and letters by those who knew him well, newspaper and
     magazine articles by anonymous authors, summaries of telephone
     conversations and interviews. All of this offers a view of his
     character and behavior as it appeared off the record. Part I,
     "The Perry Friendship," includes excerpts from a manuscript by
     Lilly Perry of Los Angeles. Part II, "A Host of Encounters,"
     offers seventy-six accounts of contacts with Sandburg, mostly
     favorable. Includes primary bibliography. Part I reprinted:
     1981.7.

16   WILLIAMS, WILBURN, Jr. "The Desolate Servitude of Language:
     A Reading of the Poetry of Melvin B. Tolson." Ph.D. diss.,
     Yale University, 316 pp., passim.
        In this study of the development of poet Melvin Beaunorus
     Tolson, accounts for Sandburg's influence on him. "A political
     radical, Tolson gravitated not to Eliot or Pound, but to more
     liberal men like Masters and Carl Sandburg."

                              1980

1   BOELIO, BOB. "A Literary Tour of Michigan." Chronicle 16
     (January):18-22.
        Brief account of the life and work of Sandburg in light of
     his residency at Harbert, Michigan.

2   CROWDER, RICHARD H. "Sandburg, Carl." In Twentieth Century
     American Literature. New York: St. Martin's, pp. 511-14.
        Survey of Sandburg's life and career with attention given
     to his critical reputation.

*3   FRIBERG, INGEGERD. "The Clash of American Dreams in Carl
     Sandburg's Poetry." Moderna Sprak 74 (January):2-30.
        Cited in 1963.8.

4   GUNTON, SHARON R., and LAURIE LANZEN HARRIS, eds. "Carl
    (August) Sandburg 1878-1967." In Contemporary Literary
    Criticism. Vol. 15. Detroit: Gale Research, pp. 466-70.
    Excerpts from 1951.17; 1976.7; 1978.13, 15; 1979.13.

5   HALLWAS, JOHN E. "Sandburg the Love Poet: 'Steamboat
    Nights': An Uncollected Poem." Notes on Modern American
    Literature 5 (June), item 1.
        Offers an uncollected poem by Sandburg.

6   HANSON, ROBERT F. "Carl Sandburg's Connemara." American Book
    Collector 1 (June):13-18.
        Description of Sandburg's home with biographical profile.

7   JONES, PETER. "Carl Sandburg 1878-1967." In Reader's Guide
    to Fifty American Poets. New York: Barnes & Noble,
    pp. 114-19.
        Reviews Sandburg's life and work and sees him as "a radical
    in poetry and in politics." Unfortunately, he was "always com-
    promised" by his subject matter. Includes excerpt of 1951.17.

8   KAWANO, AKIRA. "The Influence of Japanese Literature and
    Scandinavian Literature upon Carl Sandburg's Poems." In
    Proceedings of the 8th Congress of the International Compara-
    tive Literature Association, II; Twentieth Century Literatures
    Organization in Different Cultures and Comparative Literature
    and Theory of Literature. Edited by Bela Köpeczi and György
    M. Vajda. Stuttgart: Bieber, pp. 397-402.
        Finds in Sandburg's poetry the influence of Japanese use of
    metaphor and personification (especially from haiku) and of
    Scandinavian writers Hans Christian Andersen and Gustaf Fröding.

9   KLAUT, BARBARA. "Lady Bird Johnson Remembers." American
    Heritage 32 (December):12.
        Recalls seeing Lynda Bird Johnson and roommate singing with
    Sandburg in the Lincoln Room and then asking questions of him.

10 SLOANE, T. O'CONNOR. "Anecdote." New York Times Book Review,
    27 January, p. 38.
        Recalls a meeting between Eliot and Sandburg at the
    Harcourt offices. Eliot refers to the lack of depth in
    Sandburg's poetry (see 1980.11 for reply).

11 WERSHBA, JOSEPH. "Sandburg, Yes." New York Times Book
    Review, 6 April, p. 29.
        Quotes Sandburg on "'cerebral poets'" who go in for
    "'obscurantist lines'" and defends the poet against charges that
    his poetry has no depth (see 1980.10).

1981

1   BETTS, GLYNNE ROBINSON. Writers in Residence: American
    Authors at Home. Introduction by Christopher Lehmann-Haupt.
    New York: Viking, pp. 90–95.
        Photographs of Sandburg at Galesburg and Flat Rock, N.C.
    For him each day was "a mix of work and simple family pleasures."
    Includes photographs of his study and manuscript pages.

2   BRADLEY, SCULLEY, ed. "Carl Sandburg." In American Tradition
    in Literature. 5th ed. New York: Random House, pp. 1099–
    1101.
        Brief summary of Sandburg's life and output.

*3 CORWIN, NORMAN [LEWIS]. Date with Sandburg. Northridge:
    California State University at Northridge, Santa Susanna
    Press.
        Cited in 1963.8.

4   FEHRENBACHER, DON E. "Lincoln's Lost Letters." American
    Heritage 32 (February–March):74–75.
        Report of a cache of Lincoln's letters discovered in 1928.
    Sandburg studied the documents and called them authentic. They
    seem to prove Lincoln's love for Ann Rutledge (see 1987.2).

5   HALL, DONALD. "Robert Frost 1874–1963" and "Carl Sandburg
    1878–1967." In The Oxford Book of American Literary Anec-
    dotes. New York and Oxford: Oxford University Press,
    pp. 171–72.
        Describes an encounter between Frost and Sandburg in May
    1960 (reprinted from 1976.14) and Sandburg's comments on goats
    and being photographed, his work on Lincoln, and his regular
    appearances at Cornell College (excerpted from 1970.1).

6   No entry

7   PERRY, LILLA S. My Friend Carl Sandburg: The Biography of a
    Friendship. Edited by E. Caswell Perry. Metuchen, N.J.:
    Scarecrow Press, 224 pp.
        Draws from 147 of her letters and collection of news clip-
    pings and journal entries to recount contacts with the poet
    during his frequent visits to California. Includes material
    from part I of 1979.15.

8   TIDWELL, JOHN EDGAR. "Cultural Collaboration and Iconoclasm:
    The Literary and Cultural Criticism of Alain Locke and
    Sterling Brown." Ph.D. diss., University of Minnesota,
    215 pp., passim.
        Says that Brown's critical approach evolved from the
    critical realism of Sandburg and other poets.

9   WINTERS, DONALD EDWARD, Jr.   "The Soul of Solidarity: The
    Relationship between the I.W.W. and American Religion in the
    Progressive Era."   Ph.D. diss., University of Minnesota,
    215 pp., passim.
        The poetry of the I.W.W. (Wobblies) seems to exemplify what
    Sandburg speaks of as "the religious strain that runs through all
    real poetry.

1982

1   ANGYAL, ANDREW J.   "Carl Sandburg."   In Critical Survey of
    Poetry: English Language Series. Vol. 6. Edited by Frank N.
    MacGill. Englewood Cliffs, N.J.: Salem Press, pp. 2444–53.
        Discusses Sandburg's achievements and life, and analyzes
    his major works. Responds to criticism that he neglected form
    in favor of expression.

2   BENEDEK, YVETTE E.   "Contract, Edward Steichen (Portrait of
    Carl Sandburg)." American Photographer 8 (June):80–82.
        Photographs of the poet.

3   BRAY, ROBERT C. Rediscoveries: Literature and Place in
    Illinois. Urbana: University of Illinois Press, pp. 145–51
    and passim.
        In Chicago Poems, Sandburg presents his "incandescent
    social conscience [more] boldly and effectively" than in most
    of his later poetry. His radicalism is "a linking force between
    the nineteenth century and the later twentieth century."

4   HEYER, WILLIAM, and ANTHONY PICCIONE.   "The Shine of the
    World: A Conversation with Archibald MacLeish."
    Massachusetts Review 23 (Winter):695.
        In this transcript of a television interview conducted on
    2 October 1974 at SUNY, Brockport, New York, MacLeish says
    Sandburg was close to writing "a people's poetry." Refers to
    a contemptuous remark by Edmund Wilson "in which he just dis-
    missed him." But Sandburg is not out of favor.

5   HOWINK, EDA. Wives of Famous Men. New York: Golden Quill
    Press, pp. 156–59.
        Tribute to Sandburg's wife with biographical details.

6   JEROME, JUDSON.   "American Bards." Writer's Digest 62 (June):
    47–49.
        Includes Sandburg in a discussion of American poets
    (Whitman, Lindsay, and Ginsberg).

7 PIRON, ALICE MARIE. "Urban Metaphor in American Art and
Literature, 1910–1930." Ph.D. diss., Northeastern University,
457 pp., passim.
Discusses how Sandburg and other writers and painters in-
terpreted the industrialized American society. "Inspired by the
ideals of freedom and individualism associated with the agrarian
past, and repelled by the materialism of a society that they saw
controlled by the pecuniary values of business and the Puritan
ethic, these artists projected utopias that merged vestiges of
past ideals with realities of modern industrialism."

8 STEICHEN, PAULA. Carl Sandburg Home National Historic Site,
North Carolina. Produced by the Division of Publications,
National Park Service. Washington, D.C.: National Park
Service, 127 pp.
Sandburg spent twenty-two years of his life here. In
part I, Steichen tells of the family life at Connemara. In
part II she presents a biographical essay on the man and his
works. In part III she provides a concise tourist's guide to the
park and reference materials. If there is a secret to the success of Sandburg, it is this: "though he was easily satisfied
when it came to the necessities and comforts of life, he never
accepted the notion that there were limits, confines, to one's
capabilities, one's life itself."

1983

1 BRESNAHAN, ROGER J. "The Imaginative Geography of Midwestern
Autobiography." Society for the Study of Midwestern Literature Newsletter 12 (Fall):1–8.
General discussion of Always the Young Strangers and other
autobiographies.

2 BURNS, MARY M. "Poetry and Song." Horn Book 59 (April):180.
Review of Rainbows Are Made: Poems. The collection provides the opportunity "to relate the poet's themes and theories
to practice." His poetry is "quintessentially American." His
definition of poetry reflects "an effort to marry the transcen-
dent and the mundane and to give form to abstraction."

3 DOLLARD, PETER. "Book Review: Biography." Library Journal
108 (15 November):2155.
Review of Ever the Winds of Chance. Says that the book
reads more like "an outline of his intentions than a completed
work." At times the story reads like a "directory." Its charac-
ters lack development.

4   GRANT, GLORIA [IRENE]. "The People and Their Fate: A Study
    of Carl Sandburg's Poetry." Ph.D. diss., University of South
    Carolina, 245 pp.
        While Sandburg appreciates the public as a whole, he is yet
    greatly interested in personal awareness and responsibility and
    sees these qualities as important factors in the individual's
    fate. Notes Sandburg's attention to the reader as an important
    figure, as an individual who has in his own character the key to
    success. Considers Sandburg's early life and its influence on
    his mature work.

5   MITGANG, HERBERT. "An Unfinished Life." New York Times Book
    Review, 25 September, p. 43.
        Review of Ever the Winds of Chance. Discusses what obliga-
    tion a writer owes to his audience and himself, and concludes
    that it is a completed life story in which he follows "his muse
    to the end." Wishes Sandburg had completed his story. But the
    demand on his time was "a burden" and so his story "tantalizes
    because it hints at what might have been."

6   NEELY, MARK E., Jr. "Carl Sandburg." In Dictionary of
    Literary Biography. Vol. 17. Detroit: Gale Research,
    pp. 378-82.
        Surveys Sandburg's life and work.

7   REID, ROBERT L. "The Day Book: Poems of Carl Sandburg."
    Old Northwest 9 (March):205-18.
        Discusses four of Sandburg's poems published in the Day
    Book, a small prolabor daily newspaper published in Chicago.
    They deserve recognition because they are characteristic of his
    later poetry with its use of colloquial expressions and free-
    verse form.

8   SANDBURG, MARGARET, and GEORGE HENDRICK, eds. "Introduction."
    In Ever the Winds of Chance, by Carl Sandburg. Urbana and
    Chicago: University of Illinois Press, pp. ix-xiii.
        Suggest that the book might have been better had Sandburg
    completed it. Give the background of its reception. Although
    incomplete, the book is worth reading for what it tells about
    this formative period of Sandburg's life, his close ties to his
    family, and his friendship with Frederick Dickinson and Philip
    Green Wright.

9   SCHOENFIELD, BERNARD C. "Aiken, Agee and Sandburg: A
    Memoir." Virginia Quarterly Review 59 (Spring):299-300,
    311-15.
        After conversing with seven aspiring but cynical writers,
    Schoenfield reviewed the influence upon himself of three friends,
    among them Sandburg. Concludes that "way back then, we could
    afford to be romantic, with prospects of far horizons." Says
    that at a bar in Georgetown, "Sandburg was in his element."

10   STUTTAFORD, GENEVIEVE. "Nonfiction." Publishers Weekly 224
     (14 October):50.
         Review of Ever the Winds of Chance. Sandburg's writing is
     vivid. "The book reveals the inner turbulence of the young poet
     and socialist and describes the many forces that helped to shape
     his life and career."

11   WICHER, LINDA. Review of Rainbows Are Made: Poems. School
     Library Journal 29 (March):196.
         Calls this a "handsome" collection of "gems," a useful book
     for the elementary or secondary school library.

                              1984

1   ELLEDGE, SCOTT. E.B. White: A Biography. New York and
     London: Norton, p. 92.
         Brief mention of Sandburg's influence on White's prose
     style in 1923.

2   GREASLEY, PHILIP A[LAN]. "Beyond Brutality: Forging Mid-
     western Urban-Industrial Mythology." Mid America 11 (Winter):
     9-19.
         Includes Sandburg in a discussion of the midwestern myth of
     competition and Sherwood Anderson's Mid-American Charts.

3   HACKER, JEFFREY H. Carl Sandburg. New York: Watts, 121 pp.
         Covers Sandburg's life and work. Draws from personal
     reminiscences found in Always the Young Strangers, selections
     from the poetry, and anecdotes from his early years. Shows the
     relationship between his growth as a poet and other patterns in
     his life. Includes photographs and suggestions for further
     reading.

4   HIRSCH, JERROLD MAURY. "Portrait of America: The Federal
     Writers' Project in an Intellectual and Cultural Context
     (Folklore, Cultural Pluralism, Romantic Nationalism)." Ph.D.
     diss., University of North Carolina at Chapel Hill, 835 pp.,
     passim.
         Considers Sandburg, among other writers and artists, in
     this study of the Federal Writers' Project as an episode in
     American cultural and intellectual history.

5   NEVINS, ALLAN. "Our Poetical New England Nun." Literary
     Digest 82 (2 August):34.
         Refers to Sandburg's "shredded prose" in discussing Emily
     Dickinson's unconventional form and the reader of her poetry in
     1924.

6   REID, ROBERT L. "The Day Book Poems of Carl Sandburg." Old Northwest 9 (Spring):205–18.
Reprints four of Sandburg's poems written in 1915, 1916, and 1917 but never collected. They are topical, related to preparations for World War 1 and current Chicago news.

7   SHAPIRO, DANIEL. "The Shape of Poetry 1910–1920: Convention, Reform, and Revolution." Ph.D. diss., University of Toronto, 257 pp., passim.
Includes Sandburg in this discussion of free verse from 1912 to 1917. In 1910 it was an oddity; by 1920 it was a common tool of poetic expression. "In one decade this group of determined young writers created a modern verse distinct in character from the poetry of earlier eras, and their legacy is visible in every subsequent movement in English verse, from Modernism (in which many of them participated) onwards."

8   SMITH, CARL S. Chicago and the American Literary Imagination 1880–1920. Chicago: University of Chicago Press, pp. 61–62, 127–29, and passim.
Discusses Sandburg and his use of buildings in The People, Yes and examines similarities between the poet and the architect Louis Sullivan.

9   SPARROW, W. KEATS. "Book Reviews." North Carolina Historical Review 61 (April):257–58.
Review of Ever the Winds of Chance. Finds of primary interest "the light it sheds on the intellectual development" of Sandburg. Of secondary interest are his commentaries on history and doctrines of the Universalist church, "glimpses of turn-of-the-century luminaries," and passages of his "unpretentious, vibrant prose."

10   WAGGONER, HYATT. "Carl Sandburg." In American Poets from the Puritans to the Present. Baton Rouge and London: Louisiana State University Press, pp. 452–57.
Reprint of 1968.45.

11   WILCOX, JOHN C. "Juan Ramón Jiménez and the Illinois Trio: Sandburg, Lindsay, Masters." Comparative Literature Studies 21 (Summer):186–200.
Chronology of Jiménez's interest in Sandburg and study of analogies and parallels that help explain that interest. Jiménez was influenced by Poetry (in which Sandburg began to appear) and Cornhuskers, but Sandburg is "far too liberal and down-to-earth" for Jiménez. In reading Sandburg, he may have been subconsciously effecting to reach his opposite self and hence self-renewal.

12   WILLIAMSON, BARBARA FISHER. "Nonfiction." New York Times
     Book Review, 1 January, p. 21.
        Review of Ever the Winds of Chance. Missing here is any
     spiritual or emotional struggle, any idea of "what shaped his
     poetry or what compelled him to become a poet in the first
     place." Thus it is rather a surprise that he became a poet.
     Calls this book "a portrait of a mind expanding, testing itself,
     measuring itself as it measures others."

                                1985

1   COWLEY, MALCOLM. The Flower and the Leaf: A Complete Record
     of American Writing since 1941. Edited with an introduction
     by Donald W. Faulkner. New York: Viking, pp. 59, 193, 254,
     349.
        Says that Sandburg's early experiments in the American
     language were widely read but had "comparatively few imitators."
     Sandburg was the literary ancestor of Nelson Algren.

2   DOWNS, ROBERT B., JOHN T. FLANAGAN, and HAROLD W. SCOTT. More
     Memorable Americans, 1750-1950. New York: Libraries
     Unlimited, pp. 305-8.
        Commemoration of Sandburg's contributions to American cul-
     ture. Surveys his career and life.

3   FETHERLING, DALE, and DOUG FETHERLING, eds. "Foreword" and
     "Introduction." In Carl Sandburg at the Movies: A Poet in
     the Silent Era, 1920-1927. Metuchen, N.J.: Scarecrow Press,
     pp. v-vii, 1-14.
        Examines Sandburg's best movie columns and the atmosphere
     in which they were written. Discusses his persona, life, and
     experiences as a reporter for the Chicago Daily News.

4   GATES, ROBERT A. "Carl Sandburg: 1878-1967." In Resesrch
     Guide to Biography and Criticism. Vol. 2. Edited by Walton
     Beacham. Washington, D.C.: Research Publishing, pp. 1016-19.
        Covers chronology of Sandburg's life, primary bibliographic
     list, biographical sources, evaluation of sources, overview of
     critical sources.

5   MAROWSKI, DANIEL G., ed. "Carl (August) Sandburg 1878-1967."
     In Contemporary Literary Criticism. Vol. 35. Detroit: Gale
     Research, pp. 337-60.
        Excerpts of 1916.2, 8, 10; 1918.7; 1919.4; 1920.12, 14;
     1921.1, 9; 1922.12, 22; 1926.1, 20, 33, 41, 46; 1928.8, 11;
     1936.5, 6, 10; 1939.3, 6, 14, 16; 1948.15, 24; 1950.11, 22;
     1953.28, 36; 1955.2, 4; 1958.4; 1959.16; 1965.5; 1968.26;
     1970.6; 1971.2; 1978.16; 1979.4.

6   MOORE, JOHN. "Reviews." Journal of American Studies 19 (April):122–23.
Review of Ever the Winds of Chance. The book provides further evidence of how "the Public Man of the 1950's remained unable to illuminate those aspects of his earlier life, which may have undermined his current status." Finds in the book hints of Sandburg's intellectual, political, and poetical development.

7   MUNSON, GORHAM [B.]. The Awakening Thirties: A Memoir-History of a Literary Period. Baton Rouge and London: Louisiana State University Press, 317 pp., passim.
Covers Sandburg's early years in a number of brief references. In time Sandburg became "a sentimental humanitarian poet."

8   STEICHEN, PAULA. "Historic Houses: Carl Sandburg's Mountain Years." Architectural Digest 41 (April):226–34, 252.
Memoir by his granddaughter in which she recounts how Sandburg moved to the hills of North Carolina in 1945 and lived for the next two decades at Connemara. There he found "the solitude he needed for his work." Says that Connemara provided for Sandburg "a home surrounded by beauty, marked by space and peace."

1986

1   RAMPERSAD, ARNOLD. The Life of Langston Hughes. Vol. 1, 1902–1941: I, Too, Sing America. New York and Oxford: Oxford University Press, pp. 28, 29, 37, 44, 63, 64, 117, 158, 355, 366.
Sandburg became Hughes's "guiding star." Whitman and Sandburg freed him from the tyranny of traditional forms and "led him toward a version of literary modernism not without limitations."

1987

1   CALLAHAN, NORTH. Carl Sandburg: A Biography. University Park: Pennsylvania State University Press, 280 pp.
Reprint of 1970.1 with revisions and updated material.

2   FEHRENBACHER, DON E. Lincoln in Text and Context: Collected Essays. Stanford: Stanford University Press, pp. 185, 206, 237, 256–60, 334, 339.
Discusses Sandburg's biography of Lincoln and his opinion of Richard Henry Little's Better Angels. In The Prairie Years, "with uncommon sensibility and in evocative, often lyrical prose, Sandburg recaptured the sights, sounds, and feelings of the several worlds in which Lincoln grew up to manhood and then to

greatness." The War Years followed "more closely the rules of
historical scholarship." To read Sandburg on Lincoln is more of
an emotional than an intellectual experience. Thus, his influence on the scholarship "has never matched the popularity of his
work." Includes review of the controversy over certain Lincoln
documents that appeared in the Atlantic Monthly (see 1981.4).

3   NIVEN, PENELOPE. "Carl Sandburg." In American Poets, 1880–
     1945. 3d ser. A Bruccoli Clark Book. Edited by Peter
     Quartermain. Detroit: Gale Research, pp. 388–406.
        Covers Sandburg's life, awards, and honors, with photo-
graphs and bibliography of primary and secondary works.

4   RAMPERSAD, ARNOLD. "Langston Hughes." In Voices and Visions:
     The Poet in America. Edited by Helen Vendler. New York:
     Random House, pp. 360–62, 370–71.
        Comments on Sandburg's early influence on Hughes and quotes
from Hughes's poem, "The Fascination of Cities," in which Sandburg is mentioned.

5   SANDBURG, MARGARET, ed. The Poet and the Dream Girl: The
     Love Letters of Lilian Steichen and Carl Sandburg. Urbana and
     Chicago: University of Illinois Press, 273 pp.
        Includes 134 letters recording their relationship from
their first meeting to their June 1908 wedding. They reveal the
emergence of Sandburg's identity as a poet and political activist
and Steichen's personality. Appendices include "Juvenilia,"
"Related Letters and Socialist Prose," and "Other Poems for
Paula." The introduction and the prologue by Margaret Sandburg
explain the purpose in bringing together these letters.

Index

Index

Index

Index

Ward, Martha E., 1967.24
Wedding Procession of the Rag
  Doll and the Broom Handle
  and Who Was in It, The,
  1967.11, 15, 17, 19-20
Weeks, Edward, 1953.40
"Week's Work: Biographical
  Note, The," 1947.7
Weigel, John C., 1968.46; 1973.10
Weintraub, Stanley, 1968.47
Weirick, Bruce, 1924.12; 1952.38
Wells, Henry W., 1940.16;
  1943.12; 1964.11; 1973.11
Welsch, Roger L., 1970.16
Wershba, Joseph, 1980.11
West, Jerry, 1977.9
West, Rebecca, 1926.40-41;
  1954.15
West, Thomas Reed, 1967.25
Westerfield, Hargis, 1963.22
"Western Bookshelf, A," 1936.17
"What Does the Symbol
  Symbolize?" 1952.19
"What Makes an American?" 1953.40
"When Lincoln Rode the Circuit,"
  1926.34
Whipple, Leon, 1928.26
Whipple, T.K., 1928.27; 1963.23;
  1978.21
White, W.A., 1926.42
White, William, 1976.15
"Whitman and Sandburg," 1928.10
"Whitman Tradition in Twentieth-
  Century American Poetry,
  The," 1977.6
Whitney, Blair, 1976.16
Whitridge, Arnold, 1962.10
"Who Reads Carl Sandburg?" 1929.2
Wicher, Linda, 1983.11
"Widening Horizons in Junior
  Reading," 1955.6
Wilcox, John C., 1984.11
Wilkinson, Marguerite O.,
  1919.11; 1935.4
Williams, Ellen, 1977.10
Williams, Stanley Thomas, 1926.43
Williams, T. Harry, 1954.16
Williams, Wilburn, Jr., 1979.16
Williams, Wilfred, 1942.13
Williams, William Carlos,
  1929.11; 1951.16; 1954.17;
  1960.18; 1980.7

Williamson, Barbara Fisher,
  1984.12
Willner, Sis, 1931.6
Wilson, Arthur, 1921.9
Wilson, Edmund, 1920.15; 1962.11;
  1977.11
Wind Song, 1960.3-4, 6-7, 11, 21;
  1964.2
Winnick, R.H., 1976.14
Winterich, John T., 1968.48
Winters, Donald Edward, Jr.,
  1981.9
Witham, W. Tasker, 1947.9
Wood, Clement, 1921.10; 1922.23;
  1925.10; 1926.44
Woodburn, J.A., 1926.45
Woods, George A., 1967.26
Woolf, Leonard, 1926.46
Woolf, Samuel J., 1939.20;
  1940.17
"World of Carl Sandburg," 1960.10
Wrede, Johan, 1966.12
Wright, Philip Green, 1904.1
Wright, Quincy, 1952.39
"Wright, Sandburg Steal Chicago
  Dynamic Show," 1957.2
Wyatt, Edith F., 1920.16; 1926.47

Yatron, Michael, 1957.13;
  1959.16-17
"Years of a Poet Who Sang of
  America," 1967.8
"Young People," 1942.2
"Your Friend the Poet: Carl
  Sandburg," 1969.1
"Your Obt. Servt.," 1939.2
Yust, Walter, 1921.11; 1922.24

Zabel, Morton D., 1936.24; 1937.9
Zaturenska, Marya, 1942.3; 1946.4
Zehnpfennig, Gladys, 1963.24
Zhuralev, Igor, 1970.17
Zwaska, Caesar, 1916.15

175